Pediatric Psychology in Clinical Practice

Pediatric Psychology in Clinical Practice

Empirically Supported Interventions

Kristin H. Kroll, PhD
Medical College of Wisconsin

CAMBRIDGE
UNIVERSITY PRESS

University Printing House, Cambridge CB2 8BS, United Kingdom

One Liberty Plaza, 20th Floor, New York, NY 10006, USA

477 Williamstown Road, Port Melbourne, VIC 3207, Australia

314–321, 3rd Floor, Plot 3, Splendor Forum, Jasola District Centre, New Delhi – 110025, India

79 Anson Road, #06–04/06, Singapore 079906

Cambridge University Press is part of the University of Cambridge.

It furthers the University's mission by disseminating knowledge in the pursuit of education, learning, and research at the highest international levels of excellence.

www.cambridge.org
Information on this title: www.cambridge.org/9781108458979
DOI: 10.1017/9781108639118

Cambridge University Press © 2020

First published 2020

Printed in the United Kingdom by TJ International Ltd, Padstow Cornwall

A catalogue record for this publication is available from the British Library.

Library of Congress Cataloging-in-Publication Data
Names: Kroll, Kristin H., author.
Title: Pediatric psychology in clinical practice : empirically supported
    interventions / Kristin H. Kroll.
Description: Cambridge ; New York, NY : Cambridge University Press, 2020.
    | Includes bibliographical references and index.
Identifiers: LCCN 2019040713 (print) | LCCN 2019040714 (ebook) |
    ISBN 9781108458979 (paperback) | ISBN 9781108639118 (epub)
Subjects: LCSH: Clinical child psychology. | Child mental health services.
Classification: LCC RJ503.3 .K76 2020 (print) | LCC RJ503.3 (ebook) |
    DDC 618.92/89–dc23
LC record available at https://lccn.loc.gov/2019040713
LC ebook record available at https://lccn.loc.gov/2019040714

ISBN 978-1-108-45897-9 Paperback

....

For my daughter and husband, the light of my life and the love of my life

Contents

8 **Technological Applications and Pediatric Psychological Care** 164

Chapter

1

Introduction to Pediatric Psychological Care

1.1 Introduction

Imagine the following presenting concerns when you arrive at your office early Monday morning:

- A child arrives with a diagnosis of functional neurological symptom disorder and no known medical etiology for his apparent inability to use his legs for the past six months.
- An adolescent experiences diabetic ketoacidosis for the eighth time in one year due to nonadherence to his treatment regimen.
- An adolescent has been assessed as being "pre-diabetic" and asks for help in losing weight.
- A child refuses to see the school nurse when she needs medication because she does not want her peers to view her as "different" or "crazy."
- A pediatrician calls asking whether you will assist with a patient who has exhibited a rapid decline in respiratory functioning due to the family's lack of follow-up for specialty medical care.
- A child suffers extensive burns from an accidental house fire and has difficulty returning to the home after discharge from the hospital.
- A sibling has difficulty coping after his brother experiences severe injuries following a motor vehicle accident.
- Parents struggle with setting appropriate boundaries and expectations for their child given the child's history of significant medical trauma.
- A patient has difficulty returning to school following a traumatic brain injury due to his accurate perception that his cognitive abilities and functioning have been adversely impacted since his accident.

What do all of these diverse concerns have in common? Despite the breadth of these concerns, the aforementioned scenarios are all potential referral questions posed to pediatric psychologists. Despite this typically falling within the purview of specially trained pediatric psychologists, many traditionally trained mental health clinicians will be asked to respond to these same concerns due to a lack of access to a pediatric psychologist, an already strong rapport with their current mental health clinician, or other important factors. As such, traditionally trained mental health clinicians, such as master's-level counselors and clinical social workers, are asked to respond to these concerns with the same dedication and expertise they apply to other presenting concerns that they may have more experience with as a result of their previous graduate training or professional clinical experience.

This book was written to help traditionally trained mental health clinicians become familiar with the basic principles and strategies used in pediatric psychology. This book provides resources to help clinicians enhance their clinical practice as well as providing resources for how to find further resources in specific areas based on the presenting problems of their patients and their own burgeoning clinical interests.

1.2 Foundational Principles of Pediatric Psychological Care

The origins of pediatric psychology have been initially attributed to Lightner Witmer's first discussion in 1896 of a partnership between child psychology and pediatrics (White, 1991). In subsequent years, Logan Wright outlined the profession of pediatric psychology as psychologists working in pediatric settings, with pediatric psychology later being defined by the Society of Pediatric Psychology's Executive Committee in 1974 as "a professionally oriented group of psychologists who deal with children in interdisciplinary settings such as hospitals, pediatric practices, and developmental centers" (Kenny, 1975, p. 8).

When many lay people are first introduced to the concept of pediatric psychology, they may be easily confused with the difference between the work of traditional child psychologists and pediatric psychologists. In contrast to traditional child psychologists who work with children whose concerns are primarily psychiatric in nature, pediatric psychologists' work may span from working with children with typical developmental trajectories to children with developmental disabilities and, in particular, children with medical needs or other concerns that are not primarily psychiatric in nature (Mesibov, 1990). Due to the multidisciplinary nature of the work of pediatric psychologists, it is particularly important for clinicians working within this scope to gain the confidence and competence to interact productively with nurses, educational specialists, medical specialists, pediatricians, medical social workers, and other vital members of multidisciplinary medical teams. Simply put, a pediatric psychologist is severely hampered in their ability to provide effective care without the support of their medical colleagues.

Over the years, pediatric psychology has evolved and redefined its scope and mission from its initial origins. Currently, pediatric psychology has been defined as a "multidisciplinary field of both scientific research and clinical practice which attempts to address the psychological aspects of illness, injury, and the promotion of health behaviors in children, adolescents, and families in a pediatric health setting" (Aylward et al., 2009, p. 3). With this definition, there is great variety in how pediatric psychology is practiced in the real world, with applications ranging from clinicians serving as embedded members of multidisciplinary teams in hospital settings to clinicians in private practice providing outpatient treatment. Despite these variations in settings and other factors, most clinical approaches with children and adolescents with medical concerns typically emphasize briefer interventions that are characteristically behavioral and cognitive-behavioral in approach (Roberts et al., 2014).

With this variety in how pediatric psychology is practiced, there is also great variability in how training for pediatric psychology occurs. Some pediatric psychologists may have first started as members of clinical child psychology graduate programs and then received specialized training later on in their graduate work through their pre-doctoral internship and postdoctoral fellowship, whereas other clinicians may have trained in other graduate programs with a broader focus (i.e. clinical or counseling psychology) prior to specializing. Whatever the path to training, clinicians should minimally gain clinical expertise in pediatric psychology via traditional coursework, clinical experience, and ongoing clinical consultation and supervision.

With the different training backgrounds of many of its members, the Society of Pediatric Psychology Task Force has worked to identify 12 specific domains recommended for training: (1) lifespan developmental psychology; (2) life span developmental psychopathology; (3) child, adolescent, and family assessment methods; (4) intervention strategies, (5) research methods and systems evaluations; (6) professional, ethical, and legal issues; (7) diversity; (8) the role of multiple disciplines in service delivery systems; (9) prevention, family support, and health promotion; (10) social issues affecting children, adolescents, and families; (11) consultation and liaison roles; and (12) disease process and medical management (Spirito et al., 2003).

With the multifactorial considerations that arise as part of clinical work in pediatric psychology come novel ethical considerations that may not be recognized or typically topical for mental health providers practicing in more traditional mental health roles and settings. For example, ethical considerations that can arise as part of pediatric psychology work can include, but are certainly not limited to, an adolescent's involvement in medical decision-making, the balancing of patient confidentiality and patient safety for adolescents engaging in risky behaviors, and determining when lack of follow through on medical care constitutes grounds for a mandated report regarding abuse/neglect.

When possible, having an adolescent involved in decision-making is preferable in order to help the patient feel some locus of control in an environment that is often well outside their influence. In some states even, an adolescent must consent in order for treatment to occur; for example, an adolescent age 14 and older can refuse outpatient mental health treatment in Wisconsin until there is a court order (Department of Health Services, 2016). It can be difficult to know when an adolescent is able to actively contribute to the medical decision process. As mental health clinicians, it is recommended that an active role is taken in assessing the patient's capacity for decision-making, care is taken to actively solicit their treatment preferences, and clinicians focus on facilitating positive communication between parents, doctors, and child (McCabe, 1995).

Despite this effort to have adolescents involved in medical decision-making, there comes a time when a mental health clinician has to decide whether or not the patient's behavior warrants breaking confidentiality with the patient in order to discuss their health risk behavior with their parents. This is never an easy decision due to the concern the patient may feel betrayed and therefore may not be as forthcoming in the future with the psychotherapist with issues associated with safety. Given this concern, it is not surprising that research indicates that pediatric psychologists tend to not report when a behavior is risky to an adolescent's health when the behavior is perceived to be of low intensity and frequency, such as smoking one cigarette per month (Rae et al., 2002).

Research indicates that pediatric psychologists are typically more likely to break confidentiality when the patient is female and the behavior is smoking or sexual behavior (Rae et al., 2002). Rae and colleagues hypothesize that this increased likelihood to break confidentiality with females may be due to the perception that risky behavior is seen as more normative in males and the possible perception of the increased negative impact of pregnancy and of increased vulnerability to sexually transmitted diseases for female adolescents.

In addition to the above concerns, clinicians working with children and adolescents with medical concerns may run up against the ethical dilemma of when or if to involve state regulatory services due to concerns of medical neglect. Similar to decisions regarding the mandated reporting of suspected child abuse, clinicians must refer to their professional organization's ethical guidelines when determining whether a patient's lack of medical care or follow-up rises to the level of suspected neglect. This decision can be hard for clinicians due to the fear that mandated reporting will irrevocably alter the therapeutic relationship; however, medical neglect must be viewed through the same lens of other types of mandated reporting that patient safety trumps other concerns.

1.3 Theoretical Underpinnings and Future Directions

In the clinical world of pediatric psychology, there are numerous theories that help guide clinicians in their work. One main theory utilized to help undergird work in health promotion is Bronfenbrenner's ecological systems theory, which recognizes a factor's level of influence based on proximity to the child (Kirschman & Karazsia, 2014). With this theory, the influence of systems and environment on the individual is accounted for rather than relying solely on viewing the individual's behavior one-dimensionally without environmental context. According to Bronfenbrenner's theory, an individual is first impacted by their immediate environment, called the microsystem, which involves the nearest influences (i.e., parents, siblings, and immediate caregivers). It can be an easy mistake for a pediatric psychologist or other mental health provider to assess and monitor the impact of only this easily identifiable microsystem and to lose sight of the larger systems at play, as described below.

The next larger system is the mesosystem, which encapsulates several microsystems, and typically involves the child's school, peer group, and religious group (Kirschman & Karazsia, 2014). Within the mesosystem, pediatric psychologists' work is with the extended community of people who have direct contact with the child, such as medical providers and school staff. In the exosystem, which is the larger environment influenced by religious, culture, and social class, pediatric psychologists are not working directly with the individual patient but instead are working with larger programs and communities that indirectly influence the patient, such as injury prevention programs (Kirschman & Karazsia, 2014). Last, the largest system, the macrosystem, involves the broadest level of influence, with the work of pediatric psychologists typically focused on research and legislation.

In addition to Bronfenbrenner's theory, another prevailing theory used in pediatric psychology is social-cognitive theory, which posits that behavior change is associated with one's belief about the outcome and belief in their abilities (Wilson & Lawson, 2009). With this theory, there is an overall emphasis on assisting patients via goal-setting and self-monitoring. According to social-cognitive theory, there are a specific set of determinants, including a patient's awareness and knowledge of health risks, perceived self-efficacy in impacting change in personal health, outcome expectancies regarding costs and benefits of the respective health habits, the goals and strategies for achieving these goals, and the identified barriers and enablers of these changes (Bandura, 2004).

Based on theories such as the aforementioned, the field of pediatric psychology has established a large body of literature with clinical applications. Myriad directions for future research and clinical work have been identified in the years to come for pediatric psychology. Three particular areas that have been noted for further work are the need for the clinical application of empirically supported treatments for diverse populations, the increasing role pediatric psychologists play with regard to genetic counseling and genetic teams, and an increased emphasis on health promotion rather than illness management (Clay, Mordhurst, & Lehn, 2002; Patenaude, 2003; Roberts et al., 2012).

As the US population becomes more diverse with regard to factors including ethnicity and family structures (e.g., single-parent households or multigenerational households), there is a call for culturally sensitive therapies in which therapy is tailored to specific cultures rather than a continuance of "one size fits all" treatment protocols (Clay et al., 2002). This is particularly important given that a large proportion of the current body of research is built on studies with samples consisting of predominantly Caucasian, middle-class participants. As such, there is a lack of data about the influence of empirically supported treatments for diverse populations and a resulting lack of information about the impact of family factors, culture, health beliefs, and other cultural factors on treatment outcomes. In particular, certain groups have been grossly ignored in the research literature, such as specific ethnic populations (i.e., Native American and Middle Eastern populations), as well as a lack of detailed information pertinent to specific subgroups within larger ethnic groups (i.e., Afro-Caribbean) (McQuaid & Barakat, 2012).

In addition to the increasing need for research into the clinical applications of empirically supported treatments for diverse populations, there is also an expanding role for pediatric psychologists in work with genetics teams. In this burgeoning role, pediatric psychologists can play a direct role in patient care by helping patients to understand and cope with the results of genetic testing (Patenaude, 2003). Similarly, pediatric psychologists can help to provide developmentally appropriate explanations for children and families to help them understand the often-complicated science behind genetics testing, as well as advising genetics teams about collaboratively and productively working with patients. Although not currently a role for pediatric psychologists, there will most likely be a future role of pediatric psychologists in the role of psychiatric genetics and risk of psychiatric disorders as the science progresses (Patenaude, 2003).

Last, the field of pediatric psychology has historically demonstrated a strong focus on clinical work geared toward chronic illness management. In the future, there is a call for research that has an emphasis on health promotion, early intervention, and prevention rather than remaining focused largely on chronic illness management, with specific emphasis on intervention in the primary care setting (Roberts et al., 2012). Rather than focusing on the best way to manage chronic diseases such as diabetes mellitus, type 2, there has been a paradigm shift in how we can best prevent these diseases from occurring in the first place. Based on Bronfenbrenner's ecological systems theory, pediatric psychologists are asked to begin placing focus on the exosystem rather than just directly on the micros and mesosystems of each patient.

1.4 Anecdotal "Golden Nuggets" for Clinical Practice in Pediatric Psychology

For all clinicians, an emphasis on empirical research to guide their clinical practice is paramount. Additionally, hard-earned tips and strategies from experienced clinicians can enhance one's clinical practice and help enhance one's foundational understanding of what it means to work with children and adolescents impacted by a medical event or chronic illness. Anecdotally, the following four themes are suggested for consideration by clinicians working with varying ages and different conditions in a pediatric psychology context: partnership, collaboration, fundamentals, and confidentiality.

Regarding partnership, clinical practice in pediatric psychology requires consistent dedication to forming and developing partnerships with families, medical providers, school personnel, and other important individuals in each patient's life. In particular, emphasis should be placed on the familial relationship, as almost all aspects of medical and mental health care will be impacted in some way by family members, whether through parenting strategies, sibling communications, or interactions with extended family members.

As such, it is important to **help the patient by helping the family**, as a family in distress (such as a mother experiencing symptoms of an untreated psychiatric illness) leads to a patient in distress. It can feel futile to try to assist a young patient with their mental health or medical concerns when larger familial influences are adversely impacting the course of treatment and the patient's overall prognosis. Despite needing to maintain the boundary of not "treating" anyone other than the identified patient, it is often necessary to ensure that other family members are at the minimum provided with alternative mental health resources if their needs are beyond the scope of the clinician or beyond the parameters of the identified clinical relationship with the patient.

Alongside a relationship with the family, it is vital for mental health clinicians to **develop a working relationship with medical personnel.** Ongoing and collaborative communication is important to ensure that the mental health clinician is up to date with the most current treatment regimen and remains aware of any changes to the patient's functioning and prognosis. The last situation any mental health clinician wants to be in is to be providing clinical recommendations that are not consistent with the recommendations of the patient's medical providers, as this leads to confusion for the patients and family and possibly malpractice by the clinician for operating outside their training and identified scope. It may be helpful for readers to view the sample pediatric psychology intake template in Figure 1.1 to help identify clinical areas to discuss with the medical team, such as discussing patient's treatment adherence and transition to increased patient autonomy in managing their treatment regimen.

With a strong working relationship, a clinician is able to learn the necessary medical information that will allow the provider to provide optimum and holistic care that is individualized to each patient. This leads to the third partnership "nugget" of: **When you don't know, ask!** Even the most veteran and experienced of clinicians will not know all of the medical terminology and information that changes rapidly due to advances in medicine. Clinicians need to be comfortable asking medical team members questions to help better understand their patient's daily journey and expected prognosis, which can often be achieved only by asking clarifying questions and requesting resources to help broaden and deepen their own understanding of the patient's medical status. In turn, this comfort with asking questions can help to support other medical providers in feeling encouraged to reach out to the clinician in the future for recommendations as needed as part of the patient's overall medical care.

Given that the field of medicine and mental health is constantly evolving, one "golden nugget" that is of paramount importance is to **never stop learning**. There are always new and exciting advances in the fields of medicine and psychology that a mental health clinician should remain aware of in order to provide the most competent and evidence-based care for their patients. Memberships on medical and psychology organizations' list servs (Society of Pediatric Psychology, Cystic Fibrosis Foundation, etc.), attending regional and national conferences, auditing graduate classes, pursuing continuing education opportunities, and maintaining both formal and informal consultative relationships are wonderful ways clinicians can stay on top of the ever-evolving research literature. As research expands to become more representative of ever-changing demographics, clinicians must

Sample Pediatric Psychology Intake Template

Referred by:

1) Presenting Problem (how long, when it start, how frequent):

2) Patient Past medical history (broken bones, surgery, illness):

3) Patient Medical:

Diagnosis	Date of Diagnosis	Treatment Regimen/Surgeries

    a. Knowledge/Skills related to treatment regimen

    b. Adherence concerns

    c. Transition to independence with treatment regimen

    d. Comfort discussing diagnosis with peers and medical providers

4) Family Medical and Psychiatric History:

Diagnosis	Date of Diagnosis	Treatment Regimen/Surgeries

5) Developmental:

    a. Pregnancy/ Complications

    b. Temperament

Figure 1.1 Sample pediatric psychology intake template.

  c. Developmental milestones

  d. Pubertal development

  e. Eating/Weight

    Current height/weight: BMI:

    Recent change in height/weight?

    How feel about weight/body size?

    Any restricting/purging/binging/compensatory behaviors?

6) <u>Patient Past/Current Psychiatric:</u>
  a. Medications

  b. Outpatient care

  c. Hospitalizations

  d. Self-harm/violence/suicide

  e. History of abuse/trauma

7) <u>Heath Promotion:</u>
  a. Typical exercise pattern

  b. Cigarettes/e-cigarettes/smoking

  c. Alcohol use

  d. Illicit drugs

  e. Reckless driving, wearing seat belt

  f. Vaccinations

  g. Sexual activity/contraception

8) <u>Social:</u>
  a. People in household

Figure 1.1 (*cont.*)

      b. Relationships with people in household

      c. Stress in household/family environment (marital conflict/financial difficulties)

9) Hobbies/Extracurricular Activities:

10) Education:
      a. School: Grade:

      b. Current grades/academic performance

      c. IEP/504

      d. Special services at school

      e. Behavior problems/suspension

      f. Current academic performance

      g. Prior academic performance

      h. Relationship to teacher

      i. Relationship with peers

11) Legal Issues/Interaction with Child Protective Services

Current Psych:
      a. Appetite
      b. Sleep
      c. Crying
      d. Mood (happy, sad, angry, okay)
      e. Self-esteem/self-concept
      f. Fatigue
      g. Anhedonia
      h. Feel lonely
      i. Motivation
      j. Anxiety
      k. SI/HI
      l. Hallucinations/Paranoia
      m. OCD

      Describe Typical Day:

      Goals for Treatment

Figure 1.1 (*cont.*)

make reading the research literature a priority in order to ensure that their patients are accessing the most evidence-based care.

Partnering with families, medical organizations, and other medical providers are not the only critical partnerships that must be developed and maintained by mental health clinicians working with children and adolescents with medical issues. An important partnership is forming relationships with individuals "in the know" in order to **have an awareness of community resources**. There are numerous resources available for children with medical conditions that can help serve the psychosocial needs of patients and families. Children's hospitals and pediatric specialty medical clinics tend to have a wide swath of resources available for members of the community, including resources such as information about college scholarships, disease-specific summer camps, and parent support groups. In particular, it may be helpful to reach out to social workers embedded in specialist clinics given their knowledge of local resources and to help enhance future collaboration between providers. Grassroots medical organizations are also superb ways to learn more about community resources that may be pertinent to providing overall family support that goes beyond just the provision of therapeutic support for the pediatric patient.

Based on this writer's experiences, the second theme of "normalization" appears to arise at some point during at least one clinical interaction with most patients. Clinicians should be mindful that most children and adolescents with a medical (and/or a psychiatric) condition will at some point feel "different" or "not normal" in comparison to their peers without their particular condition. The implicit, and even explicit, message that should undergird these clinical interactions is the message that "**You are unique and different, as is everyone.**" This message can be further strengthened by being mindful of using language that conveys that the patient is seen for who they are as a person, rather than as their illness.

The **power of language** can be identified by the following change in a description of the same patient as "Katie, a volleyball player with epilepsy" as opposed to "Katie, the epileptic." This nuance not only is important for the patient hearing the description, but also helps to prevent the clinician from becoming clinically detached and unmindful of the uniqueness of each patient, regardless of similar symptomology with other patients. This emphasis on the uniqueness of each patient rather than their diagnosis can help to serve as an important model for how medical providers can actively develop rapport and convey respect during interactions with or about patients.

As part of the awareness of the theme of "normalization," it is also important to be aware of typical developmental challenges that can occur within a medical context. In particular, adolescents are developmentally tasked with learning to individuate and gain autonomy from their parents. As such, "typical" adolescent behavior can include some growing pains related to difficulty with being "adult enough" to manage their treatment regimen consistently when responsibility is first transferred to the adolescent. This "treatment nonadherence" can be determined by clinicians as being either **pathological or developmentally appropriate** given that clinician's understanding of the child's developmental stage and chronological age and, thus, will require different interventions or strategies for assistance. Most parents will wonder at some point or another whether their child's behavior is "typical," and it is good clinical practice for a clinician to be strongly grounded in developmental theory in order to answer accurately whether that child's behavior is developmentally appropriate.

Similarly, when patients exhibit frustrating behavior that tests the patience of even the best of clinicians, it is important to **validate and normalize the underlying emotion, if not the behavior**. For instance, one can validate a teenager's frustration with having to perform lengthy air clearance techniques on a daily basis with cystic fibrosis, even if they are not able to validate or reinforce the appropriateness of the resultant behavior (i.e., skipping treatments due to feelings of frustration). Likewise, a clinician can provide a safe haven for parents to discuss their frustrations and fears about a teenager's lack of adherence to important medical regimens, without reinforcing some parents' innate desire to be overprotective of their child.

The third theme of "fundamentals" refers to the necessity of remembering the basics of psychotherapy despite the complexity of medical information that will be part of a patient's history. While it is easy to become solely focused on the medical aspects of a patient's condition, clinicians should also be mindful to **utilize fundamental therapeutic interventions** from child and adolescent psychotherapy to address common developmental concerns that may be co-occuring with the medical condition. Specifically, it can be easy to fixate on the goal of helping a child improve their pulmonary functioning or reduce their blood glucose by emphasizing treatment adherence, when it may be as important (or more important) to first begin with working on positive parenting strategies, improving family communication, or other "typical" child psychotherapy interventions. Fundamental child psychotherapy strategies and interventions are at the root of pediatric psychology and should not be forgotten despite the allure of responding to a medical team's most pressing medical-related concern.

In addition to remaining cognizant of utilizing core child psychotherapy interventions, mental health clinicians should help patients and families identify and subsequently utilize their unique strengths. This **search for strengths** may be harder for some families than others, given that many families present to psychotherapy when they are in the midst of chaos rather than when they are "at their best." For some patients, it may be helpful to just highlight the fact that they showed up to the appointment despite logistical barriers and are willing to engage in a discussion with a stranger about what is not working. Even in the event of court-mandated psychotherapy, each patient and family brings their own set of strengths. It may be just that the clinician's viewpoint of what constitutes a perceived strength or aptitude needs to be adjusted based on each patient's situation and context.

As part of this search for strengths, the patient and family's most basic needs and concerns may come to light, which is critical information necessary for treatment planning. Many of the challenges faced by patients and their families may not be encountered by their gainfully employed mental health provider, such as the ability to pay for necessary medications or having consistent access to reliable transportation to appointments. As such, **consider Abraham Maslow's hierarchy of needs** (1970). When working with children and adolescents with medical concerns, ensure (to the extent possible) that basic needs are being met or at least considered as part of the treatment planning process, as inadequate food, shelter, and medical supplies may prevent adherence to even the most well-crafted treatment plan. For example, a family can be as motivated as humanly possible to adhere to an advised treatment regimen, but all of the motivation in the world cannot overcome a lack of resources to consistently buy needed medical supplies or to consistently attend appointments. Some families may be embarrassed to discuss these barriers or concerns, so it may be advisable to normalize these barriers as common concerns for many of the patients and families in one's clinical practice.

The fourth theme of "confidentiality" is particularly pertinent in a pediatric psychology context as clinicians may encounter ethical dilemmas that were not typically discussed or presented during their training in traditional graduate programs. In working with adolescent (and occasionally pre-adolescent) patients, it can be extremely difficult for clinicians to **balance the confidentiality and safety concerns of adolescents engaged in high-risk behaviors**. To prevent patients and parents from perceiving the breaking or disclosure of confidential information as a "breach of trust," it may be helpful for these concerns to be addressed in the initial intake session and during ensuing therapy sessions so that both the patient and the parent(s) are aware of how the clinician will handle the balance of confidentiality and safety regarding high-risk behaviors such as sexual activity, smoking cigarettes, illicit drug use, or risky driving practices.

For instance, some clinicians might break confidentiality only when they felt safety was threatened via unprotected sexual intercourse and may not break confidentiality if the patient is utilizing safe sexual practices. These "gray area" judgment calls should of course depend on relevant ethical principles, state licensing guidelines, the client's developmental and chronological age, and the clinician's clinical judgment; however, in the event that is not explicitly addressed, it may be helpful for an agreement to be made with each family with specific scenarios utilized to help illustrate the clinician's decision-making process with regard to risky behaviors that may be engaged in by patients. This can help to prevent a perceived "breach of trust" later on in psychotherapy by either the adolescent or parent and help both the patient and parent be more comfortable with the clinician's ethical decision-making regarding the balance of safety and confidentiality.

Similarly, decisions about what can and should be shared with medical teams and academic personnel should be an ongoing discussion that begins in the initial intake session. Depending on the context of the psychological service being provided (e.g., care from a private practice clinician versus care provided by an embedded member of a medical multidisciplinary team), there may be significant differences in how clinicians **maintain confidentiality related to mental health issues while also working collaboratively with the medical team**. This can proactively be addressed during the initial consult session with discussions about what information the clinician can (and should) relay to medical members in order to help facilitate collaborative care, such as a patient's depression interfering with their motivation for treatment adherence. Just as importantly, specific attention should also paid to what the clinician and/or family may not feel is relevant information for the medical team, such as a parent's prior and successful treatment for substance abuse twenty years ago. As psychotherapy progresses, this balance of information should continue to be revisited to ensure that there is consistent communication with the medical team that also considers the patient and family's right of confidentiality.

Summary

In the world of pediatric psychology, there is great breadth to the type of populations and concerns that are addressed, as pediatric psychologists' work may span from working with children with typical development to children with developmental disabilities. Most clinical work across these populations typically focuses on helping children with medical needs or other concerns that are not primarily psychiatric in nature. With this emphasis, pediatric psychologists practice in a variety of settings, ranging from serving as embedded members of multidisciplinary teams in hospital settings to psychologists in private practice providing outpatient treatment.

Similar to traditional mental health psychotherapy, psychologists must be aware of ethical situations that tend to arise as part of working with children and adolescents with medical problems, including but not limited to an adolescent's involvement in medical decision-making, the balancing of patient confidentiality and patient safety for adolescents engaging in risky behaviors, and the decision of when or if a clinical situation is suspicious for medical neglect. For many pediatric psychologists, Bronfenbrenner's ecological systems theory, which recognizes a factor's level of influence based on proximity to the child, and social-cognitive theory, which posits that behavior change is associated with one's belief about the outcome and belief in their abilities, are foundational principles that undergird their work.

Based on the recognition of the need for more diverse and representative research, future research in pediatric psychology will most likely focus on the creation and utilization of culturally sensitive therapies. Additionally, an emphasis on health promotion, early intervention, and prevention rather than chronic disease management will most likely achieve prominence within the future research literature.

Whether or not clinicians have received training in pediatric psychology, it may be helpful to be aware of hard-earned "tips and tricks" garnered from the daily life of a pediatric psychologist (see Table 1.1). The common themes of partnership, normalization, fundamentals, and confidentiality are all themes in pediatric psychology that underscore the importance of creating and maintaining productive relationships, remembering developmental norms for differing clinical presentations, emphasizing the fundamentals of child psychotherapy in the midst of complex medical presentations, and remaining cognizant of the ways in which confidentiality is a factor in the therapeutic process.

Table 1.1 "Golden nuggets" for clinical practice

Theme	Tip/Strategy
Partnership	Help the patient by helping the family.
	Develop a working relationship with medical team members.
	"When you don't know, ask!"
	Never stop learning.
	Be aware of community resources.
Normalization	"You are normal."
	Power of language.
	Pathological or developmentally appropriate?
	Validate the emotion, if not the behavior.
Fundamentals	Remember the fundamentals of child and adolescent psychotherapy.
	Search for strengths.
	Consider Maslow's hierarchy of needs.
Confidentiality	Transparency about balancing confidentiality and safety of adolescents.
	Mental health confidentiality and the medical team.

References

Aylward, B., Bender, J., Graves, M., Roberts, M., Roberts, M., & Steele, R. (2009). Historical developments and trends in pediatric psychology. In *Handbook of Pediatric Psychology*, 4th ed. (pp. 3–18). New York: Guilford Press.

Bandura, A. (2004). Health promotion by social cognitive means. *Health Education and Behavior, 31*(12), 143–164.

Clay, D., Mordhurst, M., & Lehn, L. (2002). Empirically supported treatments in pediatric psychology: where is the diversity? *Journal of Pediatric Psychology, 27*(4), 325–337.

Department of Health Services. (2016). State of Wisconsin Rights of Children and Adolescents in Outpatient Mental Health Treatment. Retrieved December 18, 2018, from www.dhs.wisconsin.gov/publications/p2/p20470b.pdf.

Kenny, T. (1975). Pediatric psychology: a reflective approach. *Pediatric Psychology, 3*(4), 8.

Kirschman, K. & Karazsia, B. (2014). The role of pediatric psychology in health promotion and health prevention. In M. Roberts, B. Aylward, & Y. Wu (eds.), *Clinical Practice in Pediatric Psychology* (pp. 3–16). New York: Guilford Press.

Maslow, A. (1970). *Motivation and Personality.* New York: Harper and Row.

McCabe, M. (1995). Involving children and adolescents in medical decision making: developmental and clinical considerations. *Journal of Pediatric Psychology, 21*(4), 505–516.

McQuaid, E. & Barakat, L. (2012). Introduction to Special Section: Advancing Research on the Intersection of Families, Culture, and Health Outcomes. *Journal of Pediatric Psychology, 37*(8), 827–831.

Mesibov, G. (1990). What is special about pediatric psychology. *Journal of Pediatric Psychology, 16*(3), 267–271.

Patenaude, A. (2003). Pediatric psychology training and genetics: what will twenty-first-century pediatric psychologists need to know. *Journal of Pediatric Psychology, 28*(2), 135–145.

Rae, W., Sullivan, J., Razo, N., George, C., & Ramirez, E. (2002). Adolescent health risk behavior: when do pediatric psychologists' break confidentiality? *Journal of Pediatric Psychology, 27*(6), 541–549.

Roberts M., Aylward, B., & Wu, Y. (2014). Overview of the field. In M. Roberts, B. Aylward, & Y. Wu (eds.), *Clinical Practice in Pediatric Psychology* (pp. 3–16). New York: Guilford Press.

Roberts, M., Canter, K., & Odar, C. (2012). Commentary: a call to action to secure the future of pediatric psychology – resonating to the points of Rozensky & Janicke (2012). *Journal of Pediatric Psychology, 37*(4), 369–375.

Spirito, A., Brown, R., D'Angelo, E., Delamater, A., Rodrigue, J., & Siegel, L. (2003). Society of Pediatric Psychology Task Force Report: Recommendations for the Training of Pediatric Psychologists. *Journal of Pediatric Psychology, 28*(2), 85–98.

White, S. (1991). A developmental history of the Society of Pediatric Psychology. *Journal of Pediatric Psychology, 16*(4), 395–410.

Wilson, D. & Lawson, H. (2009). Health promotion in children and adolescents. In M. Roberts & R. Steele (eds.), *Handbook of Pediatric Psychology*, 4th ed. (pp. 603–617). New York: Guilford Press.

Recommended Websites, Books, and Other Resources

Professional Organizations

Society of Pediatric Psychology – Division 54 of the American Psychological Association, www.societyofpediatricpsychology.org/

Professional Journals

Clinical Practice in Pediatric Psychology, www.societyofpediatric,psychology.org/node/193

Journal of Pediatric Psychology, www.societyofpediatricpsychology.org/node/192

Professional Publications

Maruish, M. (ed.). (2018). *Handbook of Pediatric Psychological Screening and Assessment in Primary Care.* New York: Routledge.

Rapoff, M. (2010). *Adherence to Pediatric Medical Regimens*, 2nd ed. New York: Springer US.

Roberts, M. & Steele, R. (eds.). (2018). *Handbook of Pediatric Psychology*, 5th ed. New York: Guilford Press.

Roberts, M., Aylward, B., & Wu, Y. (eds.). (2014). *Clinical Practice in Pediatric Psychology.* New York: Guilford Press.

Spirito, A. & Kazak, A. (2006). *Effective and Emerging Treatments in Pediatric Psychology.* New York: Oxford University Press.

2

Working with Young Children with Medical Concerns

2.1 Prenatal and Perinatal Medical Concerns

When identifying oneself as a mental health provider for children and adolescents, many clinicians may question the need to be informed about parental concerns prior to or immediately following birth. "I'm a child clinician – I don't work with adults" is a common response that may arise when discussing the need for awareness and information about prenatal and perinatal medical care. However, given the role that these early periods play in a child's later development, it behooves child and adolescent clinicians to be aware of the current research in this area so that they are in a better position to guide the parents of children they may already be working with, as well as to have a better understanding of how these early experiences may have impacted their current patients.

In particular, prenatal maternal mental health has long been associated with infant outcomes (Dollberg et al., 2016). Regarding prenatal maternal mental health, high anxiety has been linked with poorer parent–infant interactions (Parfitt et al., 2013). Of interest is that while many people may be aware of the impact that maternal mental health postpartum may have on a child, there is now evidence that this heightened anxiety occurring prior to birth has implications for parent–infant interactions.

Research has also consistently substantiated the impact of postpartum depression on infant development as approximately 29% of mothers with postpartum depression may exhibit an impaired mother–infant relationship (Brockington et al., 2001). This awareness of the role of early relationships is not only important for later infant development, but also important given that poor parent–infant relationships are linked with a greater risk of child abuse and neglect (Scannapieco & Connell-Carrick, 2005).

When working with families of children where the patient's mother is newly post-partum, a mental health clinician can assist in the overall care of their patient by helping to screen mothers for postpartum depression. While many parents may at first balk at discussing their own mental health at their "child's appointment," psychoeducation about the impact of parental mental health on their child's health can help to provide context for why this type of screening is important for the identified patient's overall care.

The Edinburgh Postnatal Depression Scale is a user-friendly scale that takes approximately 5 minutes to administer and has been well validated as an empirically supported measure (Cox et al., 1987; Boyce et al., 1993). For convenience, this questionnaire is available in the "Reproducible Resources" section at the end of this chapter. Once depression has been identified as an area of concern, a clinician must first perform a comprehensive risk assessment to ensure the safety of the mother and child, including follow-up questions regarding whether the mother is experiencing any thoughts of harming the baby, which can be a symptom seen in disorders such as postpartum depression, psychosis, and obsessive-compulsive disorder.

Should a mother be assessed as being a danger to herself or others, the clinician should follow their organization's policies as well as state law with regard to disclosing medical information to prevent harm to mother or child. For mothers not at imminent risk and who are assessed as being safe to engage in outpatient psychotherapy, cognitive behavioral therapy or interpersonal therapy for depression is recommended given its evidence of effectiveness for postpartum depression (Elkin et al., 1989). For assistance with assessing the nature of the mother–infant relationship, readers can utilize the Postpartum Bonding Questionnaire (Brockington et al., 2006). This self-rating scale and answer key is also available in the "Reproducible Resources" section at the end of this chapter.

In addition to helping pediatric patients by assisting in the provision of assessment and referrals for parental depression, identifying parental anxiety early in a child's life can help provide early indicators of a mother's perception of their child as being particularly vulnerable and, subsequently, modifying their parenting style due to this perception. For example, elevated anxiety is particularly prevalent in the mothers of premature babies, and maternal anxiety on discharge from the neonatal intensive care unit has been found to be predictive of higher perception by the mother of their child's vulnerability (Allen et al., 2004).

So, why is this important for child clinicians working with these children years later? While this perception of greater vulnerability may not intuitively seem to be a risk factor for future adverse outcomes at first glance, research has shown that if children are perceived by their mothers as being particularly vulnerable, preschoolers who were born premature are at risk for "vulnerable child syndrome" (Estroff et al., 1994). It has been posited due to this perception of vulnerability that parents may be less likely to set developmentally appropriate limits, which in turn may lead to future concerns, such as internalizing problems (Green & Solnit, 1964; Estroff et al., 1994).

2.2 Young Children and Routine Medical Interventions

Based on current immunization practices, children "may receive as many as 20 shots by 2 years of age and up to 5 shots in a single visit" (Farren & McEwen, 2004). Although mental health clinicians are not responsible for the actual administration of vaccines, mental health professionals can serve as an invaluable resource by implementing psychological interventions that help to minimize use of pharmacological interventions (e.g., sedation) for immunizations (Blount et al., 2003).

This assistance with distress related to this and similar procedures is important for clinicians who work with children given that the fear of needles is implicated in future health care adherence (Blount et al., 2003). Although pediatric psychologists may have the opportunity to actually be present during the administration of immunizations in some health care settings, traditionally trained mental health clinicians can significantly help in non-health care settings with the use of outpatient cognitive behavioral therapy that emphasizes breathing and relaxation exercises, positive self-talk, and behavioral rehearsal (Blount et al., 2003).

Although as a general rule most children respond well when developmentally appropriate information is provided and when the child's attention is manipulated away when the painful procedure is actually occurring, protocols for how to assist a child with pain management will vary based on the patient's age, temperament, and other factors (Blount et al., 2003). In addition to these factors, it is important for clinicians to consider the developmental age of the child when the target of the intervention is procedural pain management, as children who are younger or are delayed developmentally may benefit more from concrete interventions (e.g., distraction), while older children or more developmentally advanced children can utilize more abstract techniques (e.g., imagery) (Welkon et al., 2009). A basic recommendation for assisting with procedural pain management that appears to be consistent regardless of age and individual factors is the importance of providing specific and timely information that focuses on describing what will occur and what the child may experience during the procedure (Blount et al., 2003).

Some research supports the idea that it is advisable to also provide parental training related to a painful procedure in pediatric care, as parents' responses to a child's medical procedure can significantly impact the child's distress (Cohen et al., 2002). As anyone who has watched children interacting with their parents for any length of time has probably observed, children often look to their parents for cues on how to respond during a situation in which they are unsure of how to respond or react. For example, when a child falls on the playground and "skins" their knee, they often will look to their parent to see if they were watching and, if so, how the parent responds to their fall. If the parent remains calm and otherwise verbally or non-verbally relays the message to their child that "they're okay," the child will often treat the fall as less distressing than if the parent had shown their own fear and rushed over to the child hurriedly. Similarly, parents can assist in ensuring that painful procedures are as minimally distressing as possible by showing a similar reaction when their child looks to them for cues on how to respond.

During a painful procedure, it is advisable for the clinicians or parent to manipulate the child's attention away from the painful stimuli via distraction, with the most effective distraction techniques appearing to be when more than one sensory faculty of the patient is engaged (Welkon et al., 2009). Given this information, clinicians can help patients and parents prepare for anticipated procedures by identifying toys or activities that the patient naturally finds engaging (e.g., a game on cell phone or tablet) and accordingly having a mock "dress rehearsal" of the procedure prior to the actual procedure taking place.

During the "dress rehearsal," clinicians can help to reduce the patient's anticipatory distress by (1) providing developmentally appropriate information about the procedure, (2) clarifying any misconceptions that the patient may have and discussing expectations of the patient's role and the roles of medical providers that will be present, (3) having the patient "practice" engaging with the fun identified game/activity while the clinician "performs" the procedure, (4) modeling for the parent how to provide instructions to the child in a calm and slow voice, and (5) helping the patient to identify their planned reward/reinforcement following the completion of the procedure. This "dress rehearsal" is important in that it helps the pediatric patient have a basic understanding of what to expect, while also helping the patient to look forward to the reward they will have earned following successful completion of the procedure.

Clinical Vignette: "No Needles!"

Amy is a 6-year-old African American female who is currently in treatment with Dr. B for separation anxiety. In session today, Amy's mother noted that Amy has been having sleeping problems and has exhibited a significantly decreased appetite after finding out that she has to receive her flu shot at her next appointment with her pediatrician in one month. When asked about how she feels about the next pediatrician's appointment, Amy yells, "No needles!" and refuses to say anything further. When asked how the patient's mother has handled vaccinations in the past at the doctor's office, Amy's mother reports that she does not tell Amy until the last minute and then usually ends up "holding her down" at the doctor's office until the vaccine has been administered by the nurse.

Dr. B thanks Amy and her mother for notifying her of this noteworthy change since the previous session and outlines a treatment plan to help prepare Amy for her upcoming vaccination. Dr. B spends time providing psychoeducation to Amy's mother about the use of parental modeling and distraction to help Amy during the procedure, as well as the use of systematic exposure to the feared stimulus to help Amy become desensitized to her fear of needles. For homework, Dr. B assigns Amy and her mother the task of bringing in Amy's favorite doll and any of her favorite toys or games to the next session.

At the next session, Dr. B uses a medical doll named Bella to show Amy what to expect when she receives her flu vaccination. While Dr. B is "administering" the vaccine to the doll, Amy becomes tearful and yells, "Now Bella will be like Mikey!" When queried, Amy's mother identified that Mikey is Amy's cousin who has been diagnosed with autism spectrum disorder with accompanying intellectual and language impairments. Amy's mother then turned to Amy asked, "Why do you think Bella will be like Mikey?" Amy said, "I heard Mikey's mom say that Mikey got sick after he got a shot and that's why he has the autism." Amy's mother turned to Dr. B and explained that her sister had been vocal in blaming Mikey's diagnosis on having received his regular vaccinations and that Amy must have overheard her sister talking to her. When asked about what she thinks will happen if she gets a flu shot, Amy stated, "I'll become like Mikey and won't be able to stay in the same class with my friends."

Dr. B spoke briefly with Amy's mother and confirmed that the mother did not share her sister's misconception that vaccines were associated with autism spectrum disorder. As such, the session then focused on providing a developmentally appropriate explanation that Bella (and Amy) would not "get" autism from a shot. After Amy appeared satisfied with this explanation, the session focused on having Amy "practice" distracting herself with her games while being "administered" a shot by Dr. B, and then subsequently identifying a specific reward she would like to earn for receiving her flu shot.

Common or routine interventions or procedures that can be distressing for pediatric patients and their families may also include pill swallowing, as some researchers estimate that approximately half of their pediatric participants are unable to swallow a standard-sized pill or small capsule (Polaha et al., 2008). When working with children who have significant difficulty with pill swallowing, it is important to determine whether there are underlying medical factors contributing to this difficulty swallowing oral medication or whether a traumatic experience from choking has led to avoidant behavior on the part of the child as part of a traumatic reaction (Slifer, 2014). This avoidant reaction may begin after a child has difficulty swallowing a pill and then becomes fearful of having a similar experience in the future when swallowing pills, and thus begins to exhibit a conditioned response. Even if there was not a traumatic experience related to choking when trying to swallow a pill, some children may struggle with swallowing pills due to a disagreeable taste or other factors.

PILL-SWALLOWING LEARNING TIPS

- Model the pill-swallowing behavior for the child with the smallest placebo.

- Sit up straight; note the level position of your head and neck.

- Place the pill on the middle of your tongue and drink water.

- Show your child that your mouth is empty and that the pill has been swallowed. Tell your child to practice.

- Your child places the pill on his or her tongue and drinks water. Say, "Take a big gulp of water."

- If the pill is swallowed, praise your child's success ("You did it!"). He or she is given no rewards (stickers, money, tokens).

- Use short, repetitive commands ("Sit up straight," "keep your head straight," "put the pill in the middle of your tongue," and "drink the water").

- Be positive about and impressed by your child's new skill.

- Use the placebos (one per day) given to you to help your child swallow at home. This applies only if training is conducted over an extended period of time.

- If your child has any problems at home swallowing the placebo, you should make sure that your child is following the guidelines.

- Do nothing else to prompt pill swallowing.

- After successfully swallowing the placebos at home for 1–2 weeks, your child can be assumed to have mastered the task and be able to swallow pills for medical treatment.

Cruz-Arrieta E. *Primary Psychiatry.* Vol 15, No 7. 2008.

Figure 2.1 Pill swallowing learning tips. Reprinted from "Pill swallowing training: a brief pediatric oncology report," by Eduvigis Cruz-Arrieta of Columbia University. From E. Cruz-Arrieta, 2008, *Primary Psychiatry, 15*(7), 49–53. Copyright 2018 by E. Cruz-Arrieta

If the patient appears to be exhibiting a conditioned response to pill swallowing, a common intervention is to have the child sequentially swallow larger and larger pieces of candy, with immediate reinforcement provided to the child as they successfully work through each step (Meltzer et al., 2006). Before beginning this intervention, it is advisable that the clinician enlists the parent's support and focus on helping to prepare the parent to use behavioral strategies for pill swallowing and to emphasize the importance of parental modeling of pill swallowing (Cruz-Arrieta, 2008). See Figure 2.1 for tips for clinicians to share with parents on how to seamlessly incorporate modeling pill swallowing for their children.

2.3 Pediatric Medical Traumatic Stress

Pediatric medical traumatic stress can be defined as "a set of psychological and physiological responses of children and their families to pain, injury, serious illness, medical procedures, and invasive or frightening treatment experiences" (National Child Traumatic Stress Network, n.d.). It is important to emphasize that the designation of an event involving medical traumatic stress should be based on the patient's subjective experience, as an event may be perceived as traumatic by one child but not by another child. This phenomenon is similar to how different members of a single military unit can experience the same distressing event, but only some military members may go on to develop acute stress disorder or posttraumatic stress disorder.

Following a traumatic injury, symptoms of pediatric medical traumatic stress symptoms are observed in approximately 22–42% of pediatric patients and approximately 10–22% of parents within the first month following the injury (Price et al., 2016). Special attention should be considered when young children with comorbid psychiatric concerns experience acute medical interventions (Souders et al., 2002). This attention is warranted given the need not only to manage symptoms associated with premorbid psychiatric conditions (e.g., autism), but also to assess and help prevent medical pediatric traumatic stress given that preexisting conditions place them at greater risk for posttraumatic stress disorder (Daviss et al., 2000; Souders et al., 2002).

Medical pediatric traumatic stress is an issue that can be pertinent to all patients given the "right" circumstances, and clinicians should be particularly attentive when working with patients with autism spectrum disorder (ASD). This vigilance for medical traumatic stress and ASD is warranted in stressful situations given that the prevalence rate of ASD is increasing and the nature of some of the symptoms associated with ASD, such as deficits in social skills and communication, may exacerbate stress during an already stressful situation for families (Scarpinato et al., 2010). This need for awareness about working with patients with ASD with medical concerns/events is particularly important since ASD has high comorbidity with other medical disorders (Rattaz et al., 2013). In addition to having higher rates of comorbidity with other medical conditions, patients with ASD "might be confronted with painful situations more frequently because of challenging behaviors (e.g. agitation and self-injury)" (p. 2007).

When working with parents of children with ASD who are facing a planned medical intervention that may be perceived as stressful, clinicians can assist parents in talking with medical staff in order to provide individualized information about their child. In particular, an autism care plan can help provide medical providers with information specific to each patient to help address their individualized needs (Broder-Fingert et al., 2016). In a recent pilot study, parents of patients with autism care plans identified that they had a more positive overall hospital experience and perceived medical staff as being more attentive to their child's needs associated with their autism diagnosis (Broder-Fingert et al., 2016).

In addition to co-occurring psychiatric conditions serving as a risk factor for medical traumatic stress, research has indicated other factors that place a patient at greater risk of experiencing medical traumatic stress following a medical event. Factors that have been identified for posttraumatic stress symptoms following discharge from a pediatric intensive care unit are younger age on admission, increased number of invasive procedures, and increased medical acuity (Rennick et al., 2002).

For pediatric patients who have been identified as being at risk for medical traumatic stress based on the above factors, clinicians can help prepare patients and parents prior to planned medical interventions that may be perceived as traumatic for the patient or family. Clinicians can help parents utilize their hard-earned knowledge about their child to help reduce the possible distress by collaborating on the development of a plan for identifying the child's unique warning signs for distress, identifying "in the moment" soothing strategies, and communicating this information verbally and in written format to providers prior to the procedure. For example, clinicians can help to create a plan that identifies warning signs such as restlessness, not speaking, not maintaining eye contact, and other behavioral observations when a child is becoming distressed in order to help alert a medical staff member when to proceed slowly or pause to help the child regain composure.

In addition to focusing on prevention by being alert for a child's known early warning signs, clinicians can either help parents communicate with medical staff or speak with medical personnel directly regarding immediate management strategies. During stressful periods prior to and during painful procedures, it may be helpful for clinicians to coach parents to use simple one-step commands and give forced choices (e.g., "Would you like to sit in the chair or on my lap when you receive the vaccine?") to help manage externalizing behavior. Environmentally, clinicians can help parents and medical staff to decrease the overall sensory input that may exacerbate a stressful situation by dimming lights and reducing the overall noise level, or providing comfort via deep pressure from weighted blankets, soothing music, or a favorite toy.

These above strategies are basic guidelines that should be personalized based on each child's personality and developmental level. For the very young child under 2 years old, most interventions to help reduce stress during medical events and procedures should focus on distraction with noises, toys, and other external stimuli. As children grow to approximately 6 years old developmentally, strategies such as using a medical play doll to help children rehearse or visualize how procedures will occur may be helpful with regard to their comprehension of the medical procedure and overall coping. More complicated reward symptoms such as token economies may be particularly helpful when older children and adolescents' thought processes allow for more abstract thinking and a greater understanding of delayed rewards.

Clinicians can also assist parents in being aware of resources available at many pediatric hospitals for children such as requesting child life services, signing up for a preadmission tour, or receiving copies of social stories that can assist in preparing children for hospitalization. Child life services can be of particular assistance with helping children and adolescents with pain management via distraction techniques and other strategies (Alcock et al., 1985). Readers are encouraged to visit applicable websites in the "Recommended Websites, Books, and Other Resources" section at the end of this chapter for examples of resources that many pediatric hospitals can provide for children.

Not only are pediatric patients at risk for posttraumatic stress symptoms following medical events, but also family members of the identified patient. Traumatic stress symptoms are not solely restricted to being the psychological sequalae of a specific injury, but can also be observed in families following discharge from intensive care units. During an inpatient hospitalization, the patient, parents, and siblings are unexpectedly placed under acute stress for an undefined period of time in an unfamiliar and stimulating environment. Often without any warning, the lives of entire families are disrupted as families shift from making decisions about their regular days to suddenly making possibly life-altering situations in a stressful environment without the luxury of time or privacy. Parents of more than one child may have their level of stress exacerbated by also having to cope with caring for the unaffected child regarding both emotional and physical needs at a time when their own resources may be stretched.

Due to the overall potential impact of a medical event on an entire family system, it is advisable for clinicians to "check in" with pertinent members of the family when possible following a medical event to screen for any trauma-related symptoms that can arise as part of the sequelae of the initial injury or hospitalization. For many family members, the hospitalization itself does not allow for adequate time to process the event or its potential ramifications. Siblings may have been kept on a "need-to-know" basis and may have trouble understanding why family dynamics are changed or why their sibling is "different" from what they remember prior to the hospitalization. Clinicians can assist with helping parents to provide developmentally appropriate explanations for both siblings and patients regarding medical events, as well as assisting with providing evidence-based treatments for trauma as needed.

For further information about recommended interventions for assisting patients and families experiencing symptoms associated with pediatric medical traumatic stress, refer to the comprehensive toolkit created by the Medical Traumatic Stress Work Group of the National Child Traumatic Stress Network (n.d.) that is referenced in the "Recommended Websites, Books, and Other Resources" section.

Clinical Vignette: "Never Again!"

Mary is a 6-year-old Caucasian female with prior diagnoses of generalized anxiety disorder and cystic fibrosis. Six months ago, Mary was hospitalized for a cystic fibrosis–related pulmonary exacerbation. During that hospitalization, the patient had a peripherally inserted central catheter (PICC) line inserted at bedside to help with blood draws and medication administration. This was the first time that Mary had a PICC line placed at bedside, as she has previously had a PICC line placed while under sedation in the hospital's interventional radiology unit. During the placement of the PICC line at bedside, Mary became extremely agitated, which resulted in the PICC line placement requiring the physical assistance of multiple staff members.

Since the hospitalization, Mary has reported having nightmares about returning to the hospital and begins crying whenever she has had to attend her quarterly scheduled outpatient appointments at her pediatric cystic fibrosis clinic. Mary's father expresses concern about her reaction to appointments and is worried about her coping with future hospitalizations. A treatment plan is developed to help Mary learn relaxation skills in preparation for systemic exposure to fear-provoking stimuli to decrease her conditioned response to future outpatient medical appointments and hospitalizations.

Over the next several sessions, you provide psychoeducation to Mary and her father about pediatric medical traumatic stress and the use of sustained exposure in place of avoidant behavior in order to help decrease Mary's traumatic stress reaction, as well as the interconnectedness of her thoughts, physical symptoms, and behaviors in perpetuating this reaction. Sessions also focus on helping Mary learn relaxation and other coping skills for when she notices the onset of physiological arousal symptoms, such as elevated heart rate and increased respiratory activity.

Once Mary has learned these skills, you and Mary collaboratively create a fear hierarchy, with planned sequential exposures such as watching a video of a child in a hospital room receiving a PICC line, sitting in the waiting room of the cystic fibrosis clinic, attending a cystic fibrosis outpatient visit and receiving a flu vaccine, touring the hospital, and engaging in medical play with a teddy bear receiving a PICC line. After each completed exposure, Mary places a sticker on her fear hierarchy chart and receives a small toy. The final stage of the hierarchy is completed when Mary sits in a hospital bed and utilizes her relaxation skills when a PICC line is placed at bedside when she is hospitalized again several months later for a pulmonary exacerbation.

2.4 Feeding Concerns with Young Children

Many young children may struggle with feeding problems early in life, which if not corrected for some, can extend later on into school age and adolescence. This basic need of feeding oneself can be extremely stressful for parents due to the severity of the impact this can have on physical and mental health. This stress for families can be particularly acute given that feeding problems can lead to malnourishment and other adverse outcomes, and it is common for parents to experience feelings of guilt or shame that a child is not eating at a developmentally appropriate level. This guilt and shame may inadvertently impact how the parent interacts with the child, as it may cause the parent to change the way they feed their child. For example, many parents may cook meals for their child separate from the meals prepared for other family members due to their fear of malnutrition. This understandable response by the parent unfortunately only reinforces the control the child has and reinforces the food refusal.

Although the range and etiology of feeding disorders in young children varies greatly, a standard definition is that "pediatric feeding disorder is characterized by food refusal, disruptive mealtime behavior, rigid food preferences, suboptimal growth, and failure to master self-feeding skills commensurate with the child's developmental abilities" (Silverman & Begotka, 2018, p. 281). Typical feeding disorder behaviors that are seen clinically are behaviors such as food refusal, "pickiness" or significant food selectivity, and other behaviors that otherwise negatively impact physical health and psychosocial functioning (Lukens & Silverman, 2014).

Multifactorial causes have been identified as causing and/or exacerbating feeding disorders. Feeding disorders are particularly prevelant in patients with developmental concerns such as autism spectrum disorder and intellectual disability, as well as in patients with anatomical concerns and myriad medical concerns (e.g., tonal or muscle weakness, lung disease, prematurity). Psychosocial factors (e.g., cultural influences about feeding and financial concerns) and behavioral concerns have also been implicated in feeding disorders (e.g., learned feeding avoidance and sensory sensitivity) (Silverman & Tarbell, 2009; Morris et al., 2017).

Given the complexity and variety of feeding concerns, most interventions are multi-component in nature, with many of the interventions tending to be behaviorally oriented. Most interventions used by mental health clinicians tend to be behavioral interventions (e.g., shaping and contingency management), nutritional strategies (e.g., mealtime scheduling), and caregiver/parent training (Lukens & Silverman, 2014). Typical behavioral components employed by pediatirc psychologists in the context of feeding disorders include interventions that focus on creating a consistent environment for feeding, such as the same environment/room with consistently scheduled mealtimes, which can help prevent the "grazing" that negatively impacts the child's ability to recognize internal hunger cues. Mealtime schedules can help to promote hunger at appropriate times for meals and typically last about 20 minutes for children 5 and under. This duration changes to approximately 30 minutes for older children or if the child has oral-motor difficulties that may require the child to need extra time to eat safely (Silverman & Begotka, 2018).

In addition to helping parents set consistent mealtimes, it is also important for clincians to observe mealtimes in order to see what role parent reinforcement may be playing in perpetuating feeding difficulties or if there are other strategies that could be employed to improve the child's feeding concerns. It is very easy for parents to inadvertently reinforce maladptive feeding patterns due to frustration or a belief that they are appropriately responding to the child's cues. For example, parents may abruptly pull a spoon away from their child's mouth if the child does not immediately open their mouth or otherwise indicates a lack of interest. Although the parent may not realize it, they have inadvertently provided negative reinforcement by removing the aversive stimulus (i.e., spoon with food) based on the child's behavior. Thus, the child has now learned that when they do not want to accept a food, they only have to exhibit "behavior A" (e.g., shaking their head or not opening mouth) in order to prevent their parent from continuing to offer the non-preferred food.

Clinicians can help parents understand basic behavioral principles of conditioning by providing reinforcement strategies to help the child learn to eat new foods or to eat foods that they may not typically eat due to textures or other selective criteria (Lukens & Silverman, 2014). For many young children, their selective or "picky" eating significantly limits the range of foods they habitually consume, which can cause, at a minimum, significant stress on parents in trying to prepare separate meals for the child and can lead to significant nutritional deficiencies. Some children may eat a restricted range of foods with emphasis on certain types of textures, smells, or even specific brands of food. It is thought that this overall food acceptance may be impacted by modeling by parents and taste preferences influenced by genetics.

This type of feeding concern requires dedicated and consistent effort from parents in order to help utilize stimulus control methods to broaden the child's current meals to include new foods (Douglas, 2011). Clinicians can help parents systematically shape the patient's feeding behaviors by gradually moving from placing the new food against their child's lips, to accepting small bites before a child is allowed to eat the food they prefer, to increasing the size of the offered food (Douglas, 2011). During this work, it may be helpful to utilize a reward chart to help reinforce newly acquired behaviors as the shaping process continues.

In addition to shaping techniques, there are many other empirically supported feeding techniques that have been comprehensively described in work by Morris and colleagues (2017). Such strategies include stimulus fading, simultaneous presentation, and escape extinction. With stimulus fading, parents sequentially increase the size of the non-preferred food, such as putting larger and larger amounts of yogurt on a spoon once the child accepts the previous spoonful. Simultaneous presentation is another strategy that can be useful in which parents put a non-preferred food and preferred food on the same eating utensil at the same time, whereas escape extinction refers to the previously discussed strategy of not putting a utensil down when a child refuses until the child accepts the proferred utensil (Morris et al., 2017).

Overall, feeding disorders tend to be complex and may require coordinated interdisciplinary care that is outside the scope or resources of most outpatient mental health clincians. This delicate balance between ensuring medical stability and health while intervening with behavioral strategies is best performed when an experienced clinician is embedded within the support of an interdisciplinary team, including dieticians, physicians, speech-language pathologists, and other specialists, to help ensure safety when trying to change feeding behaviors.

It is particularly important for clinicians to know when to refer to a pediatric psychologist who specializes in feeding when the scope or severity of the feeding problem is beyond the individual clinician's experience and training. In particular, it may be advisable for traditionally trained clinicians to refer to a pediatric psychologist embedded within a multidisciplinary team when, in addition to feeding difficulites, the patient has a neurological or organic concern, developmental delay, nutritional deficiencies, malnutrition, and/or choking-swallowing problems.

Clinical Vignette: The Picky Eater

Ms. Paulette presents to your office with her son, Kevin, as a new patient after being referred by his pediatrician due to concerns about the limited range of foods that Kevin will eat, which are typically simple carbohydrates from a specific brand. In reviewing records from the pediatrician's office, it is clear that Kevin does not meet criteria for malnutrition or other imminent health concerns, but it is also clear that Ms. Paulette is distressed by constantly having to prepare meals for Kevin that are separate from the meals she prepares for other members of their family. Additionally, she reports frequently being embarrassed when she has to pack food for Kevin when he attends birthday parties and other events with his peer group of 5-year-olds, whom Ms. Paulette indicates do not exhibit the same severity of food selectivity.

Ms. Paulette reports that in addition to having been seen by the pediatrician, Kevin has also been evaluted by a speech-language pathologist who did not identify any oral-motor concerns or other factors that may be exacerbating his food selectivity. With this data in hand, you provide psychoeducation on the importance of consistency in implementing a behavioral management plan involving shaping to help Kevin broaden his current range of foods, which will require a significant time commitment from Ms. Paulette at mealtime. Ms. Paulette expresses her under-tanding of this plan and agrees to bring his preferred food to the next appointment, as well as a closely related type of food that Kevin does not currently eat willingly.

At the next appointment, Ms. Paulette and Kevin bring his preferred brand of crackers and a non-preferred brand of crackers of a similar but slightly different texture. Kevin is encouraged to eat a small piece of the non-preferred cracker prior to being allowed to eat his favorite cracker. Once Kevin has eaten the targeted piece of food, he is allowed to put a sticker on a chart. This sticker chart reinforces Kevin for trying new foods by giving him 5 minutes of extra time on his favorite video game after dinner each night for each sticker he earns that day. With this success, Ms. Paulette is urged to gradually increase the size of the target food over the next several days before implementing this same plan with a new target food.

Over the next several sessions, you continue to encourage Ms. Paulette's consistent efforts at mealtimes and Kevin's slow but steady progress in accepting new foods. By the end of the intervention, Kevin has significantly expanded the amount and variety of foods he will eat, and Ms. Paulette expresses her belief that she will be able to continue to expand his diet with the strategies she has learned from this intervention.

2.5 Toileting Concerns with Young Children

In the United States, toilet training typically occurs between 21 and 36 months of age, with males typically completing toilet training later than females (Choby & George, 2008). For many parents, toilet training can be a frustrating and difficult experience. This stress can be compounded by embarrassment for both the child and parent when a child continues to struggle with toilet training despite appearing to be developmentally ready. Difficulty with toilet training can be attributed to a range of different causes and factors, and thus requires careful assessment prior to the onset of any interventions.

In nocturnal enuresis, or "bedwetting" at night, it is common for a child's parent to have also struggled with this concern when they were children. Despite this family history of difficulty with noctural enuresis, this concern is rarely due to organic causes and typically will spontaneously remit as the child ages into adolescence (Shepard & Cox, 2018). Although this means that most children will be "cured" without requiring an official intervention, early intervention can help particularly when a child may be embarrassed and avoid certain activities, such as staying overnight at a friend's house or attending overnight camp, as result of a fear of having an "accident" away from home. Of interest, enuresis that occurs during the day tends to be more associated with compounding medical problems such as urinary tract abnormalities, and, therefore, close collaboration with a medical provider is recommended for comprehensive treatment (Mellon & McGrath, 2000). Regardless of whether enuresis occurs at night, during the day, or during both day and night, a thorough medical evaluation is recommended prior to the onset of behavioral treatment.

Once a patient has been medically assessed, a clinician can help a family utilize a urine alarm, which helps detect moisture on a child's clothing or mattress and alerts the child that enuresis has occurred. Urine alarms have been identified as the most effective intervention for nocturnal enuresis (Mellon & McGrath, 2000). Once a child has been alerted to the alarm, they are then tasked with going directly to the bathroom to void their bladder. With this practice, the child then begins to associate the feeling of a full bladder with the behavior of using the toilet. In conjunction with the use of a urine alarm, it can be helpful to use positive reinforcement for toileting, such as a sticker chart that can be used to help reinforce the child for their consisent engagement in toilet training. A sample chart has been provided for readers in the "Reproducible Resources" section.

Despite the efficacy of the urine alarm in treating nocturnal enuresis, clinicians should be mindful that this intervention can impart a significant amount of stress on families with regard to requiring significant time and energy to consistently implement. Clinicians may find it helpful to be transparent with families prior to the intervention about this reality in order to ensure that parents are fully ready to begin the intervention, rather than attempting the intervention and dropping out due to being unprepared for what was required.

When helping families intervene with nocturnal enuresis, clinicians may also want to recommend that the child decreases their fluid intake immediately before bed and to have scheduled times to use the toilet (Shepard & Cox, 2018). Furthermore, long-term remission of noctural enuresis has been shown to occur after several weeks through "dry bed training," which is a combination of behavioral interventions and the use of a urine alarm. With this training, the behavioral interventions focus on positive practice, where a child wakes to use the toilet despite lacking the urge to urinate, as well as cleanliness training, in which the child assists with cleaning linens and clothing after bedwetting occurs (Shepard & Cox, 2018).

Similar to enuresis, encopresis can be stressful and embarrassing for families and can cause added stress and work related to extra laundry from soiled bedding and reduced day care options. Unlike enuresis, a simultaneous medical and behavioral approach is typically recommended, as often encopresis can result from chronic constipation in which "walls of the rectum stretch to accommodate large amounts of retained stool (i.e. acquired mega-colon), causing reduced rectal tone and lessened urge to defecate" (Campbell et al., 2009, p. 485). For many children, their struggle with constipation and later encopresis is related to the paradoxical construction of the external anal sphincter during a bowel movement. A painful bowel movement may lead a child to paradoxically constrict their external anal sphincter, which leads to an incomplete bowel movement. As more feces build up, chronic constipation can ensue and is related to decreased rectal sensation and a weaker sphincter (McGrath et al., 2000).

An important component of clinically intervening with encopresis is the need for family education, as it is important to emphasize the physiological aspects of encopresis rather than labeling child as being "bad" or "doing this on purpose." Education about the role of constipation and the potential need for disimpaction or a "clean out" is important as well as education that the child may be ignoring the need to defecate due to fear of pain from previous instances where they have experienced pain in association with a bowel movement. Pain is a commonly reported symptom of constipation for many children, and is linked with other uncomfortable symptoms such as decreased appetite, rectal bleeding, rectal prolapse, and abdominal pain (McGrath et al., 2000). Clinicians should also collaborate with medical professionals in ensuring that the child receives resources abut how to increase regular bowel movements by increasing fluid and fiber intake and the possible use of medications (Wassom & Christopherson, 2014).

In research on the treatment for chronic constipation and fecal impaction, a combination of behavioral interventions and medical management has received empirical support. Research by Stark and colleages (1997) utilized a protocol in which parents and children were placed in separate groups and the parent group focused on psychoeducation about increasing toilet intake, toilet sitting, behavioral managment strategies (e.g., time-out and contracting), and medical management via increasing fiber intake and enema administration. The child group also received parallel psychoeducation at a more developmentally appropriate level, as well as being able to complete a sticker chart with a weekly reward for completing assigned tasks such as toilet sitting. By the end of this intervention, 86% of children had ceasing soiling (Stark et al., 1997).

In a similar study, researcher utilized laxatives plus enhanced toilet training as part of their intervention protocol (Cox et al., 1996). Laxatives were used to "clean out" the rectum and then the enhanced toilet training intervention utilized an incentive program for using the toilet. The therapist first modeled appropriate "form" for sitting on a portable toilet, as improper form can cause accidental constriction of the external anal sphincter. Approximately 15–30 minutes after eating, children were then tasked with sitting on a toilet for a total of 12 minutes. According to Cox and colleagues' protocol, the child sat on the toilet while engaging in a fun or otherwise relaxing activity before proceeding to 4 minutes of consciously tensing and relaxing their sphincter, and finally, to 4 minutes of actively attempting to have a bowel movement.

Overall, toileting concerns are a common concern for many young children that can be a source of significant stress and embarrassment for families. Depending on the concern, some families may choose to try to let their child "grow out of it," which may be successful for many cases of nocturnal enuresis. However, should toileting appear to impact patient self-esteem, cause family distress, be associated with medical concerns, or cause diurnal enuresis or encopresis, a combination of medical and behavioral interventions is recommended.

2.6 Sleeping Concerns with Young Children

In addition to feeding and toileting concerns, sleeping difficulties are common concerns for parents of young children. Research suggests that approximately 2–25% of young children between ages 1 and 5 will experience sleep disturbances, which typically include night awakenings and/or bedtime refusal (Mindell, 1999). This percentage appears to be higher with children with known psychiatric or neurodevelopmental problems. While undoubtedly stressful for the family, sleep concerns in young children are an important area for clinical intervention for other myriad reasons. Sleep problems can persist as a child gets older and can have negative implications for cognitive development, mood regulation, and quality of life (Mindell et al., 2006).

Similar to toileting and feeding concerns, most psychological interventions for pediatric sleep are behavioral. Behavioral interventions have even been found to be more effective in the long term than moderately effective sleep medications, whose efficacy diminishes once the patient stops taking them (Mindell, 1999). Psychoeducation about sleep has been found not only to be an important component of clinical interventions but also to help when used as part of prevention programs for parents both prenatally and within the first 6 months after birth. Typical psychoeducation focuses on not putting the baby to bed until they have become drowsy, having a consistent bedtime routine, as well as the provision of information about developmentally appropriate sleeping (Mindell, 1999).

Well-meaning parents can inadvertently reinforce poor sleeping habits by attempting to soothe their child by remaining with them in their room until they fall asleep or otherwise actively soothing them until the child sleeps. Poor sleeping habits can also be reinforced when parents immediately respond to night awakenings with these same efforts, which unfortunately prevents the child from learning to self-soothe on their own (Mindell & Durand, 1993).

In addition to psychoeducation, extinction has been established as an effective intervention technique for bedtime refusal. Simply put, extinction for bedtime refusal is when parents are tasked with ignoring their child's cries and tantrums once the child has been put to bed (Mindell, 1999). Although this technique is well known to be effective, it can be particularly difficult for parents to refrain from soothing their child when hearing their distress at night.

Given this difficulty, another form of extinction called graduated extinction may be less stressful for parents, and, thus, may promote greater adherence with the treatment regimen. In graduated extinction, parents are asked to wait for increasingly longer periods of time before checking on their child, such as waiting 10 minutes before checking on their child for a set duration of time and then waiting 15 minutes before intervening with their child. In research conducted by Lawton, France, and Blampied (1991), this graduated extinction occured after a set bedtime and bedtime routine were already in place. Parents then "checked in" with their child during the night as usual, with the time spent with each child tailored to each individual patient/participant. Every 4 days, the amount of time was reduced by one-seventh so that no "check ins" between bedtime and a predetermined wake time were allowed by day 28.

Some research has also supported the use of positive bedtime routines and faded bedtimes with response cost. As suggested by the name, positive bedtime routines focus on ensuring that the child enjoys quiet activities prior to a set bedtime. The strategy of faded bedtimes with response cost "involves taking the child out of bed for prescribed periods of time when the child does not fall asleep" (Mindell et al., 2006, p. 1266). When using this strategy, it is also important that bedtime is delayed until the child exhibits sleep cues, with the intent of gradually and consistently moving up their bedtime to the desired time.

Summary

Given what we know about the impact of prenatal maternal mental health on infant outcomes, it is important for all clinicians to help assess for any concerns that may potentially impact the future development of a child and the health of a parent. Clinicians who work with children and adolescents will often work with parents who are expecting or otherwise planning to grow their young families, and they can be integral in helping their current (and future) pediatric patients by assisting in providing assessment and referrals for parental mental health, particularly during the critical prenatal and postpartum periods.

As children mature and develop, they face numerous medical interventions such as vaccinations, minor surgeries (e.g., ear tube surgeries), and other procedures that may be distressing for young patients. Mental health clinicians can serve as an invaluable resource in the implementation of psychological interventions to help minimize the use of pharmacological interventions to alleviate acute anxiety and distress. For patients engaged in outpatient psychotherapy, cognitive behavioral therapy can help children and adolescents develop and learn skills such as diaphragmatic breathing and other relaxation exercises, positive self-talk, and behavioral rehearsal to help with coping with planned medical procedures. Older and more developmentally advanced children may benefit from more abstract techniques such as imagery or mindfulness, while younger children or children with developmental delays may benefit more from concrete interventions (e.g., distraction).

In addition to typical distress or anticipatory anxiety related to painful procedures, children may also experience distress related to being asked to learn to swallow "adult sized" pills as part of a medical regimen. When working with children who have significant difficulty with pill swallowing, it is important to determine whether there are underlying medical factors contributing to any difficulty the child exhibits in swallowing oral medication or whether a traumatic experience from choking has led to avoidant behavior. For most children, a common and effective intervention is to have the child sequentially swallow larger and larger pieces of candy, with immediate reinforcement provided to the child as they work through each step.

Despite the best efforts of parents, clinicians, and medical personnel, young children may experience medical traumatic stress as part of either routine care or life-saving emergency services. It is important to emphasize that the designation of an event involving medical traumatic stress should be based on the patient's subjective experience, even though clinicians should be aware of risk factors such as younger age on admission, increased number of invasive procedures, and increased medical acuity.

Many young children may struggle with feeding, toileting, and sleeping problems early in life, which can be extremely stressful for the entire family. For the most part, feeding, toileting, and sleeping interventions provided by mental health professionals tend to be behaviorally oriented. For all of these common concerns, clinical observation and psychoeducation are important components of treatment. For example, observation can help identify the role that inadvertent reinforcement may be playing in maintaining the target behavior.

When working with toileting concerns, clinicians should be mindful that, for the most part, most instances of nocturnal enuresis tend to resolve over time without intervention; however, the use of a urine alarm and other behavioral techniques can help alleviate distress or embarrassment that this concern may cause for the patient and family. Dissimilar to noctural enuresis, it is important for intervention to include simultaneous medical and behavioral approaches to occur in patients exhibiting difficulty with encopresis or daytime enuresis.

When intervening with sleeping difficulties with young children, exposure tends to be the most empirically supported treatment for bedtime refusal and nighttime awakenings. Given that this can be extremely distressing for parents to implement, graduated extinction and other behavioral interventions may be better suited for some parents.

Overall, for feeding, toileting, and sleeping concerns in young children, clinicians play a key role in providing parents with developmentally appropriate education and subsequent resources for intervention as needed.

References

Alberta Children's Hospital Research Institute. (2018). Better than a Spoonful of Sugar – How to Swallow Pills. Retrieved June 2, 2018, from http://research4kids.ucalgary.ca/pillswallowing.

Alcock, D., Feldman, W., Goodman, J., McGrath, P., & Park, J. (1985). Evaluation of child life intervention in emergency department suturing. *Pediatric Emergency Care, 1*, 111–115.

Allen, E., Manuel, J., Legault, C., Naughton, M., Pivor, C., & O'Shea, M. (2004). Perception of child vulnerability among mothers of former premature infants. *Pediatrics, 113*(2), 267–273.

Blount, R., Zempsky, W., Jaaniste, T., Evans, S., Cohen, L., Devine, K., & Zelter, L. (2003). Management of pediatric pain and distress due to medical procedures. In M. Roberts (ed.), *Handbook of Pediatric Psychology*, 3rd ed. (pp. 171–188). New York: Guilford Press.

Boston Children's Hospital. (2018). My Hospital Story. Retrieved June 9, 2018, from www.childrenshospital.org/patient-resources/family-resources/child-life-specialists/preparing-your-child-and-family-for-a-visit/my-hospital-story.

Boyce, P., Stubbs, J., & Todd, A. (1993). The Edinburgh Postnatal Depression Scale: validation for an Australian sample. *Australian and New Zealand Journal of Psychiatry, 27*, 472–476.

Brockington, I., Fraser, C., & Wilson, D. (2006). The Postpartum Bonding Questionnaire: a validation. *Archives of Women's Mental Health, 9*, 233–242.

Brockington, I., Oates, J., George, S., Turner, D., Vostanis, P., Sullivan, M., Loh, C., & Murdoch, C. (2001) A screening questionnaire for mother–infant bonding disorders. *Archives of Women's Mental Health, 3*, 133–140.

Brodert-Fingert, S., Shui, A., Ferrone, C., Iannuzzi, D., Cheng, E., Giauque, A., Connors, S., McDougle, C., Donelan, K., Neumeyer, A., & Kuhlthau, K. (2016). A pilot study of autism-specific care plans during hospital admissions. *Pediatrics, 137*(S2), e2015851R.

Campbell, L., Cox, D., & Borowitz, S. (2009). Elimination disorders. In M. Roberts & R. Steele (eds.), *Handbook of Pediatric Psychology*, 4th ed. (pp. 481–490). New York: Guilford Press.

Children's Hospital of Philadelphia. (2014). After the Injury. Retrieved June 9, 2018, from www.aftertheinjury.org/.

Choby, B. & George, S. (2008). Toilet training. *American Family Physician, 78*(9), 1059–1064.

Cohen, L., Bernard, R., & Greco, L. (2002). A child-focused intervention for coping with procedural pain: are parent and nurse coaches necessary? *Journal of Pediatric Psychology, 27*, 749–757.

Cox, D., Sutphen, J., Ling, W., Quillian, W., & Borowitz, S. (1996). Additive benefits of laxative, toilet training, and biofeedback therapies in the treatment of pediatric encopresis. *Journal of Pediatric Psychology, 21*(5), 659–670.

Cox, J., Holden, J., & Sagovsky, R. (1987). Detection of postnatal depression: development of the 10-item Edinburgh Postnatal Depression Scale. *British Journal of Psychiatry, 150*, 782–786.

Cruz-Arrieta, E. (2008). Pill-swallowing training: a brief pediatric oncology report. *Primary Psychiatry, 15*(7), 49–53.

Daviss, W., Mooney, D., Racusin, R., Ford, J., Fleischer, A., & McHugo, G. (2000). Predicting posttraumatic stress after hospitalization for pediatric injury. *Journal of* the American Academy of Child and Adolescent Psychiatry, 39(5), 576–583.

Dollberg, D., Rozenfeld, T., & Kupfermincz, M. (2016). Early parental adaptation, prenatal distress, and high-risk pregnancy. Journal of Pediatric Psychology, 41(8), 915–929.

Douglas, J. (2011). The management of selective eating in young children. In A. Southall & C. Martin (eds.), Feeding Problems in Children, 2nd ed. (pp. 174–187). Oxon: Radcliffe Publishing.

Elkin, I., Shea, M., Watkins, J., Imber, S., Sotsky, S., Collins, J., Glass, D., Pilkonis, P., Leber, W., Docherty, J., Fiester, S., & Parloff, M. (1989). National Institute of Mental Health Treatment of Depression Collaborative Research Program: general effectiveness of treatments. Archives of General Psychiatry, 46, 971–982.

Estroff, D., Yando, R., Burke, K., & Snyder, D. (1994). Perceptions of preschoolers' vulnerability by mothers who had delivered preterm. Journal of Pediatric Psychology, 19 (6), 709–721.

Farren, E. & McEwen, M. (2004). The basics of pediatric immunizations. Newborn and Infant Nursing Reviews, 4(1), 5–14.

Green, M. & Solnit, A. (1964). Reactions to the threated loss of a child: a vulnerable child syndrome. Pediatric management of the dying child, part III. Pediatrics, 34(1), 58–66.

Lawton, C., France, K., & Blampied, N. (1991). Treatment of infant sleep disturbances by graduated extinction. Child and Family Behavior Therapy, 13, 39–56.

Lukens, C. & Silverman, A. (2014). Systematic review of psychological interventions for pediatric feeding problems. Journal of Pediatric Psychology, 39(8), 903–917.

McGrath, M., Mellon, M., & Murphy, L. (2000). Empirically supported treatments in pediatric psychology: constipation and encopresis. Journal of Pediatric Psychology, 25(4), 225–254.

Medical Traumatic Stress Work Group of the National Child Traumatic Stress Network. (n.d.). Pediatric Medical Traumatic Stress: A Comprehensive Guide. Retrieved June 9, 2018, from www.icctc.org/PMM% 20Handouts/pediatric_toolkit_for_health_care_providers.pdf.

Mellon, M. & McGrath, M. (2000). Empirically supported treatments in pediatric psychology: nocturnal enuresis. Journal of Pediatric Psychology, 25(4), 193–214.

Meltzer, E., Welch, M., & Ostrom, N. (2006). Pill swallowing ability and training in children 6 to 11 years of age. Clinical Pediatrics, 45(8), 725–733.

Mindell, J. (1999). Empirically supported treatments in pediatric psychology: bedtime refusal and night wakings in young children. Journal of Pediatric Psychology, 24(6), 465–481.

Mindell, J. & Durand, V. (1993). Treatment of child sleep disorders: generalizations across disorders and effects on family members. Journal of Pediatric Psychology, 18(6), 731–750.

Mindell, J., Kuhn, B., Lewin, D., Meltzer, L., & Sadeh, A. (2006). Behavioral treatment of bedtime problems and night wakings in infants and young children. Sleep, 29(10), 1263–1276.

Morris, N., Knight, R., Bruni, T., Sayers, L., & Drayton, A. (2017). Feeding disorders. Child and Adolescent Psychiatric Clinics of North America, 26, 571–586.

National Child Traumatic Stress Network. (n.d.). Medical Trauma. Retrieved June 9, 2018, from www.nctsn.org/what-is-child-trauma/trauma-types/medical-trauma.

Parfitt, Y., Pike, A., & Ayers, S. (2013). The impact of parents' mental health on parent–baby interaction: a prospective study. Infant Behavior and Development, 36(4), 599–608.

Polaha, J., Dalton, W., & Lancaster, B. (2008). Parental report of medication acceptance among youth: implications for everyday practice. Southern Medical Journal, 101(11), 1106–1112.

Price, J., Kassam-Adams, N., Alderfer, M., Christofferson, J., & Kazak, A. (2016). Systematic review: a reevaluation and update of the integrative (trajectory) model of pediatric medical traumatic stress. Journal of Pediatric Psychology, 41(1), 86–97.

Quittner, A., Marciel, K., Modi, A., & Cruz, I. (n. d.). Encouraging Pill Swallowing in Young Children with Cystic Fibrosis (Ages 3–8 Years): A Behavioral Intervention for the CF Team. Retrieved July 1, 2018, from www.childrensal.org/workfiles/Clinical_ Services/CF/pillswallowing.pdf.

Rady Children's Hospital, San Diego. (2018). Social Stories. Retrieved June 9, 2018, from www.rchsd.org/programs-services/autism-discovery-institute/hospital-visit-tips/social-stories/.

Rattaz, C., Dubois, A., Michelon, C., Viellard, M., Poinso, F., & Baghdadli, A. (2013). How do children with autism spectrum disorders express pain? A comparison of developmentally delayed and typically developing children. *Pain, 154*, 2007–2013.

Rennick, J., Johnston, C., Dougherty, G., Platt, R., & Ritchie, J. (2002). Children's psychological responses to illness and exposure to invasive technology. *Journal of Developmental and Behavioral Pediatrics, 23*, 133–144.

Scannapieco, M. & Connell-Carrick, K. (2005). Focus on the first years: correlates of substantiation of child maltreatment for families with children 0 to 4. *Children and Youth Services Review, 27*(12), 1307–1323.

Scarpinato, N., Bradley, J., Kurbjun, K., Bateman, X., Holtzer, B., & Ely, B. (2010). Caring for the child with an autism spectrum disorder in the acute care setting. *Journal for Specialists in Pediatric Nursing, 15*(3), 244–254.

Shepard, J. & Cox, D. (2018). Elimination disorders. In M. Roberts & R. Steele (eds.), *Handbook of Pediatric Psychology*, 5th ed. (pp. 442–451). New York: Guilford Press.

Silverman, A. & Begotka, A. (2018). Psychological and behavioral disorders in dysfunctional feeding: identification and management. In J. Ongkasuwan & E. Chiou (eds.), *Pediatric Dysphagia* (pp. 281–301). New York: Springer International Publishing.

Silverman, A. & Tarbell, S. (2009). Feeding and vomiting problems in pediatric populations. In M. Roberts & R. Steele (eds.), *Handbook of Pediatric Psychology*, 4th ed. (pp. 429–445). New York: Guilford Press.

Slifer, K. (2014). *A Clinician's Guide to Helping Children Cope and Cooperate with Medical Care: An Applied Behavioral Approach*. Baltimore: Johns Hopkins University Press.

Souders, M., DePaul, D., Freeman, K., & Levy, S. (2002). Caring for children and adolescents with autism who require challenging procedures. *Pediatric Nursing, 28*(6), 555–562.

Stark, L., Opipari, L., Donaldson, D., Danovsky, M., Rasile, D., & DelSanto, A. (1997). Evaluation of a standard protocol for retentive encopresis: a replication. *Journal of Pediatric Psychology, 22*(5), 619–633.

Wassom, M. & Christophersen, E. (2014). A clinical application of evidence-based treatments in pediatric functional constipation and incontinence. *Clinical Practice in Pediatric Psychology, 2*(3), 294–311.

Welkom, J., Cohen, L., Joffe, N., & Bearden, D. (2009). Psychological approaches to acute pediatric pain management. In S. D'Alonso & K. L. Grasso (eds.), *Acute Pain: Causes, Effects and Treatment* (pp. 155–168). New York: Nova Science Publishers.

Reproducible Resources

Appendix
Edinburgh Postnatal Depression Scale (EPDS)

The Edinburgh Postnatal Depression Scale (EPDS) has been developed to assist primary care health professionals to detect mothers suffering from postnatal depression; a distressing disorder more prolonged than the 'blues' (which occur in the first week after delivery) but less severe than puerperal psychosis.

Previous studies have shown that postnatal depression affects at least 10% of women and that many depressed mothers remain untreated. These mothers may cope with their baby and with household tasks, but their enjoyment of life is seriously affected and it is possible that there are long-term effects on the family.

The EPDS was developed at health centres in Livingston and Edinburgh. It consists of ten short statements. The mother underlines which of the four possible responses is closest to how she has been feeling during the past week. Most mothers complete the scale without difficulty in less than 5 minutes.

The validation study showed that mothers who scored above a threshold 12/13 were likely to be suffering from a depressive illness of varying severity. Nevertheless the EPDS score should *not* override clinical judgement. A careful clinical assessment should be carried out to confirm the diagnosis. The scale indicates how the mother has felt *during the previous week*, and in doubtful cases it may be usefully repeated after 2 weeks. The scale will not detect mothers with anxiety neuroses, phobias or personality disorders.

Instructions for users

1. The mother is asked to underline the response which comes closest to how she has been feeling in the previous 7 days.
2. All ten items must be completed.
3. Care should be taken to avoid the possibility of the mother discussing her answers with others.
4. The mother should complete the scale herself, unless she has limited English or has difficulty with reading.
5. The EPDS may be used at 6–8 weeks to screen postnatal women. The child health clinic, postnatal check-up or a home visit may provide suitable opportunities for its completion.

EDINBURGH POSTNATAL DEPRESSION SCALE (EPDS)
J. L. Cox, J. M. Holden, R. Sagovsky
Department of Psychiatry, University of Edinburgh

Name:
Address:
Baby's age:

As you have recently had a baby, we would like to know how you are feeling. Please UNDERLINE the answer which comes closest to how you have felt IN THE PAST 7 DAYS, not just how you feel today.

Here is an example, already completed.
I have felt happy:
  Yes, all the time
  <u>Yes, most of the time</u>
  No, not very often
  No, not at all
This would mean: "I have felt happy most of the time" during the past week. Please complete the other questions in the same way.

In the past 7 days:
1. I have been able to laugh and see the funny side of things
     As much as I always could
     Not quite so much now
     Definitely not so much now
     Not at all
2. I have looked forward with enjoyment to things
     As much as I ever did
     Rather less than I used to
     Definitely less than I used to
     Hardly at all
* 3. I have blamed myself unnecessarily when things went wrong
     Yes, most of the time
     Yes, some of the time
     Not very often
     No, never
4. I have been anxious or worried for no good reason
     No, not at all
     Hardly ever
     Yes, sometimes
     Yes, very often
* 5. I have felt scared or panicky for no very good reason
     Yes, quite a lot
     Yes, sometimes
     No, not much
     No, not at all
* 6. Things have been getting on top of me
     Yes, most of the time I haven't been able to cope at all
     Yes, sometimes I haven't been coping as well as usual
     No, most of the time I have coped quite well
     No, I have been coping as well as ever
* 7. I have been so unhappy that I have had difficulty sleeping
     Yes, most of the time
     Yes, sometimes
     Not very often
     No, not at all
* 8. I have felt sad or miserable
     Yes, most of the time
     Yes, quite often
     Not very often
     No, not at all
* 9. I have been so unhappy that I have been crying
     Yes, most of the time
     Yes, quite often
     Only occasionally
     No, never
*10. The thought of harming myself has occurred to me
     Yes, quite often
     Sometimes
     Hardly ever
     Never

*J. L. Cox, MA, DM, FRCP(Edin), FRCPsych, *Professor of Psychiatry, Department of Postgraduate Medicine, University of Keele. Consultant Psychiatrist, City General Hospital, Stoke-on-Trent, formerly Senior Lecturer, Department of Psychiatry, University of Edinburgh;* J. M. Holden, BSc, SRN, HVCert, *Research Psychologist;* R. Sagovsky, MB, ChB, MRCPsych, *Research Psychiatrist, Department of Psychiatry, University of Edinburgh*

*Correspondence: *University of Keele, Thornburrow Drive, Hartshill, Stoke-on-Trent, Staffs SI7 7QB*

Figure 2.2 Edinburgh Postnatal Depression Scale.
Reprinted from Cox, J., Holden, J., & Sagovsky, R. 1987. Detection of postnatal depression: development of the 10-item Edinburgh Postnatal Depression Scale. *British Journal of Psychiatry, 150,* 782–786, reproduced with permission

(a)

Post Partum Bonding Questionnaire

Please indicate how often the following ae true for you.
   There are no 'right' or 'wrong' answers. Choose the answer which seems right in your recent experience.

Factor	Scoring	Statement	Always	Very often	Quite often	Some-times	Rarely	Never
1	0 → 5	I feel close to my baby						
1	5 → 0	I wish the old days when I had no baby would come back						
2	5 → 0	I feel distant from my baby						
2	0 → 5	I love to cuddle my baby						
2	5 → 0	I regret having this baby						
1	5 → 0	The baby does not seem to be mine						
1	5 → 0	My baby winds me up						
1	0 → 5	I love my baby to bits						
1	0 → 5	I feel happy when my baby smiles or laughs						
1	5 → 0	My baby irritates me						
2	0 → 5	I enjoy playing with my baby						
1	5 → 0	My baby cries too much						
1	5 → 0	I feel trapped as a mother						
2	5 → 0	I feel angry with my baby						
1	5 → 0	I resent my baby						
1	0 → 5	My baby is the most beautiful baby in the world						
1	5 → 0	I wish my baby would somehow go away						
4	5 → 0	I have done harmful things to my baby						
3	5 → 0	My baby makes me feel anxious						
3	5 → 0	I am afraid of my baby						
2	5 → 0	My baby annoys me						
3	0 → 5	I feel confident when caring for my baby						
2	5 → 0	I feel the only solution is for someone else to look after my baby						
4	5 → 0	I feel like hurting my baby						
3	0 → 5	My baby is easily comforted						

Figure 2.3a The Postpartum Bonding Questionnaire.
Reprinted by permission from Springer Nature from Brockington, I., Fraser, C., & Wilson, D., The Postpartum Bonding Questionnaire: a validation. *Archives of Women's Mental Health, 9,* 233–242, copyright 2006

(b)

PBQ

Statement	Always	Very often	Quite often	Some-times	Rarely	Never
I feel close to my baby		1	2	3	4	5
I wish the old days when I had no baby would come back	5	4	3	2	1	
I feel distant from my baby	5	4	3	2	1	
I love to cuddle my baby		1	2	3	4	5
I regret having this baby	5	4	3	2	1	
The baby does not seem to be mine	5	4	3	2	1	
My baby winds me up	5	4	3	2	1	
I love my baby to bits		1	2	3	4	5
I feel happy when my baby smiles or laughs		1	2	3	4	5
My baby irritates me	5	4	3	2	1	
I enjoy playing with my baby		1	2	3	4	5
My baby cries too much	5	4	3	2	1	
I feel trapped as a mother	5	4	3	2	1	
I feel angry with my baby	5	4	3	2	1	
I resent my baby	5	4	3	2	1	
My baby is the most beautiful baby in the world		1	2	3	4	5
I wish my baby would somehow go away	5	4	3	2	1	
I have done harmful things to my baby	5	4	3	2	1	
My baby makes me feel anxious	5	4	3	2	1	
I am afraid of my baby	5	4	3	2	1	
My baby annoys me	5	4	3	2	1	
I feel confident when caring for my baby		1	2	3	4	5
I feel the only solution is for someone else to look after my baby	5	4	3	2	1	
I feel like hurting my baby	5	4	3	2	2	
My baby is easily comforted		1	2	3	4	5

Scoring

→   Very often = 1   quite often = 2   sometimes = 3   rarely = 4   never = 5

←   Rarely = 1   sometimes = 2   quite often = 3   very often = 4   always = 5

Scores

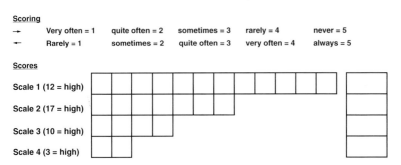

Scale 1 (12 = high)

Scale 2 (17 = high)

Scale 3 (10 = high)

Scale 4 (3 = high)

Figure 2.3b Postpartum Bonding Questionnaire scoring key.
Reprinted by permission from Springer Nature from Brockington, I., Fraser, C., & Wilson, D., The Postpartum Bonding Questionnaire: a validation. *Archives of Women's Mental Health, 9*, 233–242, copyright 2006

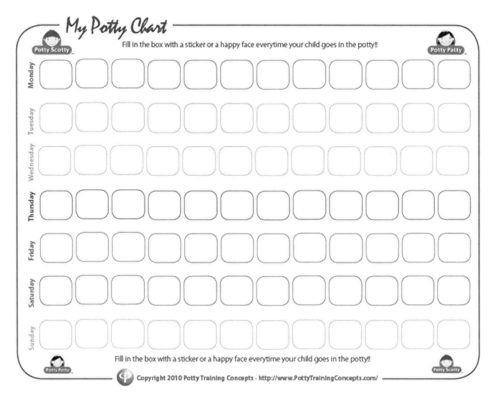

Figure 2.4 Potty training concepts.
Reprinted from *Potty Training Chart Weekly* (2019). Retrieved January 27, 2019, from www.pottytrainingconcepts.com/Potty-Training-Chart-Weekly%202.html

Recommended Websites, Books, and Other Resources
Clinical Resources
Pill Swallowing

Better than a Spoonful of Sugar – How to Swallow Pills, http://research4kids.ucalgary.ca/pillswallowing

Kaplan, B., Steiger, R., Pope, J., Marsh, A., Sharp, M., & Crawford, S. (2010). Successful treatment of pill-swallowing difficulties with head posture practice. *Paediatrics and Child Health, 15*(5), e1–e5.

Encouraging Pill Swallowing in Young Children with Cystic Fibrosis, www.childrensal.org/workfiles/Clinical_Services/CF/pillswallowing.pdf

Social Stories

Boston Children's Hospital, My Hospital Story, www.childrenshospital.org/patient-resources/family-resources/child-life-specialists/preparing-your-child-and-family-for-a-visit/my-hospital-story

Rady Children's Hospital, San Diego, Social Stories, www.rchsd.org/programs-services/autism-discovery-institute/hospital-visit-tips/social-stories/

Pediatric Medical Traumatic Stress

National Child Traumatic Stress Network – Medical Trauma, www.nctsn.org/what-is-child-trauma/trauma-types/medical-trauma

Pediatric Medical Traumatic Stress: A Comprehensive Guide, www.icctc.org/PMM%20Handouts/pediatric_toolkit_for_health_care_providers.pdf

After the Injury, www.aftertheinjury.org/

Feeding and Toileting Resources

Southall, A. & Martin C. (eds.). (2011). *Feeding Problems in Children*, 2nd ed. Oxon: Radcliffe Publishing.

Choby, B. & George, S. (2008). Toilet training. *American Family Physician, 78*(9), 1059–1064. Retrieved January 27, 2019, from www.aafp.org/afp/2008/1101/p1059.html.

Potty Training Concepts. (2019). Potty Training Chart Weekly. Retrieved January 27, 2019, from www.pottytrainingconcepts.com/.

Fact Sheets on Enuresis and Encopresis

Society of Pediatric Psychology. (2016). Fact Sheet: Enuresis in Children and Adolescents. Retrieved February 2, 2019, from www.societyofpediatricpsychology.org/enuresis.

Society of Pediatric Psychology. (2016). Fact Sheet: Encopresis in Children and Adolescents. Retrieved February 2, 2019, from www.societyofpediatricpsychology.org/encopresis.

Working with School-Age Children with Medical Concerns

3.1 School-Age Children and Common Concerns

When children first begin attending school, new concerns, hopes, and fears arise for both patients and parents as they enter this next stage of development. With this new independence also comes new risks and precautions that families should be mindful of regarding their children's safety. For all parents and clinicians, it is important to be aware of the greatest risk factors for death and injury based on age in order to help prevent future accidents or death. This is especially true given that the highest risk of death from infancy to age 19 is from injuries, with suffocation identified as the leading cause of death in children less than 1 year of age, drowning as the leading cause of death between ages 1 and 4, and death from a motor vehicle accident as the leading cause of death from ages 5 to 19 (Centers for Disease Control, 2015). Different risk factors have been identified concerning a school-age child's risk for accidental death, with males and patients with "active" temperaments at particular risk (Boles et al., 2005).

This "active" temperament is associated with a child having greater difficulty assessing risk in their home environment in contrast to other children with less active temperaments. Given this difficulty, clinicians may want to counsel parents that trying to identify and create separate (and numerous) safety rules for the home may be difficult, and that, instead, emphasis might be placed on identifying various areas of the home (e.g., kitchen) as "dangerous" (Boles et al., 2005). Naturally, it also can be helpful for clinicians to review with parents basic environmental modifications that can help reduce the risk of accidents, such as gun locks, child-resistant caps on medication bottles, pool barriers, age- and weight-appropriate car seats (e.g., rear-facing infant-only bucket seat or a front-facing convertible car seat).

Parents may overestimate their child's capabilities when they are school-age, and they may not be aware of the supervision requirements for this age despite "school age" being identified as the age of greatest risk for unintentional injuries (Bradbury et al., 1999). This risk is increased when there are more children in the family, when children are younger, when younger children have older siblings they are trying to match in capabilities, and when there is decreased parental supervision (Bradbury et al., 1999). As such, it may be advantageous for families assessed as being at risk based on these above factors to have a clinician review with them a website by the American Academy of Pediatrics with guidelines for safety counseling based on patient age, which is listed in the "Recommended Websites, Books, and Other Resources" section at the end of this chapter.

In contrast to the above role clinicians hold in helping parents to understand and subsequently utilize appropriate safety precautions, clinicians are conversely tasked with ensuring that parents do not "overprotect" or serve as "helicopter parents" to their child due to the impact this can have on a child's later functioning and self-esteem. This concept can be particularly tough for parents when their child has experienced an acute medical event or is managing a chronic illness. "Vulnerable child syndrome" was first described by Green and Solnit in 1964 in parents of children who had experienced life-threatening illnesses when their children were infants.

As observed in this syndrome, parents of the medically vulnerable child "overprotected the child, were unable to set age-appropriate limits, and displayed excessive concern in medical settings about their children's health" (Leslie & Boyce, 1996, p. 323). This behavior was not observed when these same parents interacted with siblings who had not experienced a life-threatening illness. Unfortunately, although parents were attempting to be protective of their child, this overprotection is associated with later academic underachievement, somatic complaints, and separation difficulties (Green & Solnit, 1964).

When a parent exhibits this overprotectiveness, it is important to validate their feelings while also providing realistic information and recommendations about developmentally appropriate parenting strategies. It is understandable that a loving parent can react with excessive worry and concern following a child's perceived or actual health crisis; however, clinicians must help to prevent this deleterious behavior by reframing it into a more beneficial parenting style that allows for their child to learn autonomy and experience the "national consequences" of their actions.

Psychoeducation about the adverse impact of overprotectiveness can be helpful, including information about the patient's actual rather than perceived health status and guidelines for the child's overall prognosis and functioning. Families with less education are more likely to perceive their child as vulnerable, and it is hypothesized that this association may in part be due to lower-quality interactions with medical providers from concerns such as decreased comfort when asking questions of medical providers (Anthony et al., 2003). Clinicians can take the lead in helping to facilitate questions by voicing common questions they have heard from other parents or that they themselves might have as a parent in the same situation.

On the other end of the spectrum of parenting styles, a critical parenting style is also associated with decreased self-efficacy and depression in preadolescents with a chronic medical condition such as diabetes mellitus type 1 (Armstrong et al., 2011). Finding the balance between overprotectiveness and criticalness can be difficult for parents and the clinicians who help them, but there is a need for a supportive and authoritative parenting style to encourage self-care (Armstrong et al., 2011).

Clinical Vignette: Cold and Flu Season Conundrum

Ms. R presents to therapy with her 11-year-old son, Joseph, for their first intake appointment. They had been referred by their school counselor due to Joseph's academic and social difficulties, which had been worsening over the past several years. While taking a comprehensive medical history during the intake, you learn that Joseph has been diagnosed with cystic fibrosis since infancy, as well as cystic fibrosis–related diabetes. Both of these conditions require careful daily management and supervision by Ms. R. Similar to other parents of children with cystic fibrosis, Ms. R. endorses anxiety about the patient's pulmonary functioning and chronic worry that he will become sick and experience a resultant decrease in pulmonary functioning.

Ms. R. is well educated about the importance of following a comprehensive treatment regimen to help preserve pulmonary functioning in cystic fibrosis, and she is ever watchful of keeping Joseph away from children who may be sick. Unfortunately, it becomes apparent that this wariness has led Ms. R. to pull Joseph from school for most of the month of October, despite Joseph having had his flu shot and taking recommended precautions by his doctors when he is at school. For instance, there is another student at school with cystic fibrosis, and due to infection control guidelines, they use separate entrances into the school to help prevent them from coming into close proximity of each other and potentially cross-infecting each other with certain bacteria, which can lead to increased lung decline.

In further discussion with Ms. R., she notes that she frequently pulls Joseph from school during the cold and flu season despite recommendations against this practice by her medical providers. In speaking with Joseph, it becomes clear that he feels overwhelmed by the schoolwork he misses during these lengthy absences, as well as feeling "left out" by his peers when they engage in after-school activities during this time.

Over the next several therapy sessions, you focus on building rapport with the family, as well as encouraging Ms. R. to work with an adult psychotherapist to assist with her own anxiety management. With Joseph, you focus mainly on social skills training with the aim of also helping to increase his self-efficacy in interacting positively with peers. Following consultation with Joseph's medical providers to ensure your own understanding of appropriate infection prevention measures for Joseph to take at school and to ensure your treatment plan is consistent with their recommendations, you help Joseph and Ms. R. communicate their infection control concerns with his teacher. The teacher then subsequently allows Joseph to move away from visibly sick children in the classroom while still remaining in the classroom. With the approval of the school administration, you help the patient and his mother writer a letter to the parents of his classmates that discusses the importance of children with respiratory conditions staying home from school due to Joseph's cystic fibrosis.

Following these proactive interventions, your remaining work focuses on helping Joseph and Ms. R accept the inevitability that he will get sick at some point and that missing school prevents him from leading a "normal" life with appropriate opportunities for peer interactions and academic functioning. Joseph returns to school at the height of the cold and flu season. One month later, he falls ill from a respiratory infection. In talking with Ms. R., she expresses acceptance that he was "going to get ill at some point," and that she was satisfied that Joseph's quality of life had increased due to his increased social and academic functioning.

3.2 Talking to Classmates and Peers about Chronic Illness

As children grow older and their emphasis starts to shift to their peer relationships, there can be a lot of confusion about how or when to help a child disclose their chronic illness to peers. Many parents (and clinicians) may initially desire to "protect" the child by themselves not disclosing the illness to other adults, and, thus, they are modeling to their child that it is important to keep their medical condition a secret. Despite positive intentions, this lack of disclosure can unfortunately perpetuate the child's internalization of the stigma associated with having a medical condition. Parents can unwittingly play a large role in a child's own belief about stigma related to their condition based on how they themselves discuss the medical condition, as the child can receive vastly different messages about stigma based on their parent's behavior, from the full spectrum of disclosing about the child's illness only when necessary to serving as members of advocacy groups for the medical condition.

In research examining school-age children with epilepsy's disclosure of their diagnosis to their peers, children tended to express concerns about an overall desire for normalcy, concern about peers' negative response to disclosure, difficulty communicating about a complex medical illness, concern related to their own or other's perception of the medical diagnosis, and concern related to the "invisibility" of their illness due to either a lack of visible symptoms or the lack of public communication about the disease (Benson et al., 2015). This perspective is important as research suggests that younger children may have less acceptance of their peer's chronic health conditions, which may be in part due to misconceptions they hold despite being given accurate medical information, such as believing a disease is contagious despite having been otherwise informed (Canter & Roberts, 2012).

Given this appropriate fear children may have regarding miscommunication of their medical condition, it is important for clinicians to help provide patients with developmentally appropriate vocabulary to clearly communicate with their peers and to answer relevant questions. By helping children take control over when and to whom they disclose their medical conditions, clinicians can help children minimize negative impressions or negative social consequences related to illness, such as other parents misattributing the symptoms of hypoglycemia to substance use rather than the patient's actual diagnosis of diabetes mellitus (Berlin et al., 2005). In addition to helping to prevent adverse miscommunication about symptoms, this preventative disclosure can also be crucial in an emergency, as the preexisting knowledge can help other people intervene in a medical crisis if necessary (e.g., administer epinephrine for an allergic reaction).

When children are hospitalized, they may need additional help in discussing their absence with curious classmates. Their peers may ask awkward questions such as why they were absent or what happened during the hospitalization, and may express curiosity about how the patient plans to make up work they missed. If a child experiences a prolonged hospitalization due to medical factors, working with the school to create a school intervention with peers may be helpful, particularly when these school interventions help to provide the patient's peers with information and help peers identify strategies about engaging with the patient when they return to school (Canter & Roberts, 2012).

Given that we know younger children can misconstrue or misunderstand medical information despite developmentally appropriate education, school reentry programs should not only help children learn the facts about the medical illness but also provide assistance in discussing the attitudes and fears of the children as it comes to interacting with the ill patient (Canter & Roberts, 2012). Although clinicians typically would not have the time to go to the school to assist with this intervention, they can still be active in assisting with this process by providing the teacher or school staff members with information (as permitted by the patient's family) and recommended resources to help facilitate these school interventions.

As children grow older into adolescence, they can become fearful that this disclosure could lead to a lack of understanding about the medical illness or pity for the patient. Due to this fear, most adolescents tend to disclose to those whom they feel care for them or whom they deem trustworthy, such as immediate family members, select extended family members, and close group of friends, or to those whom they feel can help with extrinsic benefits, such as academic accommodations (Kaushansky et al., 2017).

Unfortunately, despite the best efforts of clinicians, patients, parents, and school staff, sometimes disclosure about a medical condition can lead to bullying. This bullying or victimization can occur for students with and without a medical and/or mental health diagnosis, as approximately 75% of youth report experiencing bullying or victimization at least once in a school year (Glover et al., 2000). For the most part, bullying is thought to occur when an individual perceives a power differential due to physical status, higher social status, systemic power, or an awareness of another child's vulnerability (Craig et al., 2007). Children and adolescents feel less able to stop bullying the longer the bullying occurs, and increased victimization appears to occur when the child responds to bullying with anger or embarrassment.

Chronic bullying has been associated with an increase in internalizing and externalizing behaviors by the victim, as well as an increase in physical complaints. Research indicates a bidirectional relationship between victimization and both physical and mental health problems, meaning that youth with physical and mental health problems are more likely to be victimized than their health peers, and youth who are victimized are more likely to later report mental and physical health problems (Biebl et al., 2011). Most of these physical concerns tend to be somatic complaints such as sleep disturbances, headaches, and stomachaches. For clinicians, these somatic complaints can serve as key indicators for the need to query for more information regarding possible victimization if these symptoms are reported by youth.

There appear to be significant differences by gender in how effective students find certain strategies in responding to bullying. Overall, females tend to experience worse health outcomes in comparison to males following chronic victimization, and it is hypothesized that this is perhaps due to internalization associated with greater emotional involvement in peer relationships (Biebl et al., 2011). Of note, females tend to perceive the use of relational strategies as effective, such as telling a friend or adult, while males tend to report strategies such as responding to bullying with aggression or confrontation.

Bullying can take many different forms that are either direct or indirect. With the rise of technology, a new form of bullying called "cyberbullying" has become a factor. Cyberbullying encompasses a wide range of harassing and hurtful behaviors such as uploading harmful pictures or sending hurtful messages that may or may not be seen by other people. This may be perceived as more harmful by some students than the traditional forms of bullying due to the potential for it to be observed (and commented on) by a wider audience (Machackova et al., 2013).

In managing this type of bullying, technological coping strategies of blocking the bully from further contact or avoiding certain websites are recommended as first-line strategies. There is also some support for "purposeful ignoring" where the bully is discouraged by the lack of response from the victim. This appears to be somewhat effective only when the bullying behavior is associated with less severe harassment rather than severe bullying (Machackova et al., 2013). Seeking social support may also help with possibly stopping the bullying but also appears to be an effective strategy for emotional coping.

Substantial research efforts have aimed at bullying prevention programs in school, with no body of literature consistently supporting their efforts. Other approaches have focused on helping individual students respond to bullying rather than on more systemic prevention efforts. In his Changing Faces booklet, "You're in Charge," Kish (1998) identifies 10 strategies to help defuse bullying behavior about appearance, as described by Lovegrow and Rumsey (2004).

The following strategies were identified to help respond to bullying behavior: (1) "Self-Motto" (positive statement or affirmation about oneself), (2) "Body Language" (positive body language such as sustained eye contact), (3) "Get Yourself an Explanation" (providing brief explanation and reassurance to the other person regarding the perceived difference), (4) "Taking Charge of the Conversation" (ignoring the negative comment and purposefully changing the conversation), (5) "Be Assertive" (clearly indicating that the bullying comment or behavior will not be tolerated), (6) "Distraction" (thinking about something else), (7) "Armor Plating" (pretending that you are protected by a suit of armor and cannot be harmed), (8) "Humor" (finding ways to laugh at the situation or bully to defuse the situation), (9) "Take Reinforcement" (having friends or social support around when bullying taking place), and (10) "Appearance" (being aware of the difference between caring about personal hygiene versus less important concerns such as what is "in fashion") (Kish 1998; Lovegrow & Rumsey, 2004).

These strategies can help provide a framework for helping individual patients in responding to bullying they may experience. Of course, with the guiding rule of "safety first," clinicians should use their judgment in deciding whether the bullying necessitates systemic intervention to ensure safety rather than focusing on helping the patient to handle the bullying independently.

Clinical Vignette: Louie's Return

Today, you meet with Ms. J and her son, an 8-year-old boy named Louie who successfully received a lung transplant 6 months ago due to pulmonary hypertension. You have been working with his family since the transplant to help them adjust to their "new normal" following the transplant. Louie has recently expressed an interest in returning to school. His lung transplant team has given him medical clearance to return to school but urged him to wait until the end of flu season in several weeks due to his impaired immune system. Following communication with the school, it is planned that Louis will return for the first half of the school day and then finish the afternoon at home. If this transition goes well, the plan is for Louie to begin attending school full-time during the next academic year. Although Louie is excited about returning to school, he and his mother are concerned about how his peers will respond to his return, particularly given visible changes that have occurred since he last attended school, such as significant weight loss and increased acne from prednisone.

Mindful that young children may have difficulty understanding Louie's past and current medical conditions, you offer to help with the transition back to school by collaborating with his teacher and by using role-play to help Louie become more comfortable answering questions that may be posed by his curious peers. With Ms. J's permission and a release of information, you subsequently contact his teacher and provide basic education about the patient's medical condition and share classroom-friendly resources, such as videos and books about lung transplants. Given that many young children will often still have misconceptions about medical conditions despite being provided with information, you also recommend that the teacher conduct an open-ended discussion session that allows students to ask questions prior to Louie's arrival at school and to have the students "brainstorm" ways to make Louie feel included and supported in the middle of a school year.

While this is occurring, you and Louie rehearse how to provide a basic explanation about his medical condition to his peers. Due to his continued anxiety about discussing this, Louie practices explaining his medical condition to various other counselors and graduate students within the medical office, with the consent of Ms. J. Louie's self-efficacy in discussing his medical condition grows as he approaches the transition date to returning to school part-time, and during the last session before he begins school, you role-play the part of the "nosy and obnoxious" student who asks questions such as: "Are you going to die? and "Are you going to make me sick?" With only minimal coaching, Louie successfully manages responses to these questions and announces at the end of the session, "I'm ready for school now!"

3.3 Collaborating with the School System

When children are diagnosed with a chronic illness, it is important for clinicians to assist patients and families in being aware of federal legislation that can help the student receive the educational accommodations and protections for promised to every child, regardless of disability status. One such protection comes from a Section 504 plan, which must be followed by all public schools or any other school that receives financial assistance from the US federal government.

Under a Section 504 plan, a student with a disability (i.e., physical and/or mental disability) meets criteria for accommodations if the disability significantly limits a major life activity (US Department of Education, 2016). In order to become eligible for these accommodations, a student must be evaluated by the school district at no cost to the parents. For many parents, they may be unaware that they can request an evaluation. Although this request does not automatically provide for an evaluation by the school, the school does have to let the parent know if the school does not decide to evaluate the student, which can then be challenged by the parent during a due process hearing (US Department of Education, 2016).

Once a student has been identified as meeting criteria for a Section 504 plan, accommodations or recommendations are developed to help ensure that the student receives an equitable education in comparison to other children without that disability. Mental health clinicians not only can assist with helping with recommendations for psychiatric concerns but, through collaboration with the patient's medical team, can provide recommendations for physical disabilities. This collaboration is crucial given that each medical diagnosis may necessitate different school accommodations.

For example, the Section 504 plan for a student with cystic fibrosis may recommend that the child is allowed to carry a water bottle at all times to assist with hydration, to receive enzymes at lunchtime from the school nurse, and to be allowed to leave class at any time due to constipation concerns. In contrast, a Section 504 plan for a student with diabetes might include daily check-ins with the nurse for blood glucose monitoring and the allowance for the student to have snacks at school to help with managing blood glucose levels throughout the day. For further information regarding Section 504 plans, refer to the "Recommended Websites, Books, and Other Resources" section for detailed information regarding patient eligibility and the implementation of a 504 plan from the US Department of Education. Additionally, refer to the "Reproducible Resources" section for a sample 504 plan for a 12-year-old student with diabetes mellitus type 1.

For some students, an Individualized Education Program (IEP) may be preferred over a Section 504 plan. The essential practical difference between an IEP and a 504 plan is that the former is for students who need individualized instruction that requires a modification to the standard curriculum, which is in contrast to the 504 plan, which allows for accommodations so that the student can access the standard curriculum (Goldberg Center, 2007).

The more detailed IEP requires that the student's progress is reported and that measurable improvement is documented, which is not required as part of a 504 plan. However, in contrast to a 504 plan, the eligibility for an IEP is restricted to certain disabilities. In the context of this book, pediatric patients with chronic medical concerns may qualify on categories such as other health impairment, traumatic brain injury, visual impairment, hearing impairment, orthopedic impairment, or multiple disabilities (Understandingspecialeducation.com, 2016).

Similar to a 504 plan, a parent can request an evaluation by the public school system if they have concerns about their child's functioning in school.

Despite having appropriate accommodations in place, some children with and without medical problems may still struggle with school refusal. School refusal has been defined as "the child-motivated refusal to attend school and/or problems remaining in classes for an entire day" (Kearney, 2008, p. 452). Despite this one definition, school refusal can occur for numerous reasons. In order to help intervene when a child is exhibiting school refusal, a clinician must first ascertain the function of the school refusal. For example, is the school refusal tied to social anxiety in which the child is trying to avoid a perceived negative impact on their mood in attending school? The function of school refusal can also be to avoid social situations or other evaluative situations, seeking attention from "significant others" (e.g., parents), and wanting to engage in more pleasurable activities or to receive other reinforcement by being outside school (Kearney & Spear, 2014). See Figure 3.2 under the "Reproducible Resources" section for a further description of interventions based on the function of school refusal behavior.

For the first example of avoiding school due to the negative impact attendance is perceived to have on mood, interventions can include psychotropic medication and psychological interventions such as relaxation training or gradual reexposure to reduce psychological symptoms. Often, refusal can be associated with not only an attempt to prevent anxiety or other psychiatric symptoms but also an attempt on the child's part to prevent chronic pain if that has been a concern for the child. Despite this very "normal" reaction to trying to avoid pain, clinicians need to help prevent overly protective behavior (i.e., restricting school attendance) that actually leads to an overall reduction in daily functioning.

When a parent attempts to "protect" the child from pain by allowing their child to consistently miss school, the child's behavior of avoidance/refusal is reinforced through attention and/or the removal of aversive tasks (e.g., attending class or completing homework assignments), which can serve to heighten the child's focus on the perception of pain. As such, parents need to reinforce any adaptive behavior exhibited by the child, such as attending school and gym class, rather than reinforce the maladaptive coping of a child in an effort to prevent pain by restricting activities (Achiam-Montal & Lipsitz, 2014).

When working with a family on the goal of returning the child to previous school functioning, it is advantageous to partner with the school counselor or school psychologist to notify them of the current treatment plan and to possibly allow for temporary accommodations such as allowing the patient to "take breaks" to use relaxation and other coping skills at school rather than immediately calling home, or for the patient to gradually begin extending their school day based on how early they typically ask to leave school prematurely.

For example, a child who habitually leaves school by 11 AM can be encouraged to begin extending "pickup time" by 1 hour each week, with the end goal of the child leaving at the regular end of the school day at the end of the intervention. For this intervention to be successful, it is necessary to have both parents and school staff on board. Psychoeducation should be provided on the role avoidance plays in perpetuating anxiety, and the expectation of an extinction burst when exposure to the feared stimulus (i.e., school) is introduced. Otherwise, parents may panic and assume the exposure is "making things worse" if they do not have a basic understanding of the conditioning principles involved in exposure.

To ensure medical safety when working with medically complex children and adolescents, it may be helpful to speak with the child's physician to ascertain what signs/symptoms would warrant leaving school from a medical perspective, in order to prevent a medically stable child from leaving school due to somatic complaints (e.g., the child reports a mild headache or slight fatigue) that are not associated with the need for acute medical attention as opposed to fever, vomiting, or other serious medical indicators. Collaborating with the child's doctor can help to ensure the child's safety from a medical perspective, while also helping to ensure that somatic complains are not used as a means of school avoidance.

Summary

As children age and begin attending school, new concerns become present for parents and clinicians. It can be difficult to help foster a school-age child's independence while also being aware that this age has been identified as being at greatest risk for unintentional injuries. This balance between fostering independence and protecting vulnerable children from harm can be particularly difficult for parents when their child has a chronic medical illness. Clinicians can assist families in preventing the experience of adverse effects associated with "vulnerable child syndrome" by validating parents' feelings while also providing realistic information and recommendations about developmentally appropriate parenting strategies.

When attending school, many children may be confronted with questions from peers about their medical illness, particularly if the symptoms or treatments of a medical illness are visible. Parents can feel uncomfortable or unsure about advising their child on how or when to help their child disclose a chronic illness to peers. Understandably, they may be reticent for their child to disclose an illness due to concerns about how their child's peers may respond to this disclosure. However, this disclosure, though not without social risks, can help prevent patients from internalizing stigma about their condition and teach them how to clearly communicate with others about their illness.

With these disclosures, as well as an awareness of the prevalence of bullying in the school-age populations, clinicians should be alert to an increase in internalizing and externalizing behaviors, as well as an increase in physical complaints, in students. As always, clinicians should use their clinical judgment in determining whether the bullying requires immediate systemic intervention due to safety concerns or whether the patient should be coached on how to assertively manage the bullying prior to parental or school intervention.

Missing school due to a prolonged hospitalization can be stressful for both parents and children. If a child experiences a prolonged hospitalization, it can be beneficial to assist the family by working with the school to create a school intervention with peers. Additionally, clinicians can assist patients and families in being aware of federal legislation that can help the student receive suitable educational accommodations to help ensure that the student receives an equitable education in comparison to other children without a disability

Formal educational accommodations typically take the form of either an Individualized Education Program (IEP) or a Section 504 plan. The IEP is limited to helping students with certain specified disabilities and allows for modification to the standard curriculum, while the 504 plan allows for accommodations so that the student can engage in the standard curriculum. Despite appropriate academic accommodations, some students (both with and without medical problems) may still struggle with school refusal for reasons including wanting to avoid social or evaluative situations, seeking attention or more time with parents, or wanting to do something "more fun" than school. In these instances, it is important to ascertain the function of the school refusal in order to help provide a relevant clinical intervention to improve school attendance and overall academic functioning.

References

AAA. (2018). Child Passenger Safety. Retrieved December 12, 2018, from https://drivinglaws.aaa.com/tag/child-passenger-safety/

Achiam-Montal, M. & Lipsitz, J. (2014). Does parental response to children's pain moderate the association between pain severity and functional disability? An examination of noncardiac chest pain. *Journal of Pediatric Psychology, 39*(1), 35–44.

American Academy of Pediatrics. (1994). TIPP – The Injury Prevention Program. Retrieved from https://patiented.solutions.aap.org/handout-collection.aspx?categoryid=32033.

Anthony, K., Gil, K., & Schanberg, L. (2003). Brief report: parenting perceptions of child vulnerability in children with chronic illness. *Journal of Pediatric Psychology, 28*(3), 185–190.

Armstrong, B., Mackey, E., & Streisand, R. (2011). Parenting behavior, child functioning, and health behaviors in pre-adolescents with type 1 diabetes. *Journal of Pediatric Psychology, 36*(9), 1052–1061.

Benson, A., Lambert, V., Gallagher, P., Shahwan, A., & Austin, J. (2015). "I don't want them to look at me and think of my illness, I just want them to look at me and see me": child perspectives on the challenges associated with disclosing an epilepsy diagnosis to others. *Epilepsy and Behavior, 53*, 83–91.

Berlin, K., Sass, D., Davies, W., Reupert, S., & Hains, A. (2005). Brief report: parent perceptions of hypoglycemic symptoms of youth with diabetes; disease disclosure minimizes risk of negative evaluations. *Journal of Pediatric Psychology, 30*(2), 207–212.

Biebl, S., DiLalla, L., Davis, E., Lynch, K., & Shinn, S. (2011). Longitudinal associations among peer victimizations and physical and mental health problems. *Journal of Pediatric Psychology, 36*(8), 868–877.

Boles, R., Roberts, M., Brown, K., & Mayes, S. (2005). Children's risk-taking behaviors: the role of child-based perceptions of vulnerability and temperament. *Journal of Pediatric Psychology, 30*(7), 562–570.

Bradbury, K., Janicke, D., Riley, A., & Finney, J. (1999). Predictors of unintentional injuries to school-age children seen in pediatric primary care. *Journal of Pediatric Psychology, 24*(5), 423–433.

Bridges4kids.org. (2018). Article of Interest – Section 504. Retrieved December 8, 2018, from www.bridges4kids.org/articles/2004/4-04/SevierAcc.html.

Canter, K. & Roberts, M. (2012). A systematic and quantitative review of interventions to facilitate school reentry for children with chronic health conditions. *Journal of Pediatric Psychology, 37*(10), 1065–1075.

Centers for Disease Control and Prevention. (2015). CDC Childhood Injury Report. Retrieved December 1, 2018, from www.cdc.gov/safechild/child_injury_data.html.

Children with Diabetes. (2018). Sample 504 and IEP Plans. Retrieved December 18, 2018, from www.childrenwithdiabetes.com/504/.

Craig, W., Pepler, D., & Blais, J. (2007). Responding to bullying: what works? *School Psychology International, 28*(4), 465–477.

Glover, D., Gough, G., Johnson, M., & Cartwright, N. (2000). Bullying in 25 secondary schools: incidence, impact, and intervention. *Educational Research, 42*, 141–156.

Goldberg Center for Educational Planning. (2007). A Support Plan Comparison: IEP vs. 504. Retrieved December 9, 2018, from www.edconsult.org/hs-fs/hub/41331/file-14184103-pdf/docs/plan_comparison_iep_vs_504.pdf.

Green, M. & Solnit, A. (1964). Reactions to the threatened loss of a child: a vulnerable child syndrome. *Pediatrics, 34*(1), 58–66.

Kaushansky, D., Cox, J., Dodson, C., McNeeley, M., Kumar, S., & Iverson, E. (2017). Living a secret: disclosure among adolescents and young adults with chronic illness. *Chronic Illness, 13*(1), 49–61.

Kearney, C. (2008). School absenteeism and school refusal behavior in youth: a contemporary review. *Clinical Psychology Review, 28*(3), 451–471.

Kearney, C. & Spear, M. (2014). School refusal behavior. In L. Grossman and S. Walfish (eds.), *Translating Psychological Research into Practice* (pp. 83–85). Washington, DC: American Psychological Association.

Kish, V. (1998). *You're in Charge*. London: Changing Faces Publications.

Leslie, L. & Boyce, T. (1996). The vulnerable child. *Pediatrics in Review, 17*(9), 323–326.

Lovegrow, E. & Rumsey, N. (2004). Ignoring it doesn't make it stop: adolescents, appearance, & bullying. *The Cleft-Palate-Craniofacial Journal, 42*(1), https://doi.org/10.1597/03-097.5.1.

Machackova, H., Cerna, A., Seveikova, A., Dedkova, L., & Daneback, K. (2013). Effectiveness of coping strategies for victims of cyberbullying. *Cyberpsychology: Journal of Psychosocial Research on Cyberspace, 7*(3), http://dx.doi.org/10.5817/CP2013-3-5.

Understandingspecialeducation.com. (2016). Understanding the 13 Categories of Special Education. Retrieved December 9, 2018, from www.understandingspecialeducation.com/private-school.html.

US Department of Education. (2016). Parent and Educator Resource Guide to Section 504. Retrieved December 8, 2018, from www2.ed.gov/about/offices/list/ocr/docs/504-resource-guide-201612.pdf.

US Consumer Product Safety Commission. (2015). Safety Barrier Guidelines for Residential Pools. Retrieved December 12, 2018, from www.floridahealth.gov/environmental-health/swimming-pools/_documents/cpsc-safety-barriers.pdf.

Wright, P. & Wright, P. (2018). Wrightslaw. Retrieved December 4, 2018 from www.wrightslaw.com/.

Reproducible Resources
Recommended Websites, Books, and Other Resources

Requirements of Section 504 for Sam
Grade:
Birth Date:
Initial 504 Plan:
Today's Date:

Summary of Concerns and Past Interventions:

Sam is a general education student who has type 1 diabetes, which may interfere with normal school activities and requirements.

Section 504 applies to Sam because of the following:

Type 1 Diabetes, as diagnosed by a physician, is a physiological disorder that affects the endocrine system. Type 1 Diabetes places the individual at risk for hypoglycemic and hyperglycemic episodes related to metabolic dysfunction. Potential fluctuations in blood glucose impact the individual's major life activities in the area of learning, which is one of the specific major life activities described in Section 504.

Both high blood sugar levels and low blood sugar levels affect Sam's ability to learn and perform in school, as well as seriously endangering his health. Blood glucose levels must be maintained in the 80-150 range for optimal learning and testing of academic skills. Sam has a recognized disability, Type 1 Diabetes, that requires the accommodations and modifications set out in this plan to ensure that he has the same opportunities and conditions for learning and academic testing as classmates, with minimal disruption of his regular school schedule and with minimal time away from the classroom. Steps to prevent hypoglycemia and hyperglycemia, and to treat these conditions if they occur must be taken in accordance with this Plan.

Accommodations that are necessary for Sam:

1. Sam shall be permitted to use the bathroom without restriction.

2. Sam shall be permitted to have immediate access to water, including keeping a water bottle in his possession and being allowed to use the drinking fountain without restriction.

3. Sam shall be permitted to have snacks in the classroom.

4. Sam shall be permitted to leave class at any time to go to the office for diabetes related issues.

5. Sam shall have immediate access to blood glucose testing equipment and insulin, and shall be permitted to carry this equipment with him at all times.

6. Blood glucose tests may be done at any location in school, including, but not limited to the classroom, on school grounds, the cafeteria, at field trips or sites of extracurricular activities, or on the school bus.

Figure 3.1 Sample 504 plan.

7. Sam will be permitted to participate in all field trips and extracurricular activities (such as sports, clubs and enrichment programs) without restriction and with all of the accommodations and modifications set out in this plan.

8. If Sam is affected by high or low blood glucose levels at the time of regular or standardized testing, he will be permitted to take the test at another time without penalty. High blood glucose is defined as over 220 and low blood glucose as under 80.

9. If Sam needs to take breaks to use the water fountain or bathroom, do a blood glucose test, or to treat hypoglycemia or hyperglycemia during a test or a classroom assignment, he will be given extra time to finish the test or assignment without penalty.

10. Sam will not be penalized for absences or tardiness required for medical appointments, illness, visits to the office, or time necessary to maintain blood glucose control.

Signatures and Indication of Agreement:

Figure 3.1 (*cont.*)

Safety Counseling Guidelines

https://patiented.solutions.aap.org/handout-collection.aspx?categoryid=32033

Safety Barrier Guidelines for Residential Pools, www.floridahealth.gov/environmental-health/swimming-pools/_documents/cpsc-safety-barriers.pdf

Child Passenger Safety State Laws, https://drivinglaws.aaa.com/tag/child-passenger-safety/

Special Education Advocacy Resources

www.wrightslaw.com/

Wright, P. & Wright, P. (2006). *From Emotions to Advocacy – The Special Education Survival Guide*, 2nd ed. Deltaville, VA: Harbor House Law Press.

Section 504 Information

US Department of Education, Office for Civil Rights, Parent and Educator Resource Guide to Section 504, www2.ed.gov/about/offices/list/ocr/docs/504-resource-guide-201612.pdf

Prescriptive interventions based on function of school refusal behavior

---

1. Refusing school to avoid school-based stimuli that provoke negative affectivity (child-based)
   Psychoeducation regarding anxiety and its components
   Somatic management techniques such as relaxation training and deep diaphragmatic breathing
   Gradual re-exposure to school setting using anxiety and avoidance hierarchy
   Self-reinforcement of gains
2. Refusing school to escape aversive social and/or evaluative situations (child-based)
   Psychoeducation regarding anxiety and its components
   Somatic management techniques such as relaxation training and deep diaphragmatic breathing
   Cognitive restructuring to modify irrational thoughts
   Practicing coping skills in real-life social and evaluative situations
   Gradual re-exposure to school setting using anxiety and avoidance hierarchy
   Self-reinforcement of gains
3. Refusing school to pursue attention from significant others (parent-based)
   Modify parent commands toward brevity and clarity
   Establish a set morning routine prior to school as well as daytime routines as necessary
   Establish rewards for attendance and punishments for nonattendance
   Forced school attendance in specific cases
4. Refusing school to pursue tangible rewards outside of school (family-based)
   Contingency contracting that involves increasing incentives for attendance and disincentives for nonattendance
   Establish times and places for family members to negotiate problem solutions
   Communication skills training
   Escorting a youth to school and classes as necessary
   Increasing monitoring of attendance
   Peer refusal skills training (to refuse offers from others to miss school)

Figure 3.2 Prescriptive interventions based on function of school refusal behavior. Reprinted from *Clinical Psychology Review, 28*, Christopher Kearney, "School absenteeism and school refusal behavior in youth: a contemporary review," 451–471, copyright 2008, with permission from Elsevier. www.sciencedirect.com/journal/clinical-psychology-review

Sample 504 Plan Accommodations

Sevier County Tennessee School System Section 504 Plans: Examples of Program Accommodations and Adjustments, www.bridges4kids.org/articles/2004/4-04/SevierAcc.html

Working with Adolescents with Medical Concerns

4.1 Adolescents and Chronic Illness

In working with the pediatric population, clinicians will often be asked to help adolescents navigate the complex needs and demands of chronic illness, as approximately 20–30% of adolescents have been diagnosed with a chronic illness (Yeo & Sawyer, 2005). In addition to managing the medical and psychological needs of their patients, clinicians who work with adolescents with medical conditions are presented with unique developmental challenges associated with this age group.

As these adolescents begin the process of physically changing from childlike frames to their full adult bodies, numerous changes within their bodies affect not only their psychological health but also their medical health as a result of bidirectional interactions between pubertal development and chronic illnesses (Neinstein, 2001). For example, adolescents with diabetes mellitus type 1 may struggle with insulin resistance as a part of normal pubertal development despite adherence to prescribed treatment regimens (Neinstein, 2001). From a behavioral health standpoint, adolescence is a critical time for intervention both medically and psychologically as adolescents are also establishing the early lifestyle habits that may follow them for their rest of their lives, such as sleeping, dietary, and physical activity levels that will influence their health across the life span.

In addition to physical and pubertal changes that occur during this time frame, adolescents with chronic illness face the typical developmental challenges associated with sexual development, as well as potential challenges associated with reproduction, pubertal development, and sexual side effects from treatments (Neinstein, 2001; Aubin & Perez, 2015). While all adolescents are busy negotiating the physical and psychological changes that occur with sexual maturation, adolescents with chronic illness may face specific challenges that are not commonly faced by their peers, such as infertility and delayed pubertal development (e.g., delayed changes in secondary sexual characteristics or primary amenorrhea) (Neinstein, 2001).

Overall, chronic illness has been shown to have a significant impact on the physical health, social functioning, psychological health, and overall autonomy of adolescents (LeBovidge et al., 2003). Physically, adolescents with a chronic illness may have observable side effects from the medical condition or its associated treatments, such as small stature and pubertal delay in cystic fibrosis, obesity from limitations in physical activity from musculoskeletal conditions, or visible scarring from surgical procedures (Yeo & Sawyer, 2005). At a time when many adolescents are mindful of their physical appearance and overall social acceptance, it is not improbable to consider that many patients may find these visible reminders of their medical condition stigmatizing and detrimental to their overall self-esteem.

Helping patients when they are struggling with self-esteem can be difficult for even the most experienced of psychotherapists, and this can be particularly challenging when the patient may be the recipient of habitual bullying based on physical appearance or impaired physical functioning. Although strategies for building self-esteem will vary for each patient, research does appear to support the use of cognitive behavioral strategies for improving global self-esteem in depressed adolescents (Taylor & Montgomery, 2007). Although the exact mechanisms by which cognitive behavioral therapy enacts changes in self-esteem have not been identified, it can be hypothesized that by helping adolescents recognize and reframe dysfunctional thoughts about themselves, they are helping to improve their global self-esteem. For example, a therapist can work with an adolescent on using a dysfunctional thought record to review an automatic thought that may arise from a curious comment from a peer (e.g., "Karen must think I am ugly if she is asking about my scar") and subsequently reframe an underlying core belief (e.g., "I'm ugly") that may be adversely impacting their self-esteem.

Additionally, research does implicate the role of perceived competency and social support as core factors in an individual's self-esteem (Harter, 1986). Regarding perceived competency, clinicians may want to help adolescents with lower self-esteem to explore areas of interest, such as athletics, music, drama, or other hobbies in which they could potentially develop feelings of competency, as well as receiving the benefits inherent with behavioral activation. Specifically, the adolescent is actively engaging in activities (preferably outside the home) and receiving the benefits of behavioral activation, while hopefully also receiving reinforcement from others regarding their efforts or competency in a skill.

This increased perceived competency can be complemented by having the adolescent work or play in situations in which the patient is able to practice key social skills that can help with engendering more social support. Given the importance of social interactions with peers during this time frame, it is problematic for adolescents with chronic illnesses that many opportunities for peer interactions during typical social occasions (e.g., lunch period) may be limited due to reduced school attendance (LeBovidge et al., 2003). As such, mental health practitioners may want to emphasize social skills training and/or group modalities to help provide adolescents with in vivo experience to practice these important social skills.

In fact, as a result of potentially limited social interactions due to their illness, adolescents with chronic illness tend to exhibit decreased social competence (Martinez et al., 2011). Moreover, research has indicated that some chronic illnesses are associated with decreased involvement in romantic relationships in older teenagers and young adults (Collins et al., 2009). Anecdotally, many adolescents may wonder about when or, rather, if they should discuss their medical condition with someone they are interested in romantically.

Like other self-disclosures in personal relationships, adolescent patients may benefit from having a mental health provider guide them in identifying both the negative and positive consequences of disclosing this information, as well as eliciting parental support for the adolescent to have autonomy in making this decision. Should an adolescent decide to disclose their medical condition to their peer(s), clinicians can help patients learn key phrases and medical terminology to help the patient explain the condition clearly and concisely. Role-playing these conversations in psychotherapy can be helpful in promoting the adolescents' perceived self-efficacy in discussing this with their peers, as well as to clarify the patient's own understanding of their illness and overall prognosis.

In addition to the impact of their condition on social functioning and peer relationships, adolescents with chronic medical conditions also have to contend with being at increased risk for psychological symptoms (Neinstein, 2001). In particular, adolescents with chronic health conditions are at increased risk for mental health concerns if they are male, from a lower socioeconomic status, or have parents with psychiatric problems and/or criminal histories (Neinstein, 2001).

In comparison to their same-aged peers, adolescents with chronic illness tend to exhibit increased rates of suicidal ideation (Knight et al., 2015). This finding is acutely important given that approximately 17% of high schoolers already report experiencing suicidal ideation within the past 12 months (Kann et al., 2016). This increased risk for suicidal ideation appears to be associated with the severity of the adolescent's disability, and it is hypothesized that this association between suicidal ideation and disability severity may be due to increased social isolation and dependency (Burcu, 2014).

When working with adolescents who may be at increased risk due to the aforementioned factors, clinicians should consistently screen for risk factors associated with suicidality. The Columbia-Suicide Severity Rating Scale (C-SSRS) is a screening measure that has been widely used in both research and clinical settings as a result of its strong psychometric properties (Posner et al., 2011). The C-SSRS assesses both suicidal ideation and suicidal behavior and, of particular interest to clinicians, has customized versions based on different patient populations and clinical settings. Free training is offered on this measure from the Columbia Lighthouse Project, and readers can find the C-SSRS screener (lifetime/recent version) in the "Recommended Websites, Books, and Other Resources" section at the end of this chapter.

Given these increased risks for problems associated with physical, social, and psychological health, adolescents with chronic medical conditions tend to exhibit impairment in achieving developmental milestones. Specifically, adolescents with chronic medical concerns tend to have lower rates of graduating from college, finding a job, and leaving their parents' home (Zukerman et al., 2010; Pinquart, 2014). It has been hypothesized that this delay in the achievement of milestones associated with adult development may be a potential result of the reduced autonomy that may be inherent with their medical condition, as well as the possibility of the patient assuming the "sick role" as part of their overall identity (Suris et al., 2004). Of note, this delay in achieving adult milestones is significantly linked with the visibility and duration of the illness. Namely, the longer the duration and the more visible the illness, the more likely that the patient's achievement of adult developmental milestones will be delayed (Pinquart, 2014).

When working with adolescents with chronic medical conditions, it is vital for clinicians to provide psychoeducation to parents about the importance of helping patients to set and achieve developmentally appropriate goals. Many parents of adolescents with and without chronic illness feel anxious about allowing their child to face natural consequences of their actions, such as feeling ill from side effects associated with not taking their medication as prescribed. This protectiveness can be observed with traditional mental health concerns as well as medical concerns. For example, parents of a patient with social anxiety may seek to pull their child from a more traditional school format in order to prevent their child from experiencing anxiety every morning before school. Similarly, a parent of an adolescent with a medical condition may be tempted to "protect" their child with diabetes by not allowing them to attend an overnight summer camp due to a fear that their blood glucose will not be accurately monitored away from home.

In their clinical work, clinicians need to help parents understand the danger of over-protectiveness in preventing adolescents with chronic illnesses from achieving normal developmental milestones. Following this education, the clinician should utilize resources to help the patient successfully achieve these milestones, such as assisting with the creation of a 504 plan for school accommodations or teaching the adolescent time management strategies to help them learn to balance the time demands of school medical treatments.

Balancing the need to validate parents' concerns while also allowing patients to experience natural consequences is particularly complicated given that we know adolescents are more likely than children to engage in risky behaviors (e.g., substance use and unsafe sexual practices), with approximately 2–17% of adolescents trying illegal substances such as cocaine and 63% trying alcohol (Kann et al., 2016). Recent statistics suggest that rates of substance use are high in the chronic illness population, as approximately one-third of adolescents with a chronic illness use alcohol while approximately one-fifth of these patients use marijuana (Weitzman et al., 2015).

Of particular clinical interest, research has indicated that if a patient engages in one risky behavior, they are much more likely to engage in other behaviors that could also be detrimental to their physical and mental health (Dryfoos, 1993). This pattern is particularly important for adolescents with chronic illness as risky behavior can significantly impact their physical health by the very nature of the risky behavior as well as by the possibility of their risky behavior interacting with medications and laboratory tests, impairing overall self-care, and decreasing their adherence with medical regimens (Hackworth et al., 2013; Weitzman et al., 2015). For example, adolescents with chronic illness who reportedly drank alcohol were 1.79 times more likely to miss taking their medications (Weitzman et al., 2015).

To assess adolescent alcohol use, the Youth Alcohol Screening Tool of the National Institute on Alcoholism and Alcohol Abuse (2015) is recommended as a brief screener that has been validated with patients between the ages of 9 and 18 with chronic medical conditions (persistent asthma, inflammatory bowel disease, etc.) (Levy et al., 2016). This screener focuses on assessing both the patient's and their friends' use of alcohol in the past year, and information on this screener and its administration can be found in the "Recommended Websites, Books, and Other Resources" section. The patient's risk level is based on the patient's age and the number of days they disclosed drinking alcohol within the past year. Of note, research by Levy and colleagues has adjusted the risk level based on whether the patient is a youth with a chronic medical condition (YCMC) (Levy et al., 2016) (see Figure 4.1).

When an adolescent has been identified as exhibiting risky behavior, a clinician must first and foremost attend to any safety concerns, such as driving while under the influence of a substance, engaging in risky sexual behavior, or other myriad concerns that can arise. Although recommendations for intervention with risky behavior should be tailored to the specific behavior exhibited as well as each patient's level of risk, some basic guidelines for immediate intervention should include (1) increasing parental supervision, (2) removing lethal objects from immediate accessibility, (3) monitoring cell phone and social media usage, and (4) ensuring that mental health treatment is prioritized.

Regarding increasing parental supervision, it may be helpful to collaborate with the adolescent on determining how they can "earn" unsupervised time by their behavior. For example, an adolescent caught using marijuana may benefit from a behavioral contract in

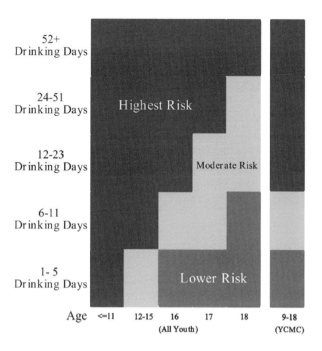

Figure 4.1 Comparison of estimated risk levels by age and response using NIAAA Youth Alcohol Screening Tool for all youth and youth with a chronic medical condition (YCMC). Reprinted from "A screening tool for assessing alcohol use risk among medically vulnerable youth," by S. Levy et al. 2016, *PLOS One, 11*(5), e0156240. Copyright 2016 by Levy et al

which they can "earn" unsupervised time with their friends after passing several random drug tests in a row (which can be bought by parents at local drugstores for a relatively low price). Similarly, an adolescent who has been sending sexually explicit pictures to other people can "earn" back their privacy by having their phone consistently monitored by their parents until they have demonstrated that they will respect the rules set forth by their parent or guardian for a specified period of consistently monitored time.

With increased parental supervision and increased monitoring or restriction of cell phone and social media usage, parents should also remove access to potentially harmful objects such as knives, guns, alcohol, and other items that can be dangerous when used impulsively when adolescents are exhibiting or engaging in risky behavior. Lastly, when an adolescent is exhibiting risky behavior, it is paramount that parents model the importance of mental health and/or substance abuse treatment. Parents should be educated on the importance of modeling this prioritization, as even the best psychotherapist in the world will struggle to get "buy in" from an adolescent if it is clear that the parent values other engagements over therapy, such as athletic games or recreational events.

4.2 Adolescents and Treatment Adherence

Despite overall improvement in problem-solving ability in comparison to children, adolescents have a "relatively poor ability to plan and prepare for different situations using abstract concepts" (Suris et al., 2004, p. 941). Given this difficulty in problem solving and planning, adolescents as a population tend to have difficulty with adhering to complex treatment regimens. This well-documented difficulty with treatment adherence is thought to be consistent with developmental changes associated with adolescence, such as decreased self-regulation, increased risk taking, and the increased perception of invulnerability (Bouchery et al., 2011).

The rates for adolescent treatment adherence, or "the extent to which a person's behavior … coincides with medical or health advice," are approximately 50% for most chronic medical conditions (Horwitz & Horwitz, 1993, p. 1863). This difficulty with treatment adherence remains a significant problem in the health care system for both adolescents and adults despite the research literature consistently demonstrating the association between treatment adherence and health outcomes (Rapoff, 2011). There are some notable factors that tend to influence adherence in adolescents. The type of medical-related tasks that must be performed for the medical condition plays a large role in adherence rates. For instance, regimens that require lifestyle changes such as increased exercise or diet alterations tend to have lower rates of adherence in comparison to medication-only treatment tasks (Rapoff, 2011).

While it may be tempting for clinicians to think of patients in the binary category of either "adherent" or "nonadherent," it may not be uncommon based on the research described above for some patients to exhibit differing rates of adherence with specific aspects of a treatment regimen. This assumption is not limited to the adolescent population. Take, for example, the scenario of an adult diagnosed with high blood pressure who has been told to take prescription medications, eat a low sodium diet, and exercise regularly. Of these three treatment recommendations, which do you think the adult patient is most likely to be adherent with in comparison to the other two treatment recommendations?

Not only do external factors, such as the type of condition or medical regimen, play a role in treatment adherence, but also intrinsic factors unique to each individual patient and family. Research has indicated that excessively anxious parents may place restrictions on the patient's behavior, and, contrary to the espoused aims of these parents, this parental anxiety and subsequent restrictive behavior is associated with decreased treatment adherence (Wamboldt & Wamboldt, 2000). Treatment adherence also tends to be lower in families facing extrinsic stressors, such as low socioeconomic status and the extra demands associated with being a single-parent household (La Greca & Bearman, 2003).

Treatment nonadherence can result from both volitional choices and nonvolitional factors (Rapoff, 2011). Volitional nonadherence may occur as a result of patients and families choosing not to take a certain medication due to deleterious side effects or the lack of knowledge about the actual impact of these medications on the patient's health (Rapoff, 2011). A teenager can perceive that the opportunity cost of checking his blood sugars before lunch is too high, as it takes up time that would otherwise be earmarked for socializing with peers, and therefore choose to skip recommended blood glucose monitoring when at school. This volitional choice therefore requires a different treatment approach from a patient whose treatment adherence is impacted by nonvolitional factors, such as the patient's inability to pay for the diabetes test strips necessary for monitoring or the teenager's symptoms of attention-deficit/hyperactivity disorder (ADHD) interfering with remembering to perform these blood glucose checks. These differing reasons for treatment adherence must be assessed in order to ensure that the root cause of this nonadherence is targeted for intervention.

Many clinicians may wonder why they, as mental health professionals, are asked to assist in promoting treatment adherence rather than just remaining focused on psychological functioning. In their role, mental health providers are equipped to help explore the biopsychosocial influences and factors that may be affecting treatment adherence, and, through the use of clinical techniques and interventions, they have a direct impact on both the patient's physical and psychological health.

Mental health providers are uniquely suited to address a number of the limiting factors that may prevent consistent treatment adherence. Similarly, another notable influence on nonadherence to medical treatment is patient depression (DiMatteo et al., 2000). With amotivation as a hallmark of depression, adherence can be significantly impacted by a patient's mood. Given their training in providing evidence-based treatment for depression, mental health clinicians are able to directly address this root cause of treatment nonadherence.

Moreover, clinicians can help to assess whether adherence may be due to nonpsychiatric factors, such as the patient and medical provider having discrepant treatment goals. For example, a medical provider may identify the main treatment goal as reducing depression by increasing the quality and duration of a patient's sleep, while a patient and family may identify that their most important goal is help the patient learn study skills in order to improve his or her grades. When patients and medical providers have differing treatment goals, frustration can ensue for both parties. As a mental health clinician, providers can help align these two seemingly disparate goals under the common goal of increasing the patient's quality of life and assist with both goals of improved sleep and academic functioning.

4.3 Assessment of Treatment Adherence

The assessment of children and adolescents' adherence to recommended treatment regimens is a complicated process that requires multimodal methods (Quittner et al., n.d.). The mental health clinician is tasked with investigating the underlying causes of this behavior in order to best identify and implement targeted interventions to increase adherence. Given this complexity and the potentially changing reasons for nonadherence, the assessment of adherence should be viewed as a process rather than as a single intervention or outcome (Quittner et al., n.d.). Unfortunately, treatment adherence is not a box that can be checked on an intake form during the initial interview, but is a concept that must be reviewed regularly as patient functioning, changes in psychiatric states, and other factors will impact adherence rates.

Multimodal methods of assessment, such as daily phone diaries, self-report questionnaires, and pharmacy refill histories, are recommended to provide both objective and subjective data regarding actual treatment adherence and the patient's perception of their adherence to the medical regimen (Quittner et al., n.d.). These differing methods of assessment have diverse strengths and weaknesses, and, collectively, the differing methods are thought to provide a more accurate clinical picture than information based on one type of assessment measure.

Assessment measures for treatment adherence can take many different forms and have differing benefits and disadvantages associated with each type. Written logs and phone diaries tend to be more accurate than self-report measures, with more objective measures (e.g., pharmacy refill histories) tending to have the highest accuracy of all measures (Quittner et al., 2007; Pai et al., 2008).

Common objective assessments that have found been to be clinically effective are electronic monitors and pharmacy refill histories (Quittner et al., 2007). There are a variety of different types of electronic monitors, and, in particular, electronic monitors may be useful in working with pediatric patients with regimens that include medications that are inhaled or are in pill form (Quittner et al., 2007). One such example of an electronic monitor is the Medication Events Monitoring System (MEMS^{TM}), which measures the time and date a pill bottle is opened (Modi et al., 2013; West Rock Company, 2016).

Despite the improved accuracy of objective measures in assessing treatment adherence, not all mental health clinicians will have access to medical resources that provide this more objective form of assessment (Lam & Fresco, 2015). Self-report questionnaires, structured interviews, and other more subjective measures also provide important information for the clinician. These methods tend to be of lower cost and provide two unique advantages over more objective measures: the ability to give immediate feedback to the patient about their adherence and the ability to more fully understand the patient's concerns associated with adherence (Lam & Fresco, 2015).

Self-report questionnaires are usually available in differing formats that may allow for both patient and parental assessment of concerns. These questionnaires tend to evaluate some or all of the following behaviors/concerns: medication or regimen adherence, barriers to adherence, and beliefs associated with adherence (Nguyen et al., 2014). Within the pediatric psychology research literature, many self-report measures may be disease-specific, such as the Disease Management Interview for Asthma or the Treatment Adherence Questionnaire-CF (Quittner et al., 2007). For more information about empirically supported disease-specific measures, refer to the website for the Society of Pediatric Psychology's recommended assessment measures, which may be found in the "Recommended Websites, Books, and Other Resources" section.

4.4 Interventions to Promote Treatment Adherence

Following the comprehensive and multimodal assessment of the potential causes of treatment nonadherence, clinicians are tasked with determining which interventions would be the most effective in helping their patients adhere to their treatment regimen or recommended lifestyle changes. While some patients and families may be nonadherent due to a lack of education about the health condition and/or recommended treatments, a reliance on an education-only intervention does not appear to be of great enough impact in helping families to promote significant and lasting behavior change (Erickson et al., 2005; Bishay & Sawicki, 2016). As such, it is imperative that the clinician assists families in taking personal information and knowledge about each individual family to create behavior change that is aligned with the patient's values and takes into context the specific impact of the medical illness and treatment on their life (Riekert et al., 2015).

Overall, the most efficacious interventions to promote treatment adherence tend to include both behavioral and multicomponent interventions (Ellis et al., 2005; Stark et al., 2005). In particular, brief multicomponent interventions have shown efficacy in promoting adherence in childhood asthma and cystic fibrosis, and these interventions typically include educational interventions to the patient and parent(s), organizational strategies, and behavioral interventions that emphasize the reinforcement of behaviors consistent with treatment adherence (Bernard & Cohen, 2004). Organizational strategies typically emphasize changing external factors such as how to make the treatment regimen simpler and can particularly help when the barrier to adherence involves forgetfulness (Hanghoi & Boisen, 2014). Meanwhile, behavioral strategies often focus on intrinsic factors unique to the individual such as increasing the patient's self-monitoring and providing reinforcement for adherence (Lemanek et al., 2001).

As part of many multicomponent interventions, motivational interviewing also has been found to be of particular assistance in promoting the self-efficacy of adolescents in making behavioral changes (Brown et al., 2003). Motivational interviewing is an empirically supported technique that "enhances a patient's intrinsic motivation to change by exploring their perspective and ambivalence" (Erickson et al., 2005, p. 1174). At its core, motivational interviewing focuses on assessing and subsequently promoting the patient's self-efficacy and motivation to change. This technique is built on the foundational principles of expressing empathy, developing discrepancy between the patient's current behavior and their goals, rolling with the resistance that may be encountered when discussing possible behavioral change, and supporting the patient's self-efficacy in being able to successfully carry out behavioral changes (Erickson et al., 2005).

When utilizing motivational interviewing techniques, it is important to keep in mind the patient's developmental level and, more specifically, the patient's ability to understand the role of causal relationships (Erickson et al., 2005). Basically, clinicians must have an overall understanding of whether their patients understand how their current behaviors are linked to future outcomes or consequences. Since this ability starts to appear by middle childhood for most patients, it is recommended that interventions with younger children focus more heavily on the behavior and its immediate consequences, such as linking the behavior of checking blood glucose with the positive consequence of earning a sticker, or on placing more emphasis on parental interventions (Erickson et al., 2005). As children become older and develop cognitively, clinicians can begin linking children's short-term behavior with future consequences/rewards. For instance, a clinician can help a patient with cystic fibrosis begin to link their improved pulmonary functioning with their overall improved athletic performance that past season in comparison to previous seasons when they had not been as consistent with their pulmonary treatments.

Motivational interviewing utilizes distinctive techniques for the purposes of trying to elicit "change talk," or any language in which the patient identifies their own reasons for change (Erickson et al., 2005). A clinician is looking to reinforce change talk in which the patient discusses why change is personally important to them. The motivation for behavior change will vary from individual to individual, so it is imperative to take the time to figure out what makes each patient decide the effort to make a change is worth it to them. Not surprisingly, many of these reasons for change may be overlooked by an adult clinician if they are not listening carefully for the patient's point of view. For example, while an adult clinician may think that a child wants to perform their cystic fibrosis treatments in order to prevent a deterioration in lung functioning, it is important to remember that a pediatric patient's motivation may be much more situation-specific, such as "I want to make sure I can go to the prom rather than possibly being in the hospital!"

In order to help elicit this "change talk," clinicians using motivational interviewing need to incorporate "OARS": using open-ended questions, affirmation, reflective listening, and summary statements (Erickson et al., 2005). The use of scaling rulers for assessing the patient's perception of the importance of making a change and their perception of their ability to make a behavioral change is helpful in assisting patients in understanding their level of motivation and belief that they can make a change. Scaling allows for differentiation of what would help increase their level of motivation or self-efficacy (Erickson et al., 2005). For example, a clinician might use the Readiness Rulers (provided courtesy of Case Western Reserve University, 2011) in Figure 4.4 in the "Reproducible Resources" section at the end of this chapter when asking a patient: "On a scale of 1 to 10 with 10 indicating the highest motivation to change, how important is it for you to regularly check your blood glucose? Why is that number not lower (i.e. less motivated)."

In some cases, adolescents are already willing and able to make a behavior change associated with their physical and/or mental health. For these patients, it is important to help them to set individualized goals. One framework in which clinicians can help set these goals is the use of "SMART" goals for behavior change (Gold & Kokotailo, 2007). This framework helps clinicians collaborate with patients in creating goals that are specific, measurable, achievable, realistic, and time-framed.

For instance, an adolescent with obesity may be motivated to lose weight; however, their goal setting (i.e., "I want to lose 10 pounds now by eating less) might not be conducive to helping them to actual achieve their overall goal of losing weight. This patient's goal is not specific (e.g., What does eating "less" look like?), measurable (i.e., How many calories per day will the patient eat to achieve weight loss?), achievable or realistic (i.e., Is losing 10 pounds healthy for their current weight, height, and overall medical stability?), or time-framed (i.e., When will this weight loss be achieved?). With the assistance of a trained clinician, a patient can revise this goal to be more attainable and measurable: "I will eat 1,800 calories per day and walk 2 miles per day with the goal of losing 1–2 pounds per week."

Another empirically supported psychological intervention for assisting adolescents in making positive behavior changes is behavioral contracting, which formalizes an agreement of the person's intention to make a behavioral change (Abraham & Michie, 2008). The research literature has identified behavioral contracting and other cognitive interventions as integral parts of empirically supported interventions for adolescents diagnosed with myriad medical conditions, such as type 1 diabetes mellitus and juvenile fibromyalgia (Wysocki et al., 1989; Degotardi et al., 2006).

When utilizing behavioral contracting, it is important to ensure that the adolescent patient is an integral part of the process in helping to define the specific behaviors that are agreed on, as well as the designated rewards and consequences. For a behavioral contract to be most effective, it is helpful to have the adolescent patient's "buy in" that this contract can be used to help them achieve their goals as well as the parents' goal of treatment adherence. One question that can be used to help spur this line of thinking into what motivates the patient is "What will the patient work for?" Parents often have an immediate reply, such as, "They will do anything to have access to their cell phone or to hang out with friends on the weekend." As such, this information can be used to help adolescent patients achieve what they desire most as part of the behavioral contract, rather than just blindly forcing them to suddenly hold the same values and motivations as their more developmentally advanced parents.

In addition to behavioral contracting, self-monitoring has been found to be an important feature of evidenced-based clinical interventions (Bakker et al., 2016). Recently, research has begun to investigate the utility of phone applications in assisting in self-monitoring and other clinical techniques to help promote pediatric behavioral change (Brannon & Cushing, 2014).

This area of focus is of particular interest given the prevalence of adolescent phone ownership, as approximately 83% of adolescents between the ages of 12 and 17 own either a cell phone or tablet computer, and approximately 58% of adolescents within this age range had previously downloaded at least one phone app (Madden et al., 2013).

Clinical Vignette: "Tired Teenager"

Ms. Q presents to her third psychotherapy session with her 16-year-old son, Timmy, who was initially referred for ADHD. In addition to ADHD, Timmy's medical history is significant for diabetes mellitus type 1, which was initially diagnosed when he was 11 years old. Although Timmy has never had significant difficulties with treatment adherence as a preadolescent, Ms. Q reports that during his past several clinical appointments with their endocrine clinic, his hemoglobin A1C (hbA1c) scores have remained high, and he has recently been hospitalized twice for diabetic ketoacidosis (DKA).

According to Ms. Q and Timmy, he has had the greatest difficulty in remembering to do his morning blood glucose checks before and after breakfast. Timmy notes that he has particular trouble remembering to eat breakfast, as he often forgets to set his alarm clock to wake up earlier, and even when he does wake up with adequate time to eat breakfast and check his blood glucose, he reports feeling unmotivated because "I don't feel sick." Timmy is able to provide an adequate rationale for why these clinical recommendations are important for both his short- and long-term health, but as he openly admits, "That's hard to remember when it's 7 o'clock in the morning!"

Given that Timmy appears to have trouble with remembering to set his alarm clock as well as having consistent difficulty with intrinsic motivation to perform his morning blood glucose checks, you propose utilizing a behavioral contract to help the patient make behavioral changes that are shaped by the application of timely positive and negative consequences. You then work with Timmy and Ms. Q to identify weekly positive and negative consequences that can be implemented consistently by Ms. Q and that are salient to Timmy.

The two target behaviors that are identified are: (1) to set his alarm clock every night when he takes his evening medications and (2) to eat and perform his morning glucose checks at 7 AM every weekday morning and at 8 AM on weekends. In exchange for performing these two tasks every day, Timmy will earn 4 hours of weekend access to the family car on Friday evenings; if not, he will be restricted from any social activities with his friends that weekend. Furthermore, it was agreed on by both Timmy and Ms. Q that it was Timmy's responsibility to have Ms. Q "sign off" when he had completed each of these two assigned tasks for the day, and it was agreed that it was Ms. Q's responsibility to implement the positive or negative consequences each Friday evening, dependent on whether both target goals had been achieved at least four times that week.

Following the joint session with Ms. Q and Timmy, you meet separately with Ms. Q to discuss the potential for an extinction burst once the contract has been implemented and the need to remain consistent in implementing both the negative and positive consequences as agreed upon in the contract.

4.5 Assisting Adolescent Patients in Transitioning from Pediatric to Adult Care

As adolescents mature into young adulthood, some clinicians will be tasked with assisting the patient in transitioning from a pediatric to an adult care center (McManus et al., 2015). Many health care clinics face difficulties about knowing *when* to transition a patient as well as *how* to transition a patient from a pediatric setting to an adult care clinic (Schwartz et al., 2014). This transition process is significant from a medical standpoint for adolescents, as the transition is typically associated with reduced follow-up visits following the adolescent patient's transition to an adult clinic (Canadian Pediatric Society, 2007). Overall, if the transition is not handled with appropriate care regarding when and how the transition occurs, patients tend to exhibit decreased treatment non-adherence (Gurvitz et al., 2007).

Research has identified numerous barriers to a successful transition, including, but not limited to, systemic processes that adversely impact the transition process and conflict within the patient's family about the timing of the transition process (Collins et al., 1997; McManus et al., 2015). Regarding the timing of the transition from a pediatric to an adult care center, there are general guidelines about the specific age range when transition should occur. In particular, a clinical report from the American Academy of Pediatrics, American Academy of Family Physicians, and American College of Physicians recommends that the actual transition should occur between ages 18 and 21 (2011). However, this clinical report emphasizes that the transition should be a process that begins in early adolescence rather than immediately prior to the actual transition.

Given the importance of handling this transition in a clinically effective manner, research has focused on identifying protocols to assist clinicians in this process. Specifically, the Six Core Elements of Health Care Transition (2.0) has been utilized to help with the transition of care in both pediatric and adult settings (Got Transition, 2014). The Six Elements of Health Care Transition are organized based on the context of the transition. In particular, the protocol changes based on whether the clinical need is to help the patient transition to an adult care provider, to help transition to an adult approach with the same previous pediatric provider, or to integrate the patient into an adult care system.

For the provider within a pediatric setting who is involved in assisting adolescents in transitioning to an adult care center, there are six recommended steps: (1) developing a policy for the transition process that involves collaboration with the adult care clinic, (2) tracking and monitoring patients, (3) readying adolescent patients for transition and orienting the patient to the adult care clinic, (4) planning the actual transition and integration into the adult care clinic, (5) officially transferring care and having an initial visit at the adult clinic, and (6) completing the actual transfer process and continuing with ongoing care in the adult clinic (Got Transition, 2014).

Based on the Six Core Elements of Health Care Transition (2.0), individual clinicians can play an important role, particularly in the middle stages of transition readiness and planning. On an individual-patient level, clinicians can begin utilizing transition readiness assessments at age 14 to help guide discussions about self-care and prioritized goals (McManus et al., 2015). Evidence-based assessments such as the Treatment Readiness Assessment Questionnaire (TRAQ) and the Successful Transition to Adulthood with Therapeutics = R_x (STARx) have been found to be of particular benefit in assessing a patient's readiness for transition (Wood et al., 2014; Cohen et al., 2015; UNC Starx Program, 2016). These evidence-based assessments have been included in the "Reproducible Resources" section.

These aforementioned assessments can be important tools in identifying the timing of the actual transition, as well as helpful in identifying areas for continued clinical attention, including the need for additional supports related to cognitive deficits that may impact the problem-solving abilities necessary for the management of chronic illness (McManus et al., 2015). This approach emphasizes the need to evaluate adolescents based on their developmental level rather than on a previously established age-based criterion (Schwartz et al., 2014).

As part of this individualized transition process, clinicians need to address health education for the patient, legal issues (e.g., capacity to consent), and the transition process for the parents/caregivers (American Academy of Pediatrics et al., 2011). For many parents, it may be difficult to relinquish responsibility for medical care given the severity of the medical condition or the parent's concerns regarding the patient's readiness to take on this responsibility. Thus, the clinician is tasked with assisting not only the adolescent patient in the transition process but also the parents' transition via education about the transition process and by addressing the family's specific concerns.

As part of the clinicians' work with assisting the adolescent in transitioning to an adult care clinic and managing their increased autonomy with regard to managing their medical care, the clinician can assist in the transfer of care process by providing salient information to adult care centers such as the most recent results of a standardized transition readiness assessment and consents for speaking with the pediatric provider (McManus et al., 2015). Given the complexity of the medical information being transferred, clinicians may find it helpful to assist their patients in utilizing "MyHealth Passport" to help convey the specifics of their medical information (Wolfstadt et al., 2001). This customizable "passport" can be accessed free of charge courtesy of the "Good 2 Go Transition Program" website at the Hospital for Sick Kids (SickKids, 2014). Refer to the "Reproducible Resources" section for an example of a medical passport.

4.6 Preparing Adolescents for the Transition to College

Given advances in medical science, the majority of children and adolescents diagnosed with a chronic condition will survive past childhood and into adulthood (Lotstein et al., 2005). Medical advances have led to increased survival rates that are particularly notable in the pediatric cancer and cystic fibrosis populations (Stark et al., 2003; Patenaude & Kupst, 2005).

During an already stressful time of transition, adolescents with chronic illness may be at increased risk for anxiety and depression during the transition to college due to medically related stressors (Wodka & Barakat, 2007). In particular, research indicates that factors such as attending medical appointments and experiencing chronic physical symptoms may adversely impact a college student's mental health by increasing symptoms of anxiety or depression (Wodka & Barakat, 2007).

To assist with navigating the hurdles of attending college with a chronic illness, it is recommended that the patient become aware of resources available within their postsecondary educational institution. Although patients with chronic illnesses may meet criteria for disability accommodations, many college students may feel uncomfortable discussing their physical or mental health problems with campus staff even for accommodations due to fears about stigma or being viewed as "different" by their peers. However, college and universities mandate that students must request accommodations for a disability prior to exhibiting impaired academic performance, and "the courts have consistently found that the burden is on the student to make that [disability] known" (Rothstein, 2013, p. 1). The Americans with Disabilities (ADA) Amendments Act of 2008 has defined a disability as "a physical or mental impairment that substantially limits one or more major life activities of such individual" (Equal Employment Opportunity Commission, 2008).

Prior to transitioning to college, it may be advantageous to have a discussion with upcoming college students about the short- and long-term "pros and cons" associated with applying for academic accommodations in order to help ensure that the student/patient is aware of applicable legislation, including privacy laws, and has given this issue due consideration prior to beginning school in order to help them make an informed decision about applying for academic accommodations. Although some patients may decide not to avail themselves of pertinent accommodations, this type of exercise can help teenagers and young adults work on clarifying their personal values regarding their health and education, as well as utilizing problem-solving skills in order to make an informed decision according to these clarified values.

For the patients who do decide to advocate for themselves by availing themselves of academic accommodations for their disability, mental health clinicians can assist their patients in becoming aware of resources available for students with disabilities as well as strategies to help support a successful transition to college such as promoting a strong relationship with their academic advisor. This strategy can be beneficial for students with chronic illness as an academic advisor can help with strategies such as enrolling in courses that accommodate frequent medical absences or exploring hybrid options of online and in-person courses to assist with reduced travel time (Houman & Stapley, 2013).

Summary

With approximately 20–30% of adolescents having a chronic illness, clinicians are tasked with assisting the adolescent in navigating the unique challenges inherent with both their diagnosis and their age, including physical maturation associated with puberty, changing psychological concerns, and the developmentally appropriate increased need for autonomy. For adolescents, chronic illness can significantly impact multiple domains of their life, including overall psychological health and social functioning. As such, adolescents with chronic medical concerns tend to be at greater risk of being delayed in or prevented from achieving developmental milestones (e.g., finding a job or graduating from college).

Consistent with other areas of their lives, adolescents with chronic illness are tasked with becoming more autonomous in their daily care, including tasks associated with often complicated medical regimens. As a result of myriad factors, adolescence tends to be associated with decreased treatment adherence in comparison to children, which is of particular concern given the well-established association between treatment adherence and health outcomes.

Thus far, the research literature has identified several empirically supported clinical interventions for assisting adolescents in becoming more adherent with their treatment regimens. Overall, the most efficacious interventions to promote treatment adherence tend to be behavioral and multicomponent interventions. Motivational interviewing also has been found to be of particular assistance in promoting the self-efficacy of adolescents in making behavioral changes.

Given that more children than ever will survive past childhood and into adulthood, not only are mental health providers asked to help adolescents become more treatment adherent, but clinicians are also tasked with assisting the patient in transitioning from a pediatric to an adult care center.

References

Abraham, C. & Michie, S. (2008). A taxonomy of behavior change techniques used in interventions. *Health Psychology, 27,* 379–387.

Adherium. (2015). Devices. Retrieved November 17, 2017, from www.smartinhaler.com/devices/.

American Academy of Pediatrics, American Academy of Family Physicians, & American College of Physicians. (2011). Supporting the health care transition from adolescence to adulthood in the medical home. *Pediatrics, 128*(1), 182–202.

Aubin, S. & Perez, S. (2015). The clinician's toolbox: assessing the sexual impacts of cancer on adolescents and young adults with cancer (AYAC). *The Journal of Sexual Medicine, 3*(3), 198–212.

Bakker, D., Kazantzis, N., Rickwood, D., & Rickard, N. (2016). Mental health smartphone apps: review and evidence-based recommendations for future developments. *JMIR Mental Health, 3*(1), e7. doi: 10.2196/mental.4984.

BC Children's Hospital. (2017). Transition to Adult Care. Retrieved November 17, 2017, from www.bcchildrens.ca/our-services/support-services/transition-to-adult-care.

Bernard, R. & Cohen, L. (2004). Increasing adherence to cystic fibrosis treatment: a systematic review of behavioral techniques. *Pediatric Pulmonology, 37*, 8–16.

Bishay, L. & Sawicki, G. (2016). Strategies to optimize treatment adherence in adolescent patients with cystic fibrosis. *Adolescent Health, Medicine, and Therapeutics, 7*, 117–124.

Bouchery, E., Harwood, H., Sacks, J., Simon, C., & Brewer, R. (2011). Economic costs of excessive alcohol consumption in the U.S., 2006. *American Journal of Preventative Medicine, 41*(5), 516–524.

Brannon, E. & Cushing, C. (2014). A systematic review: is there an app for that? Translational science of pediatric behavior change for physical activity and dietary interventions. *Journal of Pediatric Psychology, 40*(4), 373–384.

Brown, R., Ramsey, S. Strong, D., Myers, M., Kahler, C., Niaura, R., Pallonen, U., Kazura, A., Goldstein, M., & Abrams, D. (2003). Effects of motivational interviewing on smoking cessation in adolescents with psychiatric disorders. *Tobacco Control, 12*, iv3–iv10.

Burcu, E. (2014). Disability and youth suicide: a focus group study of disabled university students. *Review of Disability Studies: An International Journal, 3*(1), 33–48.

Canadian Pediatric Society. (2007). Transition to adult care for youth with special health care needs. *Paediatrics and Child Health, 12* (9), 785–788.

Case Western Reserve University. (2011). Resources. Retrieved November 17, 2017, from www.centerforebp.case.edu/resources/tools/product=5&category=47.

Cohen, S., Hooper, S., Javalkar, K., Haberman, C., Fenton, N., Lai, H., Mahan, J., Massengill, S., Phillips, A., Sawicki, G., Wood, D., Johnson, M., Benton, M., & Ferris, M. (2015). Self-management and transition readiness assessment: concurrent, predictive and discriminate validation of the Starx Questionnaire. *Journal of Pediatric Nursing, 30*, 668–676.

Collins, A., Laursen, B., Mortenson, N., Luebker, C., & Ferreira, M. (1997). Conflict processes and transitions in parent and peer relationships: implications for autonomy and regulation. *Journal of Adolescent Research, 12*, 178–198.

Collins, W., Welsh, D., & Furman, W. (2009). Adolescent romantic relationships. *Annual Review of Psychology, 60*, 631–652.

Columbia Lighthouse Project. (2016). C-SSRS for Communities and Healthcare. Retrieved December 4, 2017, from http://cssrs .columbia.edu/the-columbia-scale-c-ssrs/cssrs-for-communities-and-healthcare/#filter=.general-use.english.

Degotardi, P., Klass, E., Rosenberg, B., Fox, D., Gallelli, K., & Gottlieb, B. (2006). Development and evaluation of a cognitive-behavioral interventionfor juvenile fibromyalgia. *Journal of Pediatric Psychology, 31*(7), 714–723.

DiMatteo, M., Lepper, H., & Croghan, T. (2000). Depression is a risk factor for noncompliance with medical treatment: a meta-analysis of the effects of anxiety and depression in patient adherence. *Archives of Internal Medicine, 160*, 2101–2107.

Dryfoos, J. (1993). Common components of successful interventions with high-risk youth. In N. Bell & R. Bell (eds.), *Adolescent Risk-*

Taking (pp. 131–147). Newbury Park, CA: Sage.

East Tennessee State University. (2017). Transition Readiness Assessment Questionnaire. Retrieved November 17, 2017, from www.etsu.edu/com/pediatrics/traq/.

Ellis, D., Frey, M., Naar-King, S., et al. (2005). Use of multisystemic therapy to improve regimen adherence among adolescents with type 1 diabetes in chronic poor metabolic control: a randomized controlled trial. *Diabetes Care, 28,* 1604–1610.

Equal Employment Opportunity Commission. (2008). ADA Amendments Act of 2008. Retrieved December 1, 2017, from www.eeoc.gov/laws/statutes/adaaa.cfm.

Erickson, S., Gerstle, M., & Feldstein, S. (2005). Brief interventions and motivational interviewing with children, adolescents, and their parents in pediatric health settings. *Archives of Pediatrics and Adolescent Medicine, 159,* 1173–1180.

Family Voice. (n.d.). Kids as Self Advocates. Retrieved November 17, 2017, from www.fvkasa.org/index.php.

Gold, M. & Kokotailo, P. (2007). Motivational interviewing strategies to facilitate adolescent behavior change. *Adolescent Health Update, 20*(1), 1–10.

Got Transition. (2014). The Six Core Elements of Health Care Transition (2.0). Retrieved from http://gottransition.org/resourceGet.cfm?id=206.

Gurvitz, M., Inkelas, M., Lee, M., Stout, K., Escarce, J., & Chang, R. (2007). Changes in hospitalization patterns among patients with congenital heart disease during the transition from adolescence to adulthood. *Journal of the American College of Cardiology, 49,* 875–882.

Hackworth, N., Hamilton, V., Moore, S., Northam, E., Bucalo, Z., & Cameron, F. (2013). Predictors of diabetes self-care, metabolic control, and mental health in youth with type 1 diabetes. *Australian Psychologist, 48,* 360–369.

Hanghoj, S. & Boisen K. (2014). Self-reported barriers to medication adherence among chronically ill adolescents: a systematic review. *Journal of Adolescent Health, 54,* 121–138.

Harter, S. (1986). Processes underlying the construction, maintenance, and enhancement of the self-concept in children. In J. Suls & A. Greenwald (eds.), *Psychological Perspectives on the Self* (vol. 3, pp. 136–182). Hillsdale, NJ: Erlbaum.

Horwitz, R. & Horwitz, S. (1993). Adherence to treatment and health outcomes. *Archives of Internal Medicine, 153*(16), 1863–1868.

Houman, K. & Stapley, J. (2013). The college experience for students with chronic illness: implications for academic advising. *NACADA Journal, 33*(1), 61–69.

Kann, L., McManus, T., Harris, W., Shanklin, S., Flint, K., Hawkins, J., Queen, B., Lowry, R., Olsen, E., Chyen, D., Whittle, L., Thornton, J., Lim, C., Yamakawa, Y., Brener, N., & Zaza, S. (2016). Youth risk behavior surveillance – United States, 2015. *MMWR Surveillance Summaries, 65,* 1–174.

Knight, A., Weiss, P., Morales, K., Gerdes, M., Rearson, M., Vickery, M., & Keren, R. (2015). Identifying differences in risk factors for depression and anxiety in pediatric chronic disease: a matched cross-sectional study of youth with lupus/mixed connective tissue disease and their peers with diabetes. *Journal of Pediatrics, 167*(6), 1397–1403.

La Greca, A. & Bearman, K. (2003). Adherence to pediatric regimens. In M. Roberts (ed.), *Handbook of Pediatric Psychology,* 3rd ed. (pp. 119–140). New York: Guilford Press.

Lam, W. & Fresco, P. (2015). Medication Adherence Measures: An Overview. *BioMed Research International.* doi: 10.1155/2015/217047.

LeBovidge, J., Lavigne, J., Donenberg, G., & Miller, M. (2003). Psychological adjustment of children and adolescents with chronic arthritis: a meta-analytic review. *Journal of Pediatric Psychology, 28,* 29–39.

Lemanek, K., Kamps, J., & Chung, N. (2001). Empirically supported treatments in pediatric psychology: regimen adherence. *Journal of Pediatric Psychology, 26*(5), 253–275.

Levy, S., Dedeoglu, F., Gaffin, J., Garvey, K., Harstad, E., MacGinnitie, A., Rufo, P.,

Huang, Q., Ziemnik, R., Wisk, L., & Weitzman, E. (2016). A screening tool for assessing alcohol use risk among medically vulnerable youth. *PLOS One, 11*(5), e0156240.

Lotstein, D., McPherson, M., Strickland, B., & Newacheck, P. (2005). Transition planning for youth with special health care needs: results from the National Survey of Children with Special Health Care Needs. *Pediatrics, 115*(6), 1562–1568.

Madden, M., Lenhart, A., Cortesi, S., & Gasser, V. (2013). Teens and Mobile Apps Privacy. *Pew Internet and American Life Project.* Retrieved November 20, 2017, from www.pewinternet.org/2013/08/22/main-findings-3/.

Martinez, W., Smith, J., & Legato, L. (2011). Social competence in children with chronic illness: a meta-analytic review. *Journal of Pediatric Psychology, 36*(8), 878–890.

McManus, M., White, P., Pirtle, R., Hancock, C., Ablan, M., & Corona-Parra, R. (2015). Incorporating the six core elements of health care transition into a Medicaid managed care plan: lessons learned from a pilot project. *Journal of Pediatric Nursing, 30*, 700–713.

MINT. (2017). Welcome to the Motivational Interviewing Website! Retrieved November 17, 2017, from http://motivationalinterviewing.org/.

Modi, A., Guilfoyle, S., & Rausch, J. (2013). Preliminary feasibility, acceptability, and efficacy of an innovative adherence intervention for children with newly diagnosed epilepsy. *Journal of Pediatric Psychology, 38*(6), 605–616.

Naspitz, C. & Tinkelman, D. (2001). Barriers to measuring and achieving optimal outcomes in pediatric asthma. *Journal of Asthma and Immunology, 107*, S482–S484.

National Alliance on Mental Illness. (2017). Managing a Mental Health Condition in College. Retrieved December 1, 2017, from www.nami.org/Find-Support/Teens-Young-Adults/Managing-a-Mental-Health-Condition-in-College.

National Institute on Alcoholism and Alcohol Abuse. (2015). A Screening Tool for Assessing Alcohol Use among Medically Vulnerable Youth. Retrieved November 20, 2017, from https://pubs.niaaa.nih.gov/publications/Practitioner/YouthGuide/YouthGuide.pdf.

Neinstein, L. (2001). The treatment of adolescents with a chronic illness. *The Western Journal of Medicine, 175*(5), 293–295.

Nguyen, A., Caze, A., & Cottrell, N. (2014). What are validated self-report adherence scales really measuring? A systematic review. *British Journal of Clinical Pharmacology, 77*(3), 427–445.

Pai, A., Drotar, D., & Kodish, E. (2008). Correspondence between objective and subjective reports of adherence among adolescents with acute lymphoblastic leukemia. *Child Health Care, 37*, 225–235.

Patenaude, A. & Kupst, J. (2005). Psychosocial functioning in pediatric cancer. *Journal of Pediatric Psychology, 30*, 9–27.

Pinquart, M. (2014). Achievement of developmental milestones in young adults with and without pediatric chronic illness – a meta-analysis. *Journal of Pediatric Psychology, 39*(6), 577–587.

Posner, K., Brent, D., Lucas, C, Gould, M., Stanley, B, Brown, G., Fisher, P., Zelazny, J., Burke, A., Oquendo, M., & Mann, J. (2009, January). Columbia-Suicide Severity Rating Scale. http://cssrs.columbia.edu/the-columbia-scale-c-ssrs/cssrs-for-communities-and-healthcare/#filter=.general-use.english.

Posner, K., Brown, G., Stanley, B., Brent, D., Yershova, K., Oquendo, M., Currier, G., Melvin, G., Greenhill, L., Shen, S., & Mann, J. J. (2011). The Columbia- Suicide Severity Rating Scale (C-SSRS): initial validity and internal consistency findings from three multi-site studies with adolescents and adults. *American Journal of Psychiatry, 168*(12), 1266–1277.

Quittner, A., Assael, B., Bregenballe, V., Goldbeck, L., Hug, M., & Pypops, U. (n.d.). Aim: Identify and Evaluate Tools to Measure Adherence [scholarly project]. Retrieved September 25, 2017, from www.ecfs.eu/sites/default/files/general-content- files/working-groups/ahp-.

Quittner, A., Modi, A., Lemanek, K., Ievers-Landis, C., & Rapoff, M. (2007). Evidence-based assessment of adherence to medical treatments in pediatric psychology. *Journal of Pediatric Psychology, 33*(9), 916–936.

Rapoff, M. (2011). *Adherence to Pediatric Medical Regimens*, 2nd ed. New York: Springer.

Riekert, K., Eakin, M., Bilderback, A., Ridge, A., & Marshall, B. (2015). Opportunities for cystic fibrosis care teams to support treatment adherence. *Journal of Cystic Fibrosis, 14*(1), 142–148.

Rothstein, L. (2013). Getting Practical: ADA and Accommodation Issues on Campus. Retrieved December 1, 2017, from www.higheredcompliance.org/resources/resources/Practical-Tips-Managing-Disabiilty-Related-Issues1.pdf.

Sawicki, G., Lukens-Bull, K., Yon, X., Demars, N., Huang, I., Livingood, W., Reiss, J., & Wood, D. (2009). Measuring the transition readiness of youth with special healthcare needs: validation of the TRAQ-Transition Readiness Assessment Questionnaire. *Journal of Pediatric Psychology, 36*(2), 160–171.

Schwartz, L., Daniel, L., Brumley, L., Barakat, L., Wesley, K., & Tuchman, L. (2014). Measures of readiness to transition to adult health care for youth with chronic physical health conditions: a systematic review for measurement testing and development. *Journal of Pediatric Psychology, 39*(6), 588–601.

SickKids. (2014). Good 2 Go Transition Program. Retrieved November 17, 2017, from www.sickkids.ca/good2go.

Society of Pediatric Psychology. (2016). Assessment Resource Sheet: Measures of Adherence to Medical Treatments. Retrieved November 17, 2017, from www.societyofpediatricpsychology.org/measures_of_adherence.

Stark, L., Janicke, D., McGrath, A., et al. (2005). Prevention of osteoporosis: a randomized clinical trial to increase calcium intake in children with juvenile rheumatoid arthritis. *Journal of Pediatric Psychology, 30*, 377–386.

Stark, L., Mackner, L., Patton, S., & Acton, J. (2003). Cystic fibrosis. In M. C. Roberts (ed.),

Handbook of Pediatric Psychology, 3rd ed. (pp. 286–303). New York: Guilford Press.

Suris, J., Michaud, P., & Viner, R. (2004). The adolescent with a chronic condition: part 1: developmental issues. *Archives of Disease in Childhood, 89*, 938–942.

Taylor, T. & Montgomery, P. (2007). Can cognitive-behavioral therapy increase self-esteem among depressed adolescents? A systematic review. *Children and Youth Services Review, 29*(7), 823–839.

UNC Starx Program. (2016, June 28). Retrieved October 9, 2017, from www.med.unc.edu/transition/transition-tools/trxansition-scale.

University of Washington. (2012). Adolescent Health Transition Project. Retrieved November 17, 2017, from http://depts.washington.edu/healthtr/.

Wamboldt, M. & Wamboldt, F. (2000). Role of the family in the onset and outcome of childhood disorders: selected research findings. *Journal of the American Academy of Child and Adolescent Psychiatry, 39*, 1212–1219.

Weitzman, E., Ziemnik, R., Huang, Q., & Levy, S. (2015). Alcohol and marijuana use and treatment adherence among medically vulnerable youth. *Pediatrics, 136*, 450–457.

West Rock Company. (2016). MEMS® Cap Versatile Adherence Monitoring Cap. Retrieved November 17, 2017, from www.medamigo.com/products/mems-cap.

Wodka, E. & Barakat, L. (2007). An exploratory study of the relationship of family support and coping with adjustment: implications for college students with a chronic illness. *Journal of Adolescence, 30*, 366–376.

Wolfstadt, J., Kaufman, A., Levitin, J., & Kaufman, M. (2001). The use and usefulness of MyHealth Passport: an online tool for the creation of a portable health summary. *International Journal of Child and Adolescent Health, 3*, 499–506.

Wood, D., Sawicki, G., Miller, M., Smotherman, C., Lukens, B., Livingwood, W., Ferris, M, & Kraemer, D. (2014). The Transition Readiness Assessment Questionnaire (TRAQ): its factor structure, reliability, and validity. *Academic Pediatrics, 14*(4), 415–422.

Wysocki, T., Green, L., & Huxtable, K. (1989). Blood glucose monitoring by diabetic adolescents: compliance and metabolic control. *Health Psychology, 8*(3), 267–284.

Yeo, M. & Sawyer, S. (2005). Chronic illness and disability. *BMJ, 330*(7493), 721–723.

Zuckerman, J., Devine, K., & Holmbeck, G. (2010). Adolescent predictors of emerging adulthood milestones in youth with spina bifida. *Journal of Pediatric Psychology, 36*(3), 265–276.

Reproducible Resources

Name	John Smith
DOB	08/01/1999
Seizures	Complex partial seizures, Loss of motor control with seizures,Onset at age: 11,seizure frequency: 1X per week ,Time of day: afternoon ,Longest seizure free interval: 1 month , Etiology: CNS infection, WARNING: CALL 911 OR OTHER EMERGENCY SERVICE IF I AM HAVING A SEIZURE
Status	WARNING: IF I HAVE A SEIZURE LASTING MORE THAN 5 MINUTES, 911 SHOULD BE CALLED.
Medical	Type 1 Diabetes
Surgery	I have not had epilepsy surgery
Meds	Topiramate,Prozac
D/C Meds	Ineffective-Lorazepam
Diet Tx	Folic acid
Allergies	Latex
Blood group	AB+
Immunization	DPTP, MMR, mening, Pneumovax, HPV, Hep A, Hep B
Coverage	USA Insurance
Primary care	Dr. Good Help
Decisions	My substitute decision maker is listed under ICE
Licence	I do not have a driver's license
ICE	Mother- Jane Smith (111) 222-3333
Date Created	10/9/2017www.sickkids.ca/myhealthpassport

Figure 4.2 MyHealth Passport. Adapted from "Good 2 Go Transition Program: MyHealth Passport," by M. Kaufman, 2012 (www.sickkids.ca/myhealthpassport/)

COLUMBIA-SUICIDE SEVERITY
RATING SCALE
(C-SSRS)

Lifetime/Recent Version

Version 1/14/09

Posner, K.; Brent, D.; Lucas, C.; Gould, M.; Stanley, B.; Brown, G.; Fisher, P.; Zelazny, J.;
Burke, A.; Oquendo, M.; Mann, J.

Disclaimer:

This scale is intended to be used by individuals who have received training in its administration. The questions contained in the Columbia-Suicide Severity Rating Scale are suggested probes. Ultimately, the determination of the presence of suicidal ideation or behavior depends on the judgment of the individual administering the scale.

Definitions of behavioral suicidal events in this scale are based on those used in **The Columbia Suicide History Form***, developed by John Mann, MD and Maria Oquendo, MD, Conte Center for the Neuroscience of Mental Disorders (CCNMD), New York State Psychiatric Institute, 1051 Riverside Drive, New York, NY, 10032. (Oquendo M. A., Halberstam B. & Mann J. J., Risk factors for suicidal behavior: utility and limitations of research instruments. In M.B. First [Ed.] Standardized Evaluation in Clinical Practice, pp. 103 -130, 2003.)*

For reprints of the C-SSRS contact Kelly Posner, Ph.D., New York State Psychiatric Institute, 1051 Riverside Drive, New York, New York, 10032; inquiries and training requirements contact posnerk@nyspi.columbia.edu
© 2008 The Research Foundation for Mental Hygiene, Inc.

Figure 4.3 Columbia-Suicide Severity Rating Scale.
Reprinted from "Columbia-Suicide Severity Rating Scale," by Posner, K., Brent, D., Lucas, C., Gould, M., Stanley, B., Brown, G., Fisher, P., Zelazny, J., Burke, A., Oquendo, M., & Mann, J., January 2009 (http://cssrs.columbia.edu/the-columbia-scale-c-ssrs/cssrs-for-communities-and-healthcare/#filter=.general-use.english), and Posner, K., Brown, G. K., Stanley, B., Brent, D. A., Yershova, K. V., Oquendo, M. A., Currier, G. W., Melvin, G., Greenhill, L., Shen, S., & Mann, J. J. (2011). The Columbia-Suicide Severity Rating Scale (C-SSRS): initial validity and internal consistency findings from three multi-site studies with adolescents and adults. *American Journal of Psychiatry, 168*(12), 1266–1277

SUICIDAL IDEATION				
Ask questions 1 and 2. If both are negative, proceed to "Suicidal Behavior" section. If the answer to question 2 is "yes", ask questions 3, 4 and 5. If the answer to question 1 and/or 2 is "yes", complete "Intensity of Ideation" section below.	Lifetime: Time He/She Felt Most Suicidal		Past 1 month	
1. Wish to be Dead Subject endorses thoughts about a wish to be dead or not alive anymore, or wish to fall asleep and not wake up. *Have you wished you were dead or wished you could go to sleep and not wake up?*	Yes ☐	No ☐	Yes ☐	No ☐
If yes, describe:				
2. Non-Specific Active Suicidal Thoughts General non-specific thoughts of wanting to end one's life/commit suicide (e.g., *"I've thought about killing myself"*) without thoughts of ways to kill oneself/associated methods, intent, or plan during the assessment period. *Have you actually had any thoughts of killing yourself?*	Yes ☐	No ☐	Yes ☐	No ☐
If yes, describe:				
3. Active Suicidal Ideation with Any Methods (Not Plan) without Intent to Act Subject endorses thoughts of suicide and has thought of at least one method during the assessment period. This is different than a specific plan with time, place or method details worked out (e.g., thought of method to kill self but not a specific plan). Includes person who said, *"I thought about taking an overdose but I never made a specific plan as to when, where or how I would actually do it...and I would never go through with it."* *Have you been thinking about how you might do this?*	Yes ☐	No ☐	Yes ☐	No ☐
If yes, describe:				
4. Active Suicidal Ideation with Some Intent to Act, without Specific Plan Active suicidal thoughts of killing oneself and subject reports having <u>some intent to act on such thoughts</u>, as opposed to *"I have the thoughts but I definitely will not do anything about them."* *Have you had these thoughts and had some intention of acting on them?*	Yes ☐	No ☐	Yes ☐	No ☐
If yes, describe:				
5. Active Suicidal Ideation with Specific Plan and Intent Thoughts of killing oneself with details of plan fully or partially worked out and subject has some intent to carry it out. *Have you started to work out or worked out the details of how to kill yourself? Do you intend to carry out this plan?*	Yes ☐	No ☐	Yes ☐	No ☐
If yes, describe:				

INTENSITY OF IDEATION		
The following features should be rated with respect to the most severe type of ideation (i.e., 1-5 from above, with 1 being the least severe and 5 being the most severe). Ask about time he/she was feeling the most suicidal.		

Lifetime - *Most Severe Ideation*: _____ _____
          Type # (1-5)   *Description of Ideation*
 	
 Recent - *Most Severe Ideation*: _____ _____
          Type # (1-5)   *Description of Ideation*
	Most Severe	Most Severe

Frequency *How many times have you had these thoughts?* (1) Less than once a week (2) Once a week (3) 2-5 times in week (4) Daily or almost daily (5) Many times each day	_____	_____
Duration *When you have the thoughts how long do they last?* (1) Fleeting - few seconds or minutes (4) 4-8 hours/most of day (2) Less than 1 hour/some of the time (5) More than 8 hours/persistent or continuous (3) 1-4 hours/a lot of time	_____	_____
Controllability *Could/can you stop thinking about killing yourself or wanting to die if you want to?* (1) Easily able to control thoughts (4) Can control thoughts with a lot of difficulty (2) Can control thoughts with little difficulty (5) Unable to control thoughts (3) Can control thoughts with some difficulty (0) Does not attempt to control thoughts	_____	_____
Deterrents *Are there things - anyone or anything (e.g., family, religion, pain of death) - that stopped you from wanting to die or acting on thoughts of committing suicide?* (1) Deterrents definitely stopped you from attempting suicide (4) Deterrents most likely did not stop you (2) Deterrents probably stopped you (5) Deterrents definitely did not stop you (3) Uncertain that deterrents stopped you (0) Does not apply	_____	_____

Reasons for Ideation *What sort of reasons did you have for thinking about wanting to die or killing yourself? Was it to end the pain or stop the way you were feeling (in other words you couldn't go on living with this pain or how you were feeling) or was it to get attention, revenge or a reaction from others? Or both?*
 (1) Completely to get attention, revenge or a reaction from others   (4) Mostly to end or stop the pain (you couldn't go on
 (2) Mostly to get attention, revenge or a reaction from others   living with the pain or how you were feeling)
 (3) Equally to get attention, revenge or a reaction from others   (5) Completely to end or stop the pain (you couldn't go on
      and to end/stop the pain   living with the pain or how you were feeling)
          (0) Does not apply
	_____	_____

Version 1/14/09

Figure 4.3 (cont.)

SUICIDAL BEHAVIOR *(Check all that apply, so long as these are separate events; must ask about all types)*	Lifetime	Past 3 months

Actual Attempt:
A potentially self-injurious act committed with at least some wish to die, *as a result of act.* Behavior was in part thought of as method to kill oneself. Intent does not have to be 100%. If there is *any* intent/desire to die associated with the act, then it can be considered an actual suicide attempt. *There does not have to be any injury or harm*, just the potential for injury or harm. If person pulls trigger while gun is in mouth but gun is broken so no injury results, this is considered an attempt.
Inferring Intent: Even if an individual denies intent/wish to die, it may be inferred clinically from the behavior or circumstances. For example, a highly lethal act that is clearly not an accident so no other intent but suicide can be inferred (e.g., gunshot to head, jumping from window of a high floor/story). Also, if someone denies intent to die, but they thought that what they did could be lethal, intent may be inferred.
Have you made a suicide attempt?
Have you done anything to harm yourself?
Have you done anything dangerous where you could have died?
   What did you do?
   Did you_____ as a way to end your life?
   Did you want to die (even a little) when you_____?
   Were you trying to end your life when you _____?
   Or Did you think it was possible you could have died from_____?
Or did you do it purely for other reasons / without ANY intention of killing yourself (like to relieve stress, feel better, get sympathy, or get something else to happen)? *(*Self-Injurious Behavior without suicidal intent)*
If yes, describe:
	Yes No
	☐ ☐
	
	Total # of Attempts
	_____
		Yes No
		☐ ☐
		
		Total # of Attempts
		_____

Has subject engaged in Non-Suicidal Self-Injurious Behavior?	Yes No ☐ ☐	Yes No ☐ ☐
Interrupted Attempt: When the person is interrupted (by an outside circumstance) from starting the potentially self-injurious act *(if not for that, actual attempt would have occurred).* Overdose: Person has pills in hand but is stopped from ingesting. Once they ingest any pills, this becomes an attempt rather than an interrupted attempt. Shooting: Person has gun pointed toward self, gun is taken away by someone else, or is somehow prevented from pulling trigger. Once they pull the trigger, even if the gun fails to fire, it is an attempt. Jumping: Person is poised to jump, is grabbed and taken down from ledge. Hanging: Person has noose around neck but has not yet started to hang - is stopped from doing so. *Has there been a time when you started to do something to end your life but someone or something stopped you before you actually did anything?* If yes, describe:	Yes No ☐ ☐ Total # of interrupted _____	Yes No ☐ ☐ Total # of interrupted _____
Aborted or Self-Interrupted Attempt: When person begins to take steps toward making a suicide attempt, but stops themselves before they actually have engaged in any self-destructive behavior. Examples are similar to interrupted attempts, except that the individual stops him/herself, instead of being stopped by something else. *Has there been a time when you started to do something to try to end your life but you stopped yourself before you actually did anything?* If yes, describe:	Yes No ☐ ☐ Total # of aborted or self-interrupted	Yes No ☐ ☐ Total # of aborted or self-interrupted
Preparatory Acts or Behavior: Acts or preparation towards imminently making a suicide attempt. This can include anything beyond a verbalization or thought, such as assembling a specific method (e.g., buying pills, purchasing a gun) or preparing for one's death by suicide (e.g., giving things away, writing a suicide note). *Have you taken any steps towards making a suicide attempt or preparing to kill yourself (such as collecting pills, getting a gun, giving valuables away or writing a suicide note)?* If yes, describe:	Yes No ☐ ☐	Yes No ☐ ☐
Suicidal Behavior: Suicidal behavior was present during the assessment period?	Yes No ☐ ☐	Yes No ☐ ☐

	Most Recent Attempt Date:	Most Lethal Attempt Date:	Initial/First Attempt Date:
Actual Lethality/Medical Damage: 0. No physical damage or very minor physical damage (e.g., surface scratches). 1. Minor physical damage (e.g., lethargic speech; first-degree burns; mild bleeding; sprains). 2. Moderate physical damage; medical attention needed (e.g., conscious but sleepy, somewhat responsive; second-degree burns; bleeding of major vessel). 3. Moderately severe physical damage; *medical* hospitalization and likely intensive care required (e.g., comatose with reflexes intact; third-degree burns less than 20% of body; extensive blood loss but can recover; major fractures). 4. Severe physical damage; *medical* hospitalization with intensive care required (e.g., comatose without reflexes; third-degree burns over 20% of body; extensive blood loss with unstable vital signs; major damage to a vital area). 5. Death	*Enter Code* _____	*Enter Code* _____	*Enter Code* _____
Potential Lethality: Only Answer if Actual Lethality=0 Likely lethality of actual attempt if no medical damage (the following examples, while having no actual medical damage, had potential for very serious lethality: put gun in mouth and pulled the trigger but gun fails to fire so no medical damage; laying on train tracks with oncoming train but pulled away before run over). 0 = Behavior not likely to result in injury 1 = Behavior likely to result in injury but not likely to cause death 2 = Behavior likely to result in death despite available medical care	*Enter Code* _____	*Enter Code* _____	*Enter Code* _____

Figure 4.3 *(cont.)*

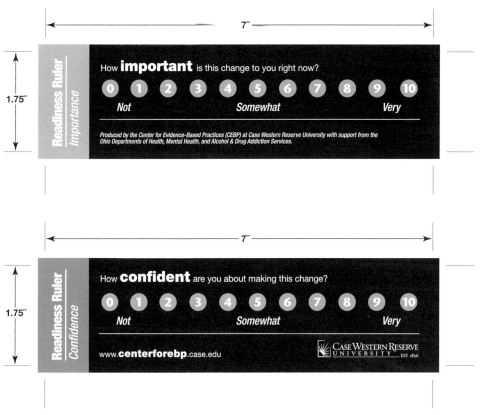

Figure 4.4 Readiness Rulers. Used with permission from Center for Evidence-Based Practices at Case Western Reserve University (2010). "Readiness Ruler." Cleveland, OH: Case Western Reserve University. A free PDF is available: www.centerforebp.case.edu/resources/tools/readiness-ruler

Family Contract for: John Jones and Mr. and Mrs. Jones

John's Tasks:	Mr. and Mrs. Jones' Tasks:
John will complete the following regimen components each day: 1) Check his blood sugar when he wakes up, before each meal (breakfast, lunch, and dinner) and before bedtime. 2) Input blood sugar data into phone application	1) Mr. and Mrs. Jones will check daily glucose readings from John's phone app. 2) Mr. and Mrs. Jones will record on log sheet whether daily glucose readings were completed each day. 3) Mr. and Mrs. Jones will pay for phone app and pay for phone

Positive Consequence:
1) If John completes all task requirements for 4 out of 7 days, he will be allowed to spend time with his friends in the basement on Friday or Saturday night until 11pm.
2) If John completes all regimen requirements on 7 out of 7 days, he can use the family car on one weekend night.

Negative Consequence:
1) If John does not complete all task requirements for at least 4 out of 7 days, he will not be allowed to spend any time with his friends on Friday or Saturday night.
2) If John does not complete all task requirements for at least 4 out of 7 days, he will have to fold two baskets of laundry on the following Sunday at 11:00am.

Effective Date: March 19, 2017
Contract will be re-negotiated on: April 9, 2017

_____   _____   _____
John   Mr. Jones   Ms. Jones

Figure 4.5 Example behavioral contract for child over 10 years old.

Patient Name: _____ Date _____ Person Completing Survey: _____

Transition Readiness Assessment Questionnaire 3.0

Direction: We would like to know how you describe your skills in the areas that are important in your care. Your answers will help us provide services and education that will be important in preparing you to transition to adult health care. There are no right or wrong answers and your answers will remain confidential and private. Please check the box ☑ that you feel best describes you.

	I do not need to do this	I do not know how but I want to learn	I am leaning to do this	I have started doing this	I always do this when I need to
TRAQ DOMAIN 1: Skills for Chronic Condition Self-Management					
1. Do you fill a prescription if you need to?					
2. Do you know the side effects or bad reactions of each medication & what to do if you are having a bad reaction?					
3. Do you pay or arrange payments for your medications?					
4. Do you take medications correctly and on your own?					
5. Do you reorder medications before they run out?					
6. Do you use and take care of medical equipment and supplies?					
7. Do you call the suppliers when there is a problem with the equipment?					
8. Do you order medical equipment before they run-out?					
9. Do you arrange payment for the medical equipment and supplies?					
10. Do you call the doctor's office to make an appointment?					
11. Do you follow-up on any referral for tests or check-ups or labs?					
12. Do you arrange for your ride to medical appointments?					
13. Do you call the doctor about unusual changes in your health (Ex. Allergic reactions)?					
14. Do you apply for health insurance if you lose your current coverage?					
15. Do you know what your health insurance covers?					
16. Do you manage your money & budget household expenses (Ex. use checking/debit card)?					

Figure 4.6 Transition Readiness Assessment Questionnaire (TRAQ).
Reprinted from www.etsu.edu/com/pediatrics/traq/. "The Transition Readiness Assessment Questionnaire (TRAQ): its factor structure, reliability, and validity," by D. Wood, G. Sawicki, M. Miller, C. Smotherman, K. Lukens-Bull, W. Livingood, M. Ferris, & D. Kraemer, 2014, *Academic Pediatrics, 14*(4), 415–422. Copyright 2014 by Academic Pediatric Association

	I do not need to do this	I do not know how but I want to learn	I am leaning to do this	I have started doing this	I always do this when I need to
TRAQ DOMAIN 2: Skills for Self-Advocacy and Health Care Utilization					
17. Do you fill out the medical history form, including a list of your allergies?					
18. Do you keep a calendar or list of medical and other appointments?					
19. Do you tell the doctor or nurse what you are feeling?					
20. Do you answer questions that are asked by the doctor, nurse or clinic staff?					
21. Do you ask questions of the doctor, nurse or clinic staff (Ex. What medications or treatments are best for you)?					
22. Do you make a list of questions before the doctor's visit?					
23. Do you request and get the accommodations & support you need at school or work?					
24. Do you apply for a job or work or vocational services?					
25. Do you get financial help with school or work?					
26. Do you help plan or prepare meals/food?					
27. Do you keep home/room clean or clean-up after meals?					
28. Do you use neighborhood stores and services (Ex. Grocery stores and pharmacy stores)?					
29. Do you call on and use community support services (Ex. After school programs) and advocacy services (Ex. Legal services) when you need them?					

Figure 4.6 (*cont.*)

STARx Transition Readiness Questionnaire (Adolescent Version)

DIRECTIONS

Patients with chronic health conditions need to have special skills and do special tasks to stay healthy.

On the following pages, please check the box underneath the answers that describe you most.

If you do not understand a question, just ask for help. We're here to help you ☺

Section 1 :

- **How often have you done the following things?**
- **Please check the box that tells how often you have done each thing in the PAST 3 MONTHS.**

In the past 3 months …	Never	Almost Never	Sometimes	Almost Always	Always	I do not take medicines right now
1. How often did you make an effort to understand what your doctor told you?	☐	☐	☐	☐	☐	
2. How often did you take your medicines on your own?	☐	☐	☐	☐	☐	☐
3. How often did you ask your doctor or nurse questions about your illness, medicines or medical care?	☐	☐	☐	☐	☐	
4. How often did you make your own appointments?	☐	☐	☐	☐	☐	
5. How often did you need someone to remind you to take your medicines?	☐	☐	☐	☐	☐	☐
6. How often did you use things like pillboxes, schedules, or alarm clocks to help you take your medicines when you were supposed to?	☐	☐	☐	☐	☐	☐
7. How often did you use the internet, books or other guides to find out more about your illness?	☐	☐	☐	☐	☐	
8. How often did you forget to take your medicines?	☐	☐	☐	☐	☐	☐
9. How often did you work with your doctor to take care of new health problems that came up?	☐	☐	☐	☐	☐	

Figure 4.7 STARx Transition Readiness Questionnaire (Adolescent Version).
Reprinted from *Journal of Pediatric Nursing, 30*, Cohen, S., Hooper, S., Javalkar, K., Haberman, C., Fenton, N., Lai, H., Mahan, J., Massengill, S., Phillips, A., Sawicki, G., Wood, D., Johnson, M., Benton, M., & Ferris, M., Self-management and transition readiness assessment: concurrent, predictive and discriminate validation of the Starx Questionnaire, 668–676, copyright 2015, with permission from Elsevier (www.med.unc.edu/transition/transition-tools/trxansition-scale/STARxAdolescentVersion.pdf)

Site ID: _____
Patient ID: _____
Date: _____

Section 2:

- Some patients know a lot about their health and some patients don't.
- How much do you know?
- Please check the answer that best describes how much you feel you know *TODAY*.

	Nothing	Not Much	A little	Some	A Lot	I do not take medicines right now
10. How much do you know about your illness?	☐	☐	☐	☐	☐	
11. How much do you know about taking care of your illness?	☐	☐	☐	☐	☐	
12. How much do you know about what will happen if you don't take your medicines?	☐	☐	☐	☐	☐	☐

Site ID: _____
Patient ID: _____
Date: _____

Section 3:

- Some patients may find it hard to do certain things.
- How easy or hard is it for you to do the following things?
- Please check the answer that best describes how you feel *TODAY*.

	Very Hard	Somewhat Hard	Neither Hard nor Easy	Somewhat Easy	Very Easy	I do not take medicines right now
13. How easy or hard is it to talk to your doctor?	☐	☐	☐	☐	☐	
14. How easy or hard is it to make a plan with your doctor to care for your health?	☐	☐	☐	☐	☐	
15. How easy or hard is it to see your doctor by yourself?	☐	☐	☐	☐	☐	
16. How easy or hard is it to take your medicines like you are supposed to?	☐	☐	☐	☐	☐	☐
17. How easy or hard is it to take care of yourself?	☐	☐	☐	☐	☐	
18. How easy or hard do you think it will be to move from pediatric to adult care?	☐	☐	☐	☐	☐	

Figure 4.7 (*cont.*)

Recommended Websites, Books, and Other Resources
Clinical Resources
Suicidality Screener

Columbia-Suicide Severity Rating Scale (C-SSRS), http://cssrs.columbia.edu/the-columbia-scale-c-ssrs/cssrs-for-communities-and-healthcare/#filter=.general-use.english

Alcohol Assessment

NIAAA Youth Alcohol Screening Tool, https://pubs.niaaa.nih.gov/publications/ Practitioner/YouthGuide/YouthGuide.pdf

Treatment Adherence Measures

Subjective Assessments, www.societyofpediatricpsychology.org/measures_of_adherence
Objective Assessments MEMS® Cap, www.medamigo.com/products/mems-cap
SmartTurbo, www.smartinhaler.com/devices/
Society of Pediatric Psychology, Evidence-Based Assessment,
www.societyofpediatricpsychology.org/measures_of_adherence

Motivational Interviewing Tools

Motivational Interviewing, Resources for Clinicians www.motivationalinterviewing.org
Case Western Reserve University, Printable Tools for Clinicians
www.centerforebp.case.edu/resources/tools/product=5&category=47

Transition Assessment

University of North Carolina School of Medicine, STARx Questionnaire,
www.med.unc.edu/transition/transition-tools/trxansition-scale
East Tennessee State University, Transition Readiness Assessment Questionnaire,
www.etsu.edu/com/pediatrics/traq/

Transition Tools

Health Passport: The Hospital for Sick Kids, Good 2 Go Transition Program,
www.sickkids.ca/good2go
Sample Medical Summary and Emergency Care Plan Got Transition,
www.gottransition.org/resourceGet.cfm?id=242

College and Chronic Illness Resources

ADA Amendments Act of 2008, www.eeoc.gov/laws/statutes/adaaa.cfm
US Department of Education, Students with Disabilities Preparing for Postsecondary
Education, www2.ed.gov/about/offices/list/ocr/transition.html

Resources for Families and Patients

University of Washington, Adolescent Health Transition Project,
www.depts.washington.edu/healthtr
Kids as Self Advocates (KASA), www.fvkasa.org
BC Children's Hospital, ON TRAC: Transitioning Responsibly to Adult Care,
www.bcchildrens.ca/our-services/support-services/transition-to-adult-care
National Alliance of Mental Illness (NAMI), Managing a Mental Health Condition in
College, www.nami.org/Find-Support/Teens-Young-Adults/Managing-a-Mental-Health-
Condition-in-College

Recommended Books and Journal Articles for Clinicians

American Psychological Association. (2002). Developing Adolescents: A Reference for Professionals. Retrieved December 1, 2017, from www.apa.org/pi/families/resources/develop.pdf.

Erickson, S., Gerstle, M., & Feldstein, S. (2005). Brief interventions and motivational interviewing with children, adolescents, and their parents in pediatric health settings. *Archives of Pediatrics and Adolescent Medicine, 159,* 1173–1180.

Gold, M. & Kokotailo, P. (2007). Motivational interviewing strategies to facilitate adolescent behavior change. *Adolescent Health Update, 20*(1), 1–10.

Rapoff, M. (2011). *Adherence to Pediatric Medical Regimens*, 2nd ed. New York: Springer.

5

Chronic Illness and the Family Unit

5.1 Navigating the Healthcare System as a Family

When facing a medical crisis or even just when faced with the relentless sequence of having regularly scheduled medical appointments associated with chronic illness, families are also stressed with having to learn how to navigate an overwhelming and complex health care system. Even for the savviest of parents, the rigmarole of insurance, co-pays, deductibles, and the dance of in-network versus out-of-network coverage can feel like an insurmountable barrier when they are already in a stressful situation with an ill child. A stressful medical event can also be compounded by the often not talked about or recognized logistical barriers of transportation, child care, and other factors that must be accounted for by parents when attending medical appointments.

Once a family has finally navigated these barriers, there is still the challenge of communicating with medical personnel and advocating for their family member. Many families may not feel comfortable with acting as equal decision makers with medical staff due to the power differential between patient and doctor. This difficulty with communicating with medical staff appears to be a particularly difficult barrier when families have a lower income, have low English proficiency, and/or lower educational achievement (Clemans-Cope & Kenney, 2007).

Given the relative luxury many mental health clinicians have in being able to develop close relationships with families over longer periods of time in contrast to the typically shorter time periods allotted for traditional medical appointments, mental health clinicians are in a unique position to have developed the relationships necessary to help assess and recognize when patients may be too embarrassed or distressed to ask questions of medical team members. When a clinician has focused on developing therapeutic rapport with the family, they can gently probe to see how comfortable a family is with communicating with medical team members.

Clinicians should be mindful of a parent's health literacy and self-efficacy in navigating the medical system. It can be easy for well-educated mental health clinicians to forget that in the United States, approximately 29% of parents are assessed as having below basic to basic health literacy (Yin et al., 2009). In this representative study, 46.4% of parents were unable to perform at least one of two medication-related tasks, such as reading a prescription drug label to ascertain what time of day it was appropriate to take the medicine. Thus, when medical teams indicate difficulty with adherence or feel that the appropriate care is not being rendered by the patient's parent, a mental health clinician can help to provide collateral information regarding whether it's possible that the "nonadherence" is actually associated with a lack of understanding or impaired communication with the patient's family rather than jumping to the conclusion that this difficulty is associated with negligence.

Health literacy assessments are one way that clinicians can try to understand a family's basic comprehension of provided medical information. Information about a navigable website for health literacy assessments can be found in the "Recommended Websites, Books, and Other Resources" section at the end of this chapter. In addition to more formalized assessments of health literacy, an informal and easy way to assess a patient's understanding of medical information is to use the "teach-back" method. With this informal method, clinicians can ask patients or parents to verbalize what they learned via questions such as: "Can you repeat back what I just said to make sure that I communicated clearly?" By emphasizing that the request is to help ensure that "you" communicated clearly, patients may be less likely to feel defensive or embarrassed when asked to ascertain their understanding of information.

If patients struggle with "repeating" what was said, clinicians can then provide clarification to prevent miscommunication. In this same manner, clinicians can determine how well a concept has been understand by patients. For example, it may be advantageous to have patients "teach" their parents how to perform diaphragmatic breathing as part of relaxation training so that clinicians can ensure the patient's understanding as well as helping the child or adolescent to feel proud of their mastery of this skill.

When working with medical providers who are struggling with patient communication, it is important to focus on teaching staff to try to stick to three main points when disseminating information, to use clear language, to use multiple modalities of communication, and to keep written information at a fifth-grade reading level (Sudore & Schillinger, 2009). For many patients and parents, it can be helpful to use visual charts or pictures in addition to verbal information to help ensure clear communication, particularly if there is a literacy concern.

5.2 Sibling Adjustment and Interventions

Given the often time-intensive nature of psychological interventions, it can be difficult to be mindful of the impact of chronic illness on family members other than the identified patient you may be treating. However, the impact of pediatric chronic illness on other family members, such as siblings, should not be overlooked given its reciprocal impact on the identified patient. Research has indicated that siblings of children with chronic illness tend to exhibit increased rates of internalizing and externalizing behaviors, with these increased rates being particularly elevated when the child's sibling has a life-threatening condition (Sharpe & Rossiter, 2002). The impact of the child's illness on their sibling also appears to be associated with the extent of the demands of daily treatment regimens, with more extensive daily regimens being associated with increased concerns for the healthy sibling.

With the stress associated with chronic illness, siblings may be at risk for "early parentification," or the taking on of responsibilities earlier than developmentally appropriate (Minuchin et al., 1967). This early parentification can be an easy trap for families to fall into due to the pressures of tasks associated with chronic illness in combination with some siblings' well-meaning intention to help reduce stress for their parents. Unfortunately, this early caretaking can be associated with increased internalizing symptoms for the caretaking sibling (Sharpe & Rossiter, 2002). Due to this stress, it is not uncommon for siblings' academic functioning to be adversely impacted, as research indicates overall poorer academic functioning and higher rates of absenteeism in siblings of children with chronic illness (Gan et al., 2017).

To help prevent this impact on a sibling's academic functioning, it is important for siblings to keep to a regular routine as much as possible, despite the upheavals of hospitalizations and acute illness that can occur within the context of chronic illness. Many parents may wonder whether it may be more beneficial for siblings to stay home from school when their sibling is experiencing medical problems; however, maintaining as normal routine as possible while also being provided developmentally appropriate information about the child's medical illness can be helpful in minimizing adverse impacts on the healthy sibling. This may also help with preventing the decreased social competence that can be observed in siblings when they are involved in fewer activities outside school (Labay & Walco, 2004).

Typically, siblings appear to cope better when provided with information about the patient's medical illness and the subsequent treatment regimen (Kramer, 1984). To help with returning to school, it may be advantageous to enlist teacher support or support from other trusted school personnel in order to provide siblings with a "safe space" to process fears and feelings of distress that may arise during the school day. This way, instead of calling their parents to pick them up early from school, siblings can first be asked to touch base with their support person at school to help them learn to work through their anxiety and fears related to their sibling rather than exhibiting avoidance by leaving school prematurely. For many siblings, fears tend to center on their sibling's disease, concerns about the future, and concern about being able to help their sibling in a crisis (Fleary & Heffner, 2013). It is important for parents and clinicians to provide developmentally appropriate information and to use the aforementioned "teach back" method to ensure that siblings have not misconstrued any significant medical information.

More formal interventions, such as psychoeducational programs and group support programs, have been demonstrated to be highly satisfactory as interventions for siblings of children with illnesses (Dolgin et al., 1997; Incledon et al., 2015). One such aforementioned program utilized a combination of interventions such as art therapy, role play, and group discussion to help siblings of children with cancer (Dolgin et al., 1997). Similarly, group support programs such as summer camps can help siblings find support from other children who are experiencing similar family stressors and provide an opportunity for children to help each other process emotions related to their sibling's illness. To assist with finding camps for children with chronic illness and their family members, refer to the "Recommended Websites, Books, and Other Resources" section for a searchable website of camp resources.

Clinical Vignette: "It's just not the right time ... It will never be the right time"

Early Monday morning, you receive a frantic call from the mother of one of your patients. Ms. H tearfully reports that her 18-year-old son, Jake, was involved in a motor vehicle accident over the weekend following his high school graduation. Ms. H notes that Jake is now medically stable, but she reports that she has been informed by doctors that he will never walk again due to a spinal cord injury sustained in the accident. Ms. H indicates that she is calling because she is unsure how to "handle the situation" with his 10-year-old brother, Richard, whom you have been treating for several months for generalized anxiety.

Ms. H reported that she and her husband have been arguing about how much medical information they should disclose to Richard about his brother's prognosis and current condition. She stated, "I think we should wait at least one month to give Richard more time to process what's happened before we tell him about Jake's paralysis.... It's just not the right time." You carefully ask Ms. H how she will know when the "right time" is to disclose that information to Richard, and she sighs heavily over the phone, saying, "It will never be the right time."

When queried about where Richard is currently staying, Ms. H reports that he has been with his aunt since they found out about the accident on Friday evening, and he has been told only that his brother was in a car accident but "will be okay." Mindful of Richard's tendency to catastrophize when he becomes anxious, you discuss with Ms. H the need to provide accurate and developmentally appropriate information in a timely manner to Richard. Ms. H declines to come into your office for a session with Richard due to her refusal to leave her eldest son's bedside except to visit Richard. As such, you rehearse with Ms. H what to disclose to Richard as soon as she visits him at his aunt's home this afternoon. You emphasize the importance of providing accurate information to Richard, such as the following: "Richard, as you know, your brother was in a car accident on Friday. He is going to be fine and come home once he is able, but he might be a little different when he does come home. He won't be able to walk anymore but he will still be the same Jake we know and love."

Ms. H asks, "What do I do after we talk? Should I keep him home from school for the next several weeks?" You encourage Ms. H to have Richard return to his regular routine as soon as possible, which includes going to school. You note that it may be helpful to ensure that Ms. H or her husband takes Richard to school as they typically do and to touch base with his teacher and school counselor prior to his return to ensure that they are aware of the circumstances and can provide additional support as needed throughout the school day.

5.3 Parental Stress

Similar to siblings of children with chronic illness, parents of a child with a medical condition are also at risk for higher rates of overall stress, which is understandable given the extra demands placed on families as part of recommended medical regimens. This parental stress appears to vary based on the specific medical condition, with higher rates seen in asthma, diabetes, and epilepsy, and with overall stress tending to be increased by the prognosis associated with their child's medical condition (Mullins et al., 2004; Cousino & Hazan, 2013).

For many child clinicians, it may seem that emphasizing parental mental health and self-care is veering into uncharted territory and is taking away precious clinical time from the needs of the patient. However, when taking a holistic viewpoint of patients' health, it is important for the mental health clinician working with a pediatric patient to take into consideration the very real impact that significant and chronic parental stress can have on patient health outcomes (Barakat et al., 2007).

Consider the scenario of a depressed mother struggling with amotivation and sleep disturbances as part of her clinical presentation. This mother will most likely have a harder time ensuring that her child's morning treatment regimen is completed due to her own interfering mental health symptoms, irrespective of her best efforts and intentions. As such, it would be futile for a child clinician to address only the child's motivation and abilities regarding treatment adherence when, developmentally, it may still be appropriate for the parent to play a leading role in monitoring and setting up the daily regimen (e.g., laying out medications or preparing insulin injections).

For parents who may be surprised at a clinician's inquiry into their own self-care and mental health, it may be beneficial to explain this line of questioning and assessment with the use of the airplane oxygen mask analogy: when an airplane in is trouble and oxygen masks are deployed, passengers are advised to secure their own masks prior to securing the mask for a dependent. This priority is to ensure that the parent remains physically able to care for their child by maintaining adequate oxygen flow rather than running the risk of the adult caregiver losing oxygen and consciousness prior to helping their dependent. Similarly, a parent should be guided to prioritize their self-care as part of the overall care of their child, rather than viewing their self-care as being in opposition to or interfering with the care of their child.

For many parents, emphasizing self-care via adequate sleep can be a reliable first step in assisting with the management of parental stress, as chronic sleep deprivation is a well-documented occurrence among caregivers of patients with chronic illness, in part due to overall stress as well as caretaking responsibilities (Meltzer & Mindell, 2006). This emphasis on sleep can help with the improvement of mood as well as overall improvement in functioning, which is important when remembering that parents of children with chronic illness have to serve multiple roles in addition to being parents (e.g., care coordinators, advocates, and insurance specialists) (Kratz et al., 2009). Sensitive to the need to ensure that parents realize that they are not "taking" their child's psychotherapy time, clinicians might want to consider educating the parents about how their modeling adequate self-care via sleep hygiene and other practices is serving as an effective means of reinforcing the importance of the skills and strategies taught in individual psychotherapy sessions with their child or adolescent.

To better assist parents with self-care and the management of parental stress, it may be helpful to assess parental stress both qualitatively and quantitatively. A qualitative assessment can help with identifying the particulars of a parent's stress that is unique to their situation, such as shame or guilt in having difficulty consistently keeping medical appointments despite their best efforts or their fear of disagreeing with doctors when they have a concern. Additionally, quantitative measures can help assess the severity of parental stress in the context of pediatric illness via comparison with published normative data. One assessment measure with strong psychometric properties that was designed to assess parental stress related to childhood illness is the Pediatric Inventory for Parents, which the authors have made available for readers in the "Reproducible Resources" section at the end of this chapter (Streisand et al., 2001).

Clinical Vignette: "Fatigued Father"

Mr. R arrives twenty minutes late with his son, Rex, to your weekly therapy appointment. They used to always be prompt for appointments, but this is the third time in a row that they have been tardy to Rex's regularly scheduled outpatient psychotherapy appointment. This trend has continued for the last month despite Mr. R's consistent apologies each time and your consistency in ending the session at the predetermined time despite the tardiness. In speaking with Mr. R prior to working individually with Rex, it becomes apparent that Mr. R is exhausted following his completion of his night-time shift. He notes that his job recently switched him to the night shift despite his protests, and he expressed guilt about not feeling that he was able to effectively assist his son with his diabetes regimen in the morning anymore due to this fatigue. Mr. R noted that his exhaustion has adversely impacted his ability to consistently monitor his son's consistency in checking his blood glucose and dosing insulin appropriately before leaving for school in the morning. He expressed feelings of shame about the school nurse calling home last week due to concerns about the patient's glucose reading at lunch time.

It is readily apparent that Mr. R has been doing his best to help his son with his medical care; however, his current job and obvious fatigue are limiting his effectiveness in the morning. You validate Mr. R for his efforts and point out that many parents struggle with the day-to-day realities of pediatric chronic illness, particularly when other areas of their life become stressful. You provide psychoeducation about the importance of parental self-care in order to ensure the overall care of a child, and he grants permission to spend additional time in session problem solving how to reduce the overall familial stress of Rex's diabetes routine. It becomes apparent that most of the morning duties, including morning psychotherapy appointments, are a significant factor in Mr. R's overall stress level.

With Mr. R's permission, you obtain a release of information to speak with Ryan's school nurse. In speaking with her, you communicate Mr. R's concern regarding his difficulty monitoring his son's morning diabetes regimen, and the school nurse notes that she would be happy to assist Rex with this if he comes to school fifteen minutes earlier than usual. This change is implemented in the patient's 504 plan, and you observe that during subsequent psychotherapy appointments, Mr. R and Rex note significant improvement in the consistency of his morning glucose measurements. Following the implementation of this strategy, you spend time working with Rex and his father on beginning to transition some of the diabetes management tasks to Rex with appropriate supervision and reinforcement via behavioral contracting. For instance, Rex utilizes a recommended phone application to help track his blood glucose, which is also viewable by his father at his convenience later in the day. After moving his regular morning psychotherapy appointments to later afternoon appointments, you are also pleased to note that Rex and his father have returned to their previous pattern of arriving on time for appointments.

5.4 Parental Illness

While the focus of most pediatric clinicians is on the child's illness or medical concerns, clinicians may also be confronted with helping their patients grapple with the realities of parental illness or death, particularly when working with medical conditions that have genetic links that may be seen as a precursor by their child of their own future. The advent of a parent's illness can be a confusing time for the entire family, and when a parent has a severe medical illness, adolescents tend to report elevated symptoms associated with post-traumatic stress (Houck et al., 2007).

Despite some parents readily identifying concerning signs or changes in behavior that are representative of their child's struggle, many parents may feel disempowered or confused about how to best help their child understand and navigate the parental illness. Given the high stakes of these conversations, parents may not feel confident in their abilities to explain their illness to their child, which may also be complicated by their own processing of the disease. Despite this understandable distress and apparent need for resources, parents, such as those with advanced cancer, have noted not feeling supported or guided by health care professionals in how to talk with their child about their illness (Phillips, 2014).

In talking to children about death and dying, it is important to be aware of how children conceptualize death at different developmental ages. Readers may find it helpful to discuss with parents an outline such as "A Child's View of Death," based on developmental age (see the "Reproducible Resources" section, Figure 5.3, provided courtesy of the Children's

Bereavement Center of South Texas). As well as being aware of the child's developmental age and overall understanding of death and dying, it is important for parents and clinicians to help the child learn the appropriate terminology about the medical condition, to give the child accurate information, and to provide the child with the resources to discuss and process their feelings.

Many parents may waver between feeling that they should "protect" their child by not disclosing information about a parent's illness until forced to by external factors such as an in-patient hospitalization or the child overhearing a conversation between adults. In examining the best way to handle an admittedly difficult situation, research identifies "measured telling" as a recommended guide for discussing parental illness with adolescents (Sheehan et al., 2014). This approach emphasizes the importance of providing accurate information that is readily understandable by the adolescent. With "measured telling," parents provide consistent, gradual information that is responsive to the adolescent's reactions, such as providing more clarification when it is clearly desired by the adolescent or, conversely, not providing more information if the adolescent indicates a need for a break from the discussion.

Rather than waiting until being forced to disclose information, this approach emphasizes the need for consistently and gradually providing predetermined information to adolescents, with ample time to allow for processing and clarification regarding concerns or questions. Prior to disclosing information about a parental illness to children, parents should be encouraged to take adequate time to process the information themselves and then to decide on the language/wording they want to use in discussing this with their adolescent.

Similar to the above recommendation for siblings of children with chronic medical illness, parents with serious illness should also try to keep their children in as regular a routine as possible. Clinicians can help parents decide how much or how little they wish to disclose to school personnel about their illness, but it can be helpful to allow patients to touch base with trusted school personnel throughout the course of the disease (Russell et al., 2014). Refer to Figure 5.2 in the "Reproducible Resources" section for a sample letter from parents to teachers or other school staff that is focused on disclosing their illness and discussing how they would like particulars about this disclosure handled at their child's school. This sample letter is provided by the Marjorie E. Korf Parenting at a Challenging Time Program, which is a useful source of information for parents with serious illness and is listed in the "Recommended Websites, Books, and Other Resources" section.

Following the death of a parent, clinicians can assist in recommending supportive interventions for both the patient and the living parent. It may be helpful for a bereaved child not only to process their loss during family therapy with the living parent, but also to have a separate space to connect with other bereaved children in a support group format (Bergman et al., 2017). Similarly, the living parent may benefit from extra support outside family therapy to provide them with space to process their grief and to manage the stress of now acting as both parents in the midst of an emotionally tumultuous time (Aamotsmo & Bugge, 2013).

During the period of bereavement following the death of a parent, the mental health clinician can help families find strategies specific to each family member that can help them cope and process their loss. Clinicians can emphasize that there is no "right" way to grieve the loss of a parent, and can help normalize the grieving process as a time of adjustment that may be different and unique for each family member.

Clinical Vignette: Paul's Passing

Joseph is a 5-year-old Caucasian male who was referred by his pediatrician for increased physical aggression at school and regression in toilet training following the sudden death of his father, Paul, from cancer 2 months ago. His older sister, Tara, is a 25-year-old college student who recently dropped out of school for the semester to return home to care for her brother following the death of her father. As legal guardian, Tara is present for the initial intake and discusses her concerns regarding Joseph's continued disciplinary infractions at school, which include biting other students, as well as his recent difficulty with bed-wetting despite having been successfully toilet trained prior to Paul's passing.

Further questioning indicates that since Paul's death, Tara has felt overwhelmed and has had difficulty deciding when and how to provide consistent discipline and boundaries for Joseph. She states, "He just lost his dad. Knowing this, it's hard to make him do something he does not want to do or to punish him when he acts out. I'm not even sure he understands what actually happened to our father as he sometimes makes comments that make me think that he thinks our dad is coming back. I try not to talk about Paul's death as I don't want to upset him."

You reassure Tara that her confusion regarding discipline versus providing comfort are normal and appropriate concerns. With her permission, you provide basic psychoeducation about the tendency for children of Joseph's age to exhibit regressive behavior after the passing of a loved one, as well as their tendency to exhibit behavioral problems when there are significant changes in discipline and routine. You discuss and provide a written handout with the following recommendations for her to follow prior to the next session: (1) Set and maintain the same behavioral limits and expectations that his father had set (e.g., restriction of privileges if he was aggressive at school), (2) validate Joseph's feelings of embarrassment and reassure him that "accidents happen" when bedwetting occurs while also requesting his help in cleaning up the soiled linens, and (3) follow up on your referral for her own mental health treatment by an adult provider.

At the next session, you review Tara's success with implementing the above recommendations. She notes that his behavior had initially worsened but then significantly improved after Tara had remained consistent in implementing consequences despite this extinction burst. Next, you spend time with Joseph developing rapport via drawing and discussing his week at school. As Joseph becomes more comfortable, you begin probing gently about his perception of his father's death. Joseph appears confused when you use the word "death" and asks, "What do you mean by death? He is in Heaven." Further questioning indicates that Joseph believes that his father is in a temporary place in Heaven and will return home once he "kills the cancer."

After discussing this development with Tara and learning more about their religious faith, it is agreed that you and Tara will speak with Joseph together to explain death as being when "dad's body stopped working and he went to join your grandparents in Heaven. He is not coming back to Earth, but you will see him again when it is time for you to go to Heaven." Joseph becomes tearful but is able to soothe himself by drawing his feelings after the discussion. Tara agrees to continue this discussion by "checking in" with Joseph during the week and encouraging him to ask further questions about death, dying, and Heaven.

The following week, Tara reports that she learned that Joseph had believed that you could "catch cancer" and as a result was afraid for her to go to the doctor for her annual physical. You provide education about the "magical thinking" that is characteristic of his developmental age and spend time discussing Joseph's fears and misconceptions regarding cancer. You encourage Tara to continue to welcome questions from Joseph about cancer and death, as well as continuing to pursue her own self-care.

Summary

In working with pediatric patients with acute or chronic medical illnesses, clinicians are also tasked with helping the family system as a whole due to the significant impact family functioning may have on a patient. Amid all of the stress that can result from medical problems, many families may become overwhelmed when tasked with also having to learn how to navigate a complex and confusing health care system. Figuring out insurance coverage, making appointments with specialists, understanding treatment regimens, and other logistical concerns are all factors that can make the most medically savvy individual feel overwhelmed and frustrated. And when that feeling is coupled with the stress of being concerned for a loved one, it is a recipe for worsening an already stressful situation. This frustration can easily be misinterpreted during communications with medical team members as "nonadherence" when it may often actually be associated with a lack of understanding or poor health literacy. Mental health clinicians can help bridge the gap between a medical provider's dissemination of information and the family's actual comprehension of the provided information.

The entire family unit is affected by a patient's medical care and treatment, and this extends to impacting the siblings and parents of patients. Siblings of children with chronic illness tend to exhibit increased rates of internalizing and externalizing behaviors, with higher rates seen in siblings of a child with a life-threatening condition or a condition that requires an intensive daily treatment regimen. Siblings may be at risk for early parentification if they are too early and actively involved in assisting in their sibling's care. Overall, when examining the research literature, siblings appear to cope best when provided with information about the child's medical illness and the subsequent treatment regimen at a developmentally appropriate level, rather than being "protected" and not provided with information.

Siblings are not the only family members significantly affected by a pediatric patient's medical concerns, as parents of a child with a medical condition are also at risk for higher rates of overall stress. Although parents may not be the identified patient of a mental health clinician, clinicians can help to improve a patient's overall health outcome by monitoring and intervening as needed in the event that parental stress is adversely impacting family functioning.

Clinicians may be called on to help their patients grapple with the realities of parental illness or death as well as to assist siblings and parents with coping with a patient's illness. For many adolescents, coping with parental illness or death is accompanied by elevated symptoms associated with posttraumatic stress. In addition to helping with elevated psychiatric symptoms that may occur as a result of these adverse events, clinicians can help parents communicate with their child in order to understand and process death and dying in developmentally appropriate ways, can help patients learn the appropriate terminology and accurate information about their parent's medical condition, and can provide them with the resources to discuss and process their feelings. Parents will have many questions about how to best help their children during this stressful time, and clinicians can provide key recommendations to assist with the children's adjustment to a "new normal."

References

Aamotsmo, T. & Bugge, K. (2013). The healthy parent's role in the family when the other parent is in the palliative phase of cancer: challenges and coping in parenting young children. *Palliative and Supportive Care, 12*(4), 1–13.

Barakat, L., Patterson, C., Weinberger, B., Simon, K., Gonzalez, E., & Dampier, C. (2007). A prospective study of the role of coping and family functioning in health outcomes for adolescents with sickle cell disease. *Journal of Pediatric Hematology Oncology, 29,* 752–760.

Bergman, A., Axberg, V., & Hanson, E. (2017). When a parent dies – a systematic review of the effects of support programs for parentally bereaved children and their caregivers. *BMC Palliative Care, 16*(39), 1–15.

Boston University. (2018). Health Literacy Tool Shed. Retrieved November 16, 2018, from https://healthliteracy.bu.edu/.

Clemans-Cope, L. & Kenney, G. (2007). Low income parents' reports of communication problems with health care providers: effects of language and insurance. *Public Health Reports, 122*(2), 206–216.

Cousino, M. & Hazan, R. (2013). Parenting stress among caregivers of children with chronic illness: a systematic review. *Journal of Pediatric Psychology, 38*(8), 809–828.

Dolgin, M., Somer, E., Zaidel, N., & Zaizov, R. (1997). A structured group intervention for siblings of children with cancer. *Journal of Child and Adolescent Group Therapy, 1,* 3–18.

Fleary, S. & Heffer, R. (2013). Impact of growing up with a chronically ill sibling on well siblings' late adolescent functioning. *ISRN Family Medicine, 2013,* Article ID 737356.

Gan, L., Lum, A., Wakefield, C., Nandakumar, B., & Fardell, J. (2017). School experiences of siblings of children with chronic illness: a systematic literature review. *Journal of Pediatric Nursing, 33,* 23–32.

Houck, C., Rodrigue, J., & Lobato, D. (2007). Parent–adolescent communication and psychological symptoms among adolescents with chronically ill parents. *Journal of Pediatric Psychology, 32*(1), 596–604.

Incledon, E., Williams, L., Hazell, T., Heard, T. Flowers, A., & Hisock, H. (2015). A review of factors associated with mental health in siblings of children with chronic illness. *Journal of Child Health Care, 19*(2), 182–194.

Kramer, R. (1984). Living with childhood cancer: impact on the healthy siblings. *Oncology Nursing Forum, 11,* 44–51.

Kratz, L., Uding, N., Trahms, C., Villareale, N., & Kieckhefer, G. (2009). Managing childhood chronic illness: parent perspectives and implications for parent–provider relationships. *Families, Systems & Health 27* (4), 303–313.

Labay, L. & Walco, G. (2004). Brief report: empathy and psychological adjustment in siblings of children with cancer. *Journal of Pediatric Psychology, 29*(4), 309–314.

Meltzer, L. & Mindell, J. (2006). Impact of a child's chronic illness on maternal sleep and daytime functioning. *JAMA Internal Medicine, 166*(16), 1749–1755.

Minuchin, S., Montalvo, B., Guerney, B., Rosman, B., & Schumer, F. (1967). *Families of the Slums.* New York: Basic Books.

Mullins, L., Fuemmeler, B., Hoff, A., Chaney, J., Van Pelt, J., & Ewing, C. (2004). The relationship of parental overprotection and perceived child vulnerability to depressive symptomotology in children with type 1 diabetes mellitus: the moderating influence of parenting stress. *Children's Health Care, 33,* 21–34.

NeedyMeds.org. (2018). Retreats, Camps and Recreational Programs for Chronic/Serious/Life Threatening Illnesses – Children. Retrieved November 12, 2018, from www.needymeds.org/camps.taf?_function= list_disease&disease_id=345&disease= Chronic/Serious/Life%20Threatening% 20Illnesses-Children.

Phillips, F. (2014). Adolescents living with a parent with advanced cancer: a review of the literature. *Psycho-Oncology, 23,* 1323–1339.

Russell, K., Adams, P., Moore, C., Convery, M., Shea, S., & Rauch, P. (2014). Marjorie E. Korf Parenting at a Challenging Time Program. Toolkit to Help Educators Support Children of Parents with Serious Illness. Retrieved November 17, 2018, from www.mghpact.org/assets/media/documents/MGH-Cancer-Educator-Toolkit.pdf.

SeriousFun Children's Network. (n.d.). Our Camps & Programs. Retrieved November 12, 2018, from www.seriousfunnetwork.org/camps-and-programs.

Sharpe, D. & Rossiter, L. (2002). Siblings of children with a chronic illness: a meta-analysis. *Journal of Pediatric Psychology, 27*(8), 699–710.

Sheehan, S., Drauker, C., Christ, G., Mayo, M., & Parish, S. (2014). Telling adolescents a parent is dying. *Journal of Palliative Medicine, 17*(5), 512–520.

Sibling Support Project. (n.d.) Sibling Support Project. Retrieved November 13, 2018, from www.siblingsupport.org/.

Streisand, R., Braniecki, S., Tercyak, K., & Kazak, A. (2001). Childhood illness-related parenting stress: the Pediatric Inventory for Parents. *Journal of Pediatric Psychology, 26*(3), 155–162.

Sudore, R. & Schillinger, D. (2009). Interventions to improve care for patients with limited health literacy. *Journal of Clinical Outcomes Management, 16*(1), 20–29.

Yin, H., Johnson, M., Mendelson, A., Abrams, M., & Dreyer, B. (2009). The health literacy of parents in the United States: a nationally representative study. *Pediatrics, 124*(3), S289–S298.

Reproducible Resources

PEDIATRIC INVENTORY FOR PARENTS

Below is a list of difficult events which parents of children who have (or have had) a serious illness sometimes face. Please read each event carefully, and circle HOW OFTEN the event has occurred for you <u>in the past 7 days</u>, using the 5 point scale below. Afterwards, please rate how DIFFICULT it was/or generally is for you, also using the 5 point scale. <u>Please complete both columns for each item.</u>

EVENT	HOW OFTEN? 1=Never, 2=Rarely, 3=Sometimes, 4=Often, 5=Very often	HOW DIFFICULT? 1=Not at all, 2=A little, 3=Somewhat, 4=Very much, 5=Extremely
1. Difficulty sleeping	1 2 3 4 5	1 2 3 4 5
2. Arguing with family member(s)	1 2 3 4 5	1 2 3 4 5
3. Bringing my child to the clinic or hospital	1 2 3 4 5	1 2 3 4 5
4. Learning upsetting news	1 2 3 4 5	1 2 3 4 5
5. Being unable to go to work/job	1 2 3 4 5	1 2 3 4 5
6. Seeing my child's mood change quickly	1 2 3 4 5	1 2 3 4 5
7. Speaking with doctor	1 2 3 4 5	1 2 3 4 5
8. Watching my child have trouble eating	1 2 3 4 5	1 2 3 4 5
9. Waiting for my child's test results	1 2 3 4 5	1 2 3 4 5
10. Having money/financial troubles	1 2 3 4 5	1 2 3 4 5
11. Trying not to think about my family's difficulties	1 2 3 4 5	1 2 3 4 5
12. Feeling confused about medical information	1 2 3 4 5	1 2 3 4 5
13. Being with my child during medical procedures	1 2 3 4 5	1 2 3 4 5
14. Knowing my child is hurting or in pain	1 2 3 4 5	1 2 3 4 5
15. Trying to attend to the needs of other family members	1 2 3 4 5	1 2 3 4 5
16. Seeing my child sad or scared	1 2 3 4 5	1 2 3 4 5
17. Talking with the nurse	1 2 3 4 5	1 2 3 4 5
18. Making decisions about medical care or medicines	1 2 3 4 5	1 2 3 4 5
19. Thinking about my child being isolated from others	1 2 3 4 5	1 2 3 4 5
20. Being far away from family and/or friends	1 2 3 4 5	1 2 3 4 5
21. Feeling numb inside	1 2 3 4 5	1 2 3 4 5
22. Disagreeing with a member of the health care team	1 2 3 4 5	1 2 3 4 5

Figure 5.1 Pediatric Inventory for Parents.
Reprinted from Streisand, R., Braniecki, S., Tercyak, K., & Kazak, A., "Childhood Illness-Related Parenting Stress: The Pediatric Inventory for Parents," *Journal of Pediatric Psychology*, 2001; 26(3):155–162, by permission of the Society of Pediatric Psychology

EVENT	HOW OFTEN? 1=Never, 2=Rarely, 3=Sometimes, 4=Often, 5=Very often	HOW DIFFICULT? 1=Not at all, 2=A little, 3=Somewhat, 4=Very much, 5=Extremely
23. Helping my child with his/her hygiene needs	1 2 3 4 5	1 2 3 4 5
24. Worrying about the long term impact of the illness	1 2 3 4 5	1 2 3 4 5
25. Having little time to take care of my own needs	1 2 3 4 5	1 2 3 4 5
26. Feeling helpless over my child's condition	1 2 3 4 5	1 2 3 4 5
27. Feeling misunderstood by family/friends as to the severity of my child's illness	1 2 3 4 5	1 2 3 4 5
28. Handling changes in my child's daily medical routines	1 2 3 4 5	1 2 3 4 5
29. Feeling uncertain about the future	1 2 3 4 5	1 2 3 4 5
30. Being in the hospital over weekends/holidays	1 2 3 4 5	1 2 3 4 5
31. Thinking about other children who have been seriously ill	1 2 3 4 5	1 2 3 4 5
32. Speaking with my child about his/her illness	1 2 3 4 5	1 2 3 4 5
33. Helping my child with medical procedures (e.g. giving shots, swallowing medicine, changing dressing)	1 2 3 4 5	1 2 3 4 5
34. Having my heart beat fast, sweating, or feeling tingly	1 2 3 4 5	1 2 3 4 5
35. Feeling uncertain about disciplining my child	1 2 3 4 5	1 2 3 4 5
36. Feeling scared that my child could get very sick or die	1 2 3 4 5	1 2 3 4 5
37. Speaking with family members about my child's illness	1 2 3 4 5	1 2 3 4 5
38. Watching my child during medical visits/procedures	1 2 3 4 5	1 2 3 4 5
39. Missing important events in the lives of other family members	1 2 3 4 5	1 2 3 4 5
40. Worrying about how friends and relatives interact with my child	1 2 3 4 5	1 2 3 4 5
41. Noticing a change in my relationship with my partner	1 2 3 4 5	1 2 3 4 5
42. Spending a great deal of time in unfamiliar settings	1 2 3 4 5	1 2 3 4 5

Figure 5.1 (cont.)

SAMPLE LETTER #1: FROM THE PARENT TO THE CLASSROOM TEACHER AND/OR OTHER EDUCATORS

This template is for the initial letter that you write to your child's teacher, the principal or another contact person at school. Your intention is to notify the school about your diagnosis and start a dialog about what will happen next.

Dear (name of educator):

Include basic information:

I am writing to let you know that I have been diagnosed with (name of illness). (Child's name) knows that I (am sick, have X type of cancer) and we have told (him/her) that treatment will involve (type of treatment) over the next (X period of time). At home, we refer to the illness as (words used by the child to understand the diagnosis) and to the upcoming treatment as (words used by the child to understand the treatment plan).

Include requests regarding your child:

It would be very helpful if you could let (me/us) know if you observe any behavioral changes in (child's name). We would also appreciate learning in advance about any school work that may involve cancer, illness, or death, in case these assignments are upsetting to (child's name).

Depending on how your child has been handling school in the past, you might want to say

EITHER (if your child has been doing well):

Our clinical team has reassured us that children who are doing well in school generally continue to do well but might benefit from some accommodations (e.g., reduced workload) at certain times.

OR (if your child has been struggling):

Our clinical team has advised us that for children who are already struggling with academic or behavioral concerns, this can be a particularly difficult time.

Include the family's privacy choices:

Depending on whether you want to share information with other members of the school community, you may want to say

EITHER (if you don't want to share information):

We have decided that at this point we prefer that this information not be shared with other children or their parents.

OR (if you do want to share information):

We think it might be helpful to (child's name) and the rest of our family to share this news with (other parents in the class, the school community). We (plan to write a letter to them, would like to discuss with you the best way of doing this).

Figure 5.2 Sample letter #1: from the parent to the classroom teacher and/or other educators.
Reprinted from Russell, K., Adams, P., Moore, C., Convery, M., Shea, S., & Rauch, P. (2014). "Sample letter 1: from the parent to the classroom teacher and/or other educators," in "Toolkit to help educators support children of parents with serious illness." Retrieved November 20, 2018, from www.mghpact.org/assets/media/documents/MGH-Cancer-Educator-Toolkit.pdf. Copyright 2014 by Marjorie E. Korff PACT Program/PACT Boston

Include your child's privacy choices:

Depending on whether your child wants the teacher to check in with him/her, you may want to say

EITHER (if the choice is not to talk about it):

(Child's name) has told us that (he/she) wants school and social activities to be places where he does not need to worry about my health, and (he/she) would prefer not to discuss the illness at school.

OR (if the choice is to talk about it, at least occasionally):

(Child's name) has told us it would be all right for you to check in with (him/her) about how (he/she) is doing and whether (he/she) needs any special help.

Describe plans for further communication:

I hope we can work together to help (child's name) cope as well as possible during my illness.

If you have decided to designate caring others to manage communication and offers of help, you may want to inform the school staff:

Given the challenges of my treatment, our family has designated (name and contact number of the "Minister of Information") as the person to whom other people in the community can direct questions about my illness. (Name and contact number of the "Captain of Kindnesses") has offered to help us out by accepting and organizing any offerings of support from the school community.

I hope we can talk soon and figure out the best way to keep in touch during this time. Thank you very much for your support of (child's name) and our family.

Sincerely,

(Parent's name)

Figure 5.2 *(cont.)*

Children's Bereavement Center
OF SOUTH TEXAS

A CHILD'S VIEW OF DEATH

These are broad outlines describing a child's perception of death. Children and adults grieve differently. As children grow and mature their understanding of death and human relationships change. At every developmental stage, children may need to re-grieve or re-experience their losses.

Developmental State (Age)	Child's Perception of Death	Frequently Observed Behaviors	How to Help
Infant/ Toddler (birth-3 years)	• No understanding of death • Limited understanding of time	• Children sense when the adults around them are sad or preoccupied • May demonstrate an increased need for touching or holding • Increased separation anxiety • Somatic concerns, such as problems with feeding and/or digestion	• Offer abundant love • Meet their increased attachment needs, to include eye contact, loving facial expressions, touching, rocking, singing • Offer the child a transitional object, such as a soft blanket or stuffed animal
Preschool (3-5 yrs)	• Death seen as reversible or temporary • Children may think they are at fault • Children absorb only as much as they can understand • Confusion about what is real/not real • "Magical thinking" is common • Their understanding is very literal • Children at this age do not typically comprehend metaphor • Their emotions are difficult for them to understand and verbalize	• May act out or relieve anxiety through fantasy instead of talking to you • May feel at fault or guilty • May fear being left alone • Regressive behavior is common (may act as they did when they were younger, such as thumb sucking or bed wetting) • May not understand sadness around them • Repeated explanations may be needed • Behavioral changes common (may become withdrawn) • Will take breaks from grieving by resorting to playing	• Help child identify and understand own feelings • Accept regressive behavior • Reaffirm that the child is not at fault • Help child grasp what's real and not real • "The body stop working" is a helpful first definition of death • Be clear that dying is not the same as sleeping • Reassure child that he/she will be cared for; demonstrate that care with closeness and love

Figure 5.3 A Child's View of Death.
Reprinted from Children's Bereavement Center of South Texas. (2009). A Child's View of Death. Retrieved November 20, 2018, from www.hcisd.com/cms/lib4/TX01001784/Centricity/Domain/1243/Childs-view-of-death.pdf. Courtesy of Children's Bereavement Center of South Texas

School Age (6-7yrs)	• Beginning to see death as final, universal, but only for others ("not me") • Neither believes nor denies that he/she will die • May believe he/she can escape by being good or trying hard • Death often viewed as an actual person, spirit, or being (such as the "boogey man")	• Feelings may be shared with you or held in and may be out of the child's control • Coping may take the form of gathering information, becoming an expert about the disease or condition • May regress to a younger stage, earlier needs and actions • Repeated explanations may be needed to help understanding • May see changes in behavior: some children become aggressive, others withdraw.	• Allow child to talk or not talk as needed • Answer questions honestly and concretely • Respect their "need to know." Having information gives a child some sense of control • Art and poetry are helpful outlets for emotional expression • Work with child's teachers at school to help grieving process and watch for isolation from classmates
School Age (7-11yrs)	• Understands death as permanent and irreversible • Child may begin to question own mortality, asking "Am I next?" • Vivid ideas of what occurs after death • May be concerned with details of what happens after a person dies	• Feelings may be talked about, expressed or kept to themselves • Regressive behavior common (including increased separation anxiety) • Relationship with friends important • May see changes in behavior and moods. Grades in school may suffer • May take on role of person who died, seeking to "repair" the loss	• Support child's style or coping • Be available, supportive • Acknowledge importance of friends • Do not ask child to be strong, brave, grown-up, in-control, or to comfort others • Help with good-byes • Say " I don't know" when you do not know the answers
Adolescent 12+yrs	• Full awareness of own mortality • Attitudes toward death similar to adults • Possible "survivor guilt" if sibling or friend dies • Relationship with siblings and friends can be quite intense at this age	• Range of emotions may include anger, sorrow and guilt. Mood changes are common • Expression of "might have been", "Why?" And "If only" • Increased reliance on peers • Striving for independence, yet often fragile inside • Grades and extracurricular activities may suffer	• " I'm here if you need me" • Understanding that friends are important; find support groups if possible • Respect adolescent's need to work through independently • Encourage journaling, diaries, art, and poetry as means of expressing strong emotions

Figure 5.3 *(cont.)*

Recommended Websites, Books, and Other Resources
Clinical Resources
Health Literacy Assessment
Health Literacy Tool Shed, https://healthliteracy.bu.edu/

Summer Camps for Patients with Chronic Illnesses and Their Family Members
NeedyMeds.org, www.needymeds.org/camps.taf?_function=list_disease&disease_id=345&disease=
Chronic/Serious/Life%20Threatening%20Illnesses-Children

Serious Fun Children's Network, www.seriousfunnetwork.org/camps-and-programs

Sibling Support
Sibling Support Project, Resources for Siblings of Patients with Various Health Concerns,
www.siblingsupport.org/

Parent Illness
Marjorie E. Korff PACT Program: Parenting at a Challenging Time, www.mghpact.org/assets/media/
documents/MGH-Cancer-Educator-Toolkit.pdf

Recommended Books
Vadasy, P. & Meyer, D. (1996). *Living with a Brother or Sister with Special Needs: A Book for Sibs.*
Seattle: Washington University Press.

Cline, F. & Greene, L. (2007). *Parenting Children with Health Issues.* Golden, CO: Love and Logic
Institute.

Abrams, M. & Dreyer, B. (2008). *Plain Language Pediatrics: Health Literacy Strategy and
Communication Resources for Common Pediatric Topics.* Elk Grove Village, IL: American Academy
of Pediatrics.

6 Psychological Guidelines for Specific Medical Conditions

6.1 Cystic Fibrosis

Cystic fibrosis is a progressive genetic disease that affects multiple organ systems, with particularly noteworthy impact on the lungs, pancreas, and reproductive systems (Quittner et al., 2009). There have been significant medical advances that have recently increased the average life expectancy of a patient with cystic fibrosis, as the average life expectancy is 47 years for patients born in 2016 in comparison to the average life time expectancy of 43 years for patients born between 2012 and 2016 (Marshall, 2017).

Cystic fibrosis is also often complicated by CF-related diabetes, as approximately 50% of patients with cystic fibrosis will develop CF-related diabetes (CFRD) by age 30 (Jacobs et al., 2016). The risk of the development of CF-related diabetes increases from childhood to adolescence, which is also unfortunately when difficulty with treatment adherence tends to increase (Jacobs et al., 2016). For many families, the diagnosis of CF-related diabetes can be overwhelming as now they are being tasked to manage two medical illnesses that are very time-intensive and require rigorous oversight.

Treatments for cystic fibrosis are very time-intensive for patients and families, as typical estimates of the daily amount of time for performing treatments (e.g., airway clearance techniques and medications) was reported as approximately 74.6 minutes by children with cystic fibrosis and approximately 56.9 minutes by parents (Ziaian et al., 2006). With this already intensive regimen, a family's stress level can be exacerbated by adding the demands of a diabetes treatment regimen, such as blood glucose monitoring and carbohydrate counting. Given the complexity of these regimens, time management problems and treatment adherence concerns are typical presenting concerns of families with children with both cystic fibrosis and CF-related diabetes.

Mental health clinicians can easily be overwhelmed by the sheer amount of medical knowledge applicable for both medical conditions and not know where to start in order to have an adequate amount of knowledge to assist these patients. First, it may be helpful for clinicians to secure releases of information to speak with both cystic fibrosis and endocrine clinic providers in order to have a basic understanding of each patient's treatment regimen and perceived adherence. For cystic fibrosis, treatment regimens typically include airway clearance therapies, antibiotics, nutritional supplementation, and taking enzymes with food (Stark et al., 1995). By working with each patient's cystic fibrosis provider, a mental health clinician can easily gain detailed information about the patient's current treatment plan, as well any patterns that may have emerged regarding hospitalizations, which can often be indicative of a patient's treatment adherence.

In addition to complex and time-intensive daily treatment regimens, children and adolescents with cystic fibrosis must adhere to strict infection control guidelines in order to help prevent the spread of pathogens (e.g., *Pseudomonas aeruginosa*) among patients with cystic fibrosis (Duff & Latchford, 2010). The Infection Prevention and Control Guideline for Cystic Fibrosis: 2013 Update indicated the need for there to be a minimum of 6 feet distance between patients with cystic fibrosis to prevent the transmission of CF-related pathogens (Saimen et al., 2014). Clinicians working with children and adolescents with cystic fibrosis should be aware of these guidelines to help protect the health of their patients. At a minimum, clinicians should wipe down areas of their office with disinfecting towelettes that may have been touched by patients with cystic fibrosis and ensure that patients with cystic fibrosis do not sit near each other in waiting rooms to help prevent cross-contamination among patients.

Given these parameters, it is important for clinicians to work with schools to ensure that these infection control guidelines are met, particularly if there is more than one student with cystic fibrosis at the school. Should more than one student at a particular school have cystic fibrosis, schools can help ensure that these students do not meet face-to-face by having students use different stairwells, participate in different gym classes, and other strategies. Having a 504 plan is advantageous in that it can confirm that students have the recommended accommodations they need to remain healthy at school and prevent unnecessary hospitalizations for pulmonary exacerbations. Refer to the "Recommended Websites, Books, and Other Resources" section at the end of this chapter for resources regarding school accommodations for cystic fibrosis.

The clinical needs of children and adolescents with cystic fibrosis tend to vary significantly by developmental age. In younger patients (e.g., pre-school age), the goals of psychological treatments tend to focus on implementing behavioral management programs and parent behavior training to assist with overall treatment refusal and nutritional concerns (Jelalian et al., 1998; Bernard & Cohen, 2004). As patients with cystic fibrosis age, patients tend to show increased levels of anxiety and depression, as well as decreased treatment adherence. In particular, increased depression rates are observed in approximately 8–29% of children and adolescents with cystic fibrosis (Quittner et al., 2016).

The Cystic Fibrosis Foundation/European Cystic Fibrosis Social International Committee on Mental Health in Cystic Fibrosis recommends annual screenings of both patients and at least one caregiver as a result of these increased rates of mental health symptoms in both patients and caregivers (Quittner et al., 2016). It is recommended that patients ages 12 and older, as well as caregivers, should be assessed for anxiety and depression with the Patient Health Questionnaire-9 (PHQ-9) and Generalized Anxiety Disorder-7 (GAD-7) (Kroenke & Spitzer, 2002; Spitzer et al., 2006; Quittner et al., 2016). The PHQ-9 and GAD-7 are within the public domain and are listed in the "Reproducible Resources" section at the end of this chapter.

With the use of these assessments, it is recommended that clinicians utilize a "stepped approach" based on symptom severity scores, with the first step focusing on education and subsequently proceeding as needed to evidence-based psychological intervention and pharmacotherapy (Quittner et al., 2016). Evidence-based psychological approaches that are recommended for pediatric patients with cystic fibrosis are cognitive behavioral therapy (CBT) or interpersonal psychotherapy (IPT) for anxiety or depression, as well as behavioral approaches for distress associated with medical procedures. If needed for severe symptoms, pharmacotherapy is also recommended in conjunction with psychotherapy, with specific recommendations of the use of selective serotonin reuptake inhibitors such as citalopram, escitalopram, sertraline, or fluoxetine (Quittner et al., 2016).

In addition to providing more traditional psychological and/or psychiatric approaches, mental health clinicians can assist with overall mental health by partnering with patients and their families to increase physical activity. Despite the well-known physical and psychological benefits of exercise and physical activity, patients with cystic fibrosis tend to be less physically active than their peers (Williams et al., 2010). In conjunction with the guidance of the patient's physical therapist and/or pulmonologist, the mental health clinician can assist in providing basic education and safety precautions for exercise recommendations for adolescents with cystic fibrosis.

Current research suggests that adolescents should typically exercise between three to five times per week when the severity of their CR-related lung disease falls within the mild to moderate range, while adolescents may need to exercise five times per week when their lung disease falls into the severe category (Williams et al., 2010; see Table 6.1). Education should

Table 6.1 General exercise and training recommendations

	Patients with mild to moderate CF lung disease	Patients with severe CF lung disease
Recommended activities	Cycling, walking, hiking, aerobics, running, rowing, tennis, swimming, strength training, climbing, roller-skating, (trampolining)	Ergometric cycling, walking, strengthening exercises, gymnastics, and day-to-day activities
Method	Intermittent and steady-state	Intermittent
Frequency	3–5 times per week	5 times per week
Duration	30–45 minutes	20–30 minutes
Intensity	70%–85% HRmax; 60%–80% peak VO_2; LT; GET	60%–80% HRmax; 50%–70% peak VO_2; LT; GET
Oxygen supplementation	Indicated, if SaO_2 drops below 90% during exercise	Indicated, if SaO_2 drops below 90% during exercise (cave: resting hypoxia)
Activities to avoid	Bungee-jumping, high diving, and scuba diving	Bungee-jumping, high diving, scuba diving, and hiking in high altitude
Potential risks associated with exercise, and training	Dehydration Hypoxemia Bronchoconstriction Pneumothorax Hypoglycemia[a] Hemoptysis Esophageal bleedings Cardiac arrhythmias Rupture of liver and spleen Spontaneous fractures[b]	

Note: HRmax: maximum heart rate; peak VO_2: peak oxygen consumption; LT: lactate threshold; GET: gas exchange threshold; SaO_2: oxygen saturation.
[a] Depending on the existence of an impaired glucose tolerance.
[b] Depending on the existence of untreated CF-related bone disease.
Source: From Williams et al., 2010, www.hindawi.com/journals/ijpedi/2010/670640/cta/.

be provided to patients and their family about safety precautions when exercising for patients with cystic fibrosis, with predominant emphasis on the impact of hot weather on sodium and chloride loss, the adverse impact of exercise in high altitudes, and awareness of symptoms of exercise-induced hypoxemia (Williams et al., 2010).

Clinical Vignette: "No one else deals with this!"

Chris is a 15-year-old Caucasian male who presents with his mother to the first intake appointment. His mother expresses concern about his pattern of declining treatment adherence and recent statements about "being alone." Over the past two years, Chris's scores on pulmonary functioning tests have consistently and significantly dropped, and he has been hospitalized four times due to pulmonary exacerbations. Per his mother, his cystic fibrosis interdisciplinary team has warned Chris that if this trend continues, he is on track to needing a lung transplant before he turns 18 years old. In discussing treatments with Chris, it is apparent that he is knowledgeable about how to perform the various treatment tasks (e.g., taking multiple prescription medications, airway clearance techniques) and that a lack of knowledge about how to complete treatments is not a main factor contributing to nonadherence. He also appears to be aware of both the short- and long-term implications of treatment nonadherence with cystic fibrosis. It is apparent is that the patient's frustration with having to do treatments is interfering with his daily adherence, as he notes, "I don't want to do it – it's not fair. No other teen I know has this stupid disease! None of my friends have to deal with this."

During the next scheduled session, you work with Chris and his mother on implementing a behavioral contract in which Chris earns weekly rewards (i.e., extended curfew and time with friends) for the successful completion of treatment tasks. Chris fails to complete the required tasks one week, and his mother calls asking for your recommendation in whether to allow him to attend a party despite not having fulfilled his part of the contract. You remind his mother about the need for consistent boundary setting and remind her about the expected extinction burst when a new behavioral change is required. His mother agrees to stick to the contract and Chris is not allowed to go to the party.

The following week, Chris and his mother arrive for the appointment. His mother indicated that she did indeed hold to the consequences defined in the contract, and Chris notes that he is on track to successfully complete all tasks this week. The remainder of the session focuses on helping Chris process his feelings about being "alone" with cystic fibrosis. With his mother's permission, Chris is encouraged to seek out positive blogs about cystic fibrosis as well as online peer support groups specific to cystic fibrosis.

Over the next several months, you continue to help Chris seek out positive and age-appropriate online support from other teenagers diagnosed with cystic fibrosis. Additionally, you help his mother continue to remain consistent in administering positive and negative consequences in association with his performance of his cystic fibrosis treatment regimen.

6.2 Diabetes Mellitus Type 1

Type 1 diabetes mellitus affects approximately 13,000 children and adolescents in the United States, with approximately 200,000 children and adolescents collectively having been diagnosed with either type 1 or type 2 diabetes mellitus (Ogden et al., 2010). During a time when many families may struggle with developmentally appropriate conflicts over curfews and homework completion, families of pediatric patients with diabetes also have to contend with managing the complications of a chronic and potentially life-threatening

Table 6.2 Warning signs of conditions associated with type 1 diabetes mellitus

Hypoglycemia	Hyperglycemia	Diabetic ketoacidosis (DKA)
Dizziness	Increased urination	Abdominal pain
Physical weakness	Excessive thirst	Shortness of breath
Sweating	Weight loss	Confusion
Irritability	Muscle cramps	Vomiting
Difficulty concentrating	Nausea	Dehydration
Anxiety	Blurred vision	Coma

disease. As part of their daily regimen, children and adolescents with type 1 diabetes mellitus are tasked with performing daily glucose monitoring, making alterations to their insulin dosage via injection or insulin pump, monitoring their carbohydrate intake, and checking their urine for ketones (American Diabetes Association, 2011).

These complex and invasive treatment-related tasks are required due to the significant short- and long-term complications that can arise without the proper management of type 1 diabetes mellitus. In particular, if type 1 diabetes is not well managed, the patient is at increased risk for serious medical complications such as amputations, vision loss, and stroke (Loghmani, 2005). It is imperative for mental health clinicians to understand the basics of daily treatment regimens for diabetes mellitus to assist with treatment adherence, as well as to have an awareness of early warning signs to assist in the prevention of the dangerous condition of diabetic ketoacidosis (see Table 6.2). Diabetic ketoacidosis (DKA) is a medical emergency that can lead to coma and/or death, and this condition is the leading cause of death in pediatric diabetes (Yau & Sperling, 2017). Refer to the "Recommended Websites, Books, and Other Resources" section for more information about recommended books to assist clinicians in gaining fundamental knowledge about diabetes mellitus type 1.

For patients with type 1 diabetes, glycemic control is managed by insulin treatment (Switzer et al., 2012). As children get older, they have to perform not only daily calculations for insulin dosing but also other calculations associated with carbohydrate counting. Carbohydrate counting is an important aspect of the diabetes regimen, and it is recommended that patients with type 1 diabetes consistently attempt to have their daily intake follow these ratios: 50–55% of their food intake consisting of carbohydrates, 30–35% consisting of fats, and 10–15% consisting of protein (Smart et al., 2014).

For carbohydrate counting, insulin dosing, and other diabetes-related calculations, patients need to have adequate numeracy skills for the successful performance of these important tasks (Mulvaney et al., 2013). A patient will find it very difficult to perform the basic calculations necessary for diabetes management if they have fundamental deficits in mathematical calculations. Mental health clinicians are tasked with assessing whether deficits in numeracy are present and, if these deficits are present, with providing specific recommendations for educational interventions or alternative clinical recommendations to help overcome this concern (Mulvaney et al., 2013).

Clinicians may find it helpful to utilize empirically supported assessments focused upon diabetes-related numeracy rather than relying on a patient's reported performance in mathematics in school given that diabetes-related numeracy requires the application of mathematical concepts in a "real world" setting rather than just mathematical computations in a classroom setting. The Diabetes Numeracy Test is an empirically supported assessment that clinicians may find helpful in their clinical practice, as this diabetes-related numeracy assessment was first normed on adults but has also been found to be a reliable and valid assessment for the adolescent population (Huizinga et al., 2008; Mulvaney et al., 2013). Refer to the "Recommended Websites, Books, and Other Resources" for information regarding websites for diabetes numeracy.

Alongside the physical symptoms of type 1 diabetes mellitus and the general logistical stress of managing diabetes treatment, children and adolescents with type 1 diabetes mellitus are also at risk for certain psychological symptoms, including, most notably, a two-fold risk for depressive symptoms in comparison to their same-aged peers, as well as an increased risk for low self-esteem (Nichols et al., 2007). Some research also suggests an increased risk of cognitive processing problems with type 1 diabetes, of which the greatest risk for these difficulties occurs in children and adolescents with early-onset diabetes and/or when child has experienced continuing episodes of hypoglycemia (Ryan et al., 1984; Holmes & Richman, 1985).

Research has also suggested that there are higher rates of disordered eating in patients with type 1 diabetes in contrast to healthy peers (Young-Hyman & Davis, 2010). In addition to typical disordered eating presentations, patients with type 1 diabetes and disordered eating patterns may engage in a behavior termed "diabulimia," in which patients manipulate insulin doses in order to lose weight by skipping doses or "under-dosing" (Davidson, 2014). As such, clinicians may also find it helpful to purposefully include a dedicated portion of the intake and assessment time to assessing for disordered eating and insulin manipulation.

Psychological interventions for pediatric diabetes often tend to focus on more family-based interventions. Families with young children diagnosed with type 1 diabetes may benefit from parenting training, as an authoritative parenting style is associated with greater glycemic control and treatment adherence in young children (Davis et al., 2001). Moreover, Behavioral Family Systems for Diabetes (BFST-D) has demonstrated efficacy in promoting family communication and problem solving for adolescents with type 1 diabetes, with this intervention mainly focusing on the components of problem-solving, communication training, cognitive restructuring, and functional-structural family therapy (Wysocki et al., 2006).

Clinical Vignette: Lunch Room Scandal

Margaret is an 8-year-old female Caucasian female whom you have been seeing for several months for emotional distress and impairment in functioning related to generalized anxiety disorder. Margaret has recently been diagnosed with type 1 diabetes mellitus, and her father notes during the session that he received a letter from the school this past week informing him that she has not been going to the school nurse as scheduled to perform her blood glucose monitoring before lunch. When queried, Margaret reports that last week, one of her peers saw her performing her glucose check with the school nurse before lunch and spread a rumor to her classmates that Margaret was purposely using a needle to make herself bleed in order to avoid peers and to spend time with the nurse.

Margaret noted that she learned of this rumor after several of her friends came up to her to ask why she was mad at them and would go to such lengths to avoid them. Thus, she reported that she has not met with the school nurse to perform her glucose checks in order to prevent her friends from becoming upset with her for "avoiding" them. In speaking with Margaret, it becomes apparent that she has not told any of her classmates about being diagnosed with diabetes. She reports some hesitation with disclosing her diagnosis to her classmates due to a fear that they will think she is "weird" or "different," but she also notes that it would be a relief not to hide this diagnosis from her friends due to the stress this induces.

Over the next several sessions, your work with Margaret focuses on normalizing and processing her feelings of "being different" and the "unfairness" of having diabetes when none of her friends have this condition. She was able to identify other areas in which her friends may struggle that she does not, such as shyness, bereavement, and sibling conflict, and subsequently relate this to the premise that "everyone struggles with something." You work with Margaret closely on practicing how to explain developmentally appropriate information about diabetes to her friends and assist with providing video resources that Margaret's teacher can show to the class about diabetes mellitus type 1. Margaret reports feeling relieved following her conversations with her close friends about diabetes, and she stated that her friends now help to remind her to report to the school nurse every day for blood glucose monitoring before lunch.

6.3 Obesity

Children and adolescents in the United States meet criteria for being classified as overweight and obese at a rate of approximately one in three individuals, with the highest rates occurring in ethnic minority populations (Taveras et al., 2013). Obesity is diagnosed when a patient's body mass index (BMI) falls at or above 95th percentile for their age and gender (Mullen & Shield, 2003). Over the past several decades, the United States has seen a rapid increase in pediatric obesity, from less than 5% of children and adolescents in 1963 to 17% of the pediatric population from 2004 to 2014 (Barlow, 2007; Centers for Disease Control and Prevention, 2017b). This increase in the obesity rate appears to have been influenced by changes in dietary habits over time as well as other factors.

For some patients, obesity can in part be attributed to endogenous influences, such as hormonal factors associated with certain diseases, and lifestyle factors related to diet and exercise (Crocker & Yanovski, 2009). In particular, there are significant risk factors for obesity from medical conditions such as Cushing's syndrome, growth hormone deficiency, and hypothyroidism. Obesity related to side effects of medications is also an important factor for mental health clinicians to recognize as some psychotropic medications are significantly associated with weight gain (e.g., lithium and olanzapine) (Crocker & Yanovski, 2009). This issue is particularly pertinent for mental health clinicians as it may be a contributing factor as to why some patients are nonadherent with medication once it has been prescribed.

Should actual weight gain or the patient's perception of potential weight gain be identified as a side effect or barrier to the patient's adherence to psychotropic medication, clinicians can help patients discuss alternatives or options with their prescriber by roleplaying medical conversations or directly contacting the provider. If weight gain is an unavoidable consequence of a necessary medication, clinicians can help patients to develop strategies for incorporating healthy behavioral changes, such as increased exercise and healthier food choices, into their daily lifestyle.

In addition to medically related causes for obesity, environmental factors such as parental modeling of eating and the weight status of a patient's parents also impacts the child or adolescent's food intake and physical activity and, subsequently, the patient's weight status (Mullen & Shield, 2003). This can make treatment complex and multifactorial as treatment approaches will therefore need to include both parents and the patient. When working with children and adolescents with obesity, it is important for mental health clinicians not only to assess symptoms associated with the patient's physical health but also to assess for psychological symptoms that are often comorbid with obesity (Cooperman, 2003; Stark et al., 2012). Given that both the physical health and mental health needs of a patient with obesity should be assessed, mental health clinicians must work collaboratively with physicians to assess for obesity-related medical problems as well as to screen for medical causes for obesity (Mullen & Shield, 2003; Stark et al., 2012).

According to the Expert Committee Recommendations on the Assessment, Prevention, and Treatment of Child and Adolescent Overweight and Obesity, the overall treatment approach depends on a patient's weight category, specific medical risks, and other factors (Barlow, 2007). Although the specific treatment approach is dependent on a patient's treatment categorization based on their BMI and other factors, the emphasis of most treatment approaches is typically on maintaining rather than losing weight (Children's Hospital Association, 2012). However, this traditional focus can differ when the patient's BMI is over 95% and/or when other medical condition(s) are a factor, but again, this is dependent on the patient's age, response to treatment, and other factors (Barlow, 2007). Refer to the "Recommended Websites, Books, and Other Resources" section for information about these recommendations and descriptions of weight categories and recommended treatment approaches.

In clinical work with children and adolescents with obesity, it is imperative that mental health clinicians emphasize behavioral changes that involve the entire family rather than solely asking for changes within the pediatric patient. This emphasis is critical in that many of the changes asked of the individual patient in relation to nutrition and physical activity are largely influenced by other family members. For instance, choices made by the patient's parents and siblings help determine which groceries are bought at the store and are subsequently available in the home and whether physical activity is prioritized in the family. As such, mental health clinicians can assist families in setting familial behavioral goals such as reviewing food labels together, engaging in family walks, and performing other goal-congruent activities (Mullen & Shield, 2003).

When assisting families in creating strategic goals for increasing physical activity, it is important for clinicians to work collaboratively with pediatricians and other medical providers. In particular, physicians are necessary for the assessment of patients with chronic health conditions prior to increasing physical activity in order to identify any medical contraindications and to provide physical activity recommendations based on this assessment (Philpott, Houghton, & Luke, 2010). This collaboration is vital to help ensure that all behavioral goals and recommendations are aligned with keeping the patient physically safe as they work to achieve their physical activity and weight goals.

Although recommendations for each patient will vary based on the patient's medical needs and other factors, it is generally recommended that children and adolescents between the ages of 6 and 17 engage in at least 60 minutes per day of aerobic activity, with at least three days per week including activities that strengthen muscles and bones (US Department of Health and Human Services, 2008). Recommendations to tailor physical activity goals should also be based on the patient's developmental age, as school-age children may prefer "play" activity while adolescents may derive more benefit from "peer-enhanced" interventions (Children's Hospital Association, 2012). For example, it may be helpful to support adolescents becoming involved in group sports or group fitness classes not only to assist in promoting physical activity but also to help with promoting social skills and decreasing social isolation.

In addition to physical activity recommendations, mental health clinicians can help the family utilize stimulus control strategies specific to the patient such as limiting "screen" time (e.g., time on electronic devices) as well as stimulus control strategies for the entire family, including removing high-caloric foods from the home entirely (Wilfley et al., 2007). Mental health clinicians are uniquely positioned to help reduce a significant risk factor for obesity in children and adolescents by assisting with the promotion of beneficial sleep practices, as research has shown that the overall risk for obesity significantly increases with decreased sleep and children also exhibit decreased physical activity in association with delayed bedtimes (Gupta et al., 2002). General recommendations for sleep hygiene can be found in the "Recommended Websites, Books, and Other Resources" section, and a sample daily sleep and exercise log for clinical use is available in the "Reproducible Resources" section.

Clinical Vignette: Comorbid Concerns

Nick is a 14-year-old African American male patient who has been diagnosed with major depressive disorder, recurrent, moderate, and obesity. Despite consistent engagement in psychotherapy for the past year, Nick has continued to struggle with recurrent depressive episodes. Although psychoeducation has been provided about the efficacy of psychopharmacology in the treatment of depression, Nick and his father are reluctant to pursue psychiatric services at this time based upon their religious beliefs. Given this, you discuss the efficacy of a treatment protocol that is not in conflict with their beliefs and that would be advantageous for both of Nick's diagnoses of depression and obesity: increased physical activity.

Following this change in treatment plan, Nick was examined by his pediatrician and cleared for participation in a physical activity program. As such, it is agreed that Nick and his father will begin a scheduled program of walking for 20 minutes on Mondays, Wednesdays, and Fridays immediately following school at a park adjacent to their home. With assistance from you, Nick and his father identify the following potential barriers to this plan: (1) inclement weather and (2) Nick's father having to work overtime unexpectedly. After identifying these potential barriers to adhering to the physical activity program, you assist Nick and his father in utilizing problem-solving skills to identify solutions to their barriers: (1) the use of a calisthenics program provided by his pediatrician in place of walking in the park in the event of inclement weather and (2) the plan to walk on a Saturday for 20 minutes should Nick's father be unable to walk with his son on one of the three days that had been identified for physical activity.

In later sessions, you work with Nick and his father on revising his physical activity by increasing frequency and duration of physical activity sessions, as well as starting to have Nick begin to engage in physical activity once per week independently. Additionally, you work with Nick and his father on scheduling nutritious "sit down" dinners that they conjointly prepare together at least once per week. This strategy was chosen to help increase Nick's overall social support from his father and to provide Nick with an example of his father modeling healthy lifestyle behaviors.

6.4 Asthma

Asthma is one of the most common pediatric illnesses in the United States, as approximately 8.4% children and adolescents under the age of 18 were diagnosed with current asthma in the United States in 2017 (Centers for Disease Control and Prevention, 2017c). Asthma typically presents with a patient having an underlying inflammation with observable symptoms of wheeziness, coughing, and other symptoms when triggered by different environmental factors (McQuaid & Abramson, 2009).

Over the past several decades, the prevalence rate of asthma has significantly increased in the United States (Platts-Mills et al., 2000). There are several hypotheses for why this increase in prevalence rate has been observed, with one hypothesis being that the interaction of decreased physical activity with the overall increased exposure to indoor allergens has increased the overall prevalence rate of asthma (Platts-Mills et al., 2000). Furthermore, this decreased physical activity is associated with obesity, which, like asthma, has been found to disproportionately affect children from lower-income and ethnic minority communities.

In addition to higher prevalence rates of asthma in ethnic minority populations, asthma mortality is also higher in ethnic minority populations, with particular risk observed in African American and Puerto Rican populations (Hunninghake et al., 2006). This uneven prevalence rate across ethnic groups is thought to be a result of both health care disparities and the role of genetic factors (McQuaid & Abramson, 2009).

Similar to other chronic diseases, asthma appears to have a significant effect on pediatric patients' academic functioning (Centers for Disease Control and Prevention, 2013). When reviewing the impact of asthma on daily academic functioning, research indicates that approximately 49% of children and adolescents with asthma missed at least one day of school during the school year due to asthma in 2010 (Centers for Disease Control and Prevention, 2013). While some absences may be unavoidable, there are behavioral strategies and resources that clinicians can utilize to assist patients in reducing this occurrence and, subsequently, to reduce the impact of missing school on the patient.

One direct strategy that clinicians can use when working with a patient is to help ensure that patients have a written asthma action plan that specifically delineates asthma-related information that can help prevent asthma exacerbations from taking place, as well as to provide information about how to manage symptoms if they do occur at school. Written asthma action plans have been found to have "reduced the mean number of acute care visits, school absenteeism, nocturnal awakenings, and symptoms" (Zemek et al., 2008, p. 162). Asthma action plans tend to be either symptom-based plans or peak-flow based plans, and research has indicated that symptom-based action plans tend to be preferred by children and are associated with a 27% lower risk of exacerbation of asthma symptoms (Zemek et al., 2008). Refer to the "Reproducible Resources" section for a sample symptom-based asthma action plan provided by AllerMates.

Clinicians can also assist patients in learning about allergen avoidance and helping children learn to navigate how to avoid or reduce the exposure to allergens in social situations without causing undue distress or embarrassment. For instance, a child with severe asthma can role-play with a mental health clinician how to explain to their peers why they are playing indoors during severe cold weather instead of continuing to play outside during recess. In addition to helping patients learn how to effectively avoid allergens, clinicians can also assist with overall stress management that in and of itself can impact asthma. For approximately 15–30% of individuals diagnosed with asthma, stress can serve as an antecedent for asthma episodes (McQuaid & Abramson, 2009). By learning evidence-based strategies for anxiety management, not only can patients influence the impact of anxiety on their mental health, but, for some, the frequency of asthma episodes may also be lessened.

Pediatric psychologists are tasked with assisting with overall asthma education, the identification and resolution of psychosocial barriers that may arise during treatment, and the implementation of targeted interventions for the management of asthma by the patient and family members (McQuaid & Abramson, 2009). Recommended interventions that focus on increasing problem-solving abilities by patients and their families have demonstrated efficacy, as well as overall interventions that are family-based (Walders et al., 2000).

6.5 Food Allergies

In the United States, approximately 4–9% of children have been diagnosed with food allergies (Branum & Lukacs, 2008). The highest prevalence rate for pediatric allergies is in the very young, as some children will experience a dissipation of allergic reactions once they are between the ages of 4 and 6 years old (Sampson, 2000). Food allergies are the most frequent causes of anaphylaxis, with some 30,000 cases across all age ranges annually presenting to emergency departments within the United States (Yocum et al., 1999).

With most pediatric food allergies, families are tasked with recognizing warning signs of an allergic reaction and responding immediately after recognizing anaphylaxis (Dinakar, 2012). With this first step, vigilance by the patient's family is necessary to help prevent the child or adolescent from accidentally ingesting the identified food allergen. To assist parents in communicating with adults in other settings in which the patient might consume food (i.e., school or peer's homes), a reproducible "Food Allergy Awareness Letter" (Bostic, n.d.) has been kindly provided by its author and is listed in the "Reproducible Resources" section.

In addition to avoiding food allergens, patients and their families must be alert to early warning signs in order to be able to respond in a timely manner should anaphylaxis occur (Dinakar, 2012). Administering intramuscular epinephrine is a crucial task that must be performed by the patient and/or parent in the event of food-induced anaphylaxis (Muraro et al., 2014b). Unfortunately, significant knowledge and skills deficits appear when researchers have examined the parental administration of epinephrine, as one study indicated that only 32% of the parents of pediatric patients with a severe food allergy were able to demonstrate accurate administration of epinephrine and only 55% of the parents in the sample were found to be carrying epinephrine that had not expired (Sicherer et al., 2000).

This necessary vigilance can be difficult to manage as it can be easy for parents to veer from helpful vigilance to hypervigilance, as well as to have difficulty with helping children naturally transition into taking increasing responsibility for the awareness and avoidance of food allergens. For many clinicians, a significant clinical intervention may be helping to provide parents with education and guidance into allowing their child to garner more responsibility for managing their medical condition as developmentally appropriate. Parents' natural anxiety for their child taking on this responsibility will need to be validated and helped into being channeled in more productive ways, such as teaching the child how to read food labels or restaurant menus, rather than allowing for natural anxiety to prevent children from learning how to independently keep themselves safe while living with a food allergy.

It is not uncommon for children with food allergies to be anxious or fearful about eating away from home. Indeed, this anxiety can be somewhat adaptive in moderation as it can help foster caution when eating unknown foods; however, this aforementioned anxiety can extend to the avoidance of other social activities such as eating at a restaurant due to the patient's and/or their parents' fears of them accidentally ingesting food that could trigger an allergic reaction (Bollinger et al., 2006).

Clinicians can assist patients in learning to be mindful but not afraid when eating outside the home in order to be able to engage in "normal" social activities that revolve around eating. A helpful analogy for teaching the importance of remaining safe but unafraid with a medical condition is asking parents if they always buckle their child in with a seat belt when they get in a vehicle. Then after the parents' (hopefully) affirmative answer to this question, ask whether they also make the patient wear a helmet and then wrap the child in "bubble wrap" prior to entering a vehicle as well. When parents respond in the negative, point out that teaching the child to inquire about ingredients and to make careful food selections is like wearing a seat belt, but that avoiding all social activities due to fear of accidental ingestion is akin to "bubble wrapping" the child.

Similarly, with regard to trying to prevent all injuries despite parents' best efforts at "bubble wrapping," the ability to prevent ingestion of an allergen is often miscarried, as approximately 50% of children with a food allergy will accidentally eat food that then triggers an allergic reaction (Nowak-Wegrzyn et al., 2001). This acceptance of the possibility of an allergic reaction despite preventative efforts is also a source of clinical intervention for both parents and patients alike.

When working with families of patients with a food allergy, it is recommended that interventions include an emphasis on providing parental support, as maternal anxiety is associated with the patient's distress with having a pediatric food allergy (LeBovidge et al., 2009). Despite the small sample size in one study that examined this recommendation, there is some evidence for the effectiveness of cognitive behavioral therapy in helping mothers of children with food allergies in reducing anxiety and depression, as well as improving their overall quality of life (Knibb, 2015).

Clinical Vignette: The Sleepover

Maria is a 13-year-old Latina female whom you have been seeing for several months for social skills training. Today, Maria bounds into your office and says, "I have been invited to my first sleepover!" Ms. L, Maria's mother, winces on hearing her daughter's words and looks down at the ground. Maria continues, "We're going to order pizza and watch a movie!" Ms. L interjects, "Maria, can you wait in the waiting room while we talk in private for a couple of minutes?" Maria frowns but acquiesces to her mother's instruction. Ms. L continues, "I'm not going to let Maria go to the sleepover in several weeks. I know she is excited but I am worried that she will eat something that has peanuts in it and then will die. I am worried that it is not safe for her to go other people's homes and eat without my supervision."

You begin by validating Ms. L's feelings regarding her fear for her daughter given her peanut allergy. Following this, you then discuss the need to help "protect" Maria by teaching her developmentally appropriate ways for her to begin to understand how to prevent accidental peanut ingestion, as well as what to do should accidental ingestion occur. Ms. L agrees to the plan of you providing education about food allergies to Maria, including how to read food labels and how to recognize the signs and symptoms of a severe allergic reaction, as well as asking her medical providers to teach Maria how to correctly administer epinephrine in the event of an emergency. Following this education, sessions will then focus on role-playing how to ask food providers whether peanut products are present in food, how to decline certain foods if it is unclear whether peanuts are present, and how to talk to her peers about the reality of having a food allergy.

Over the next several sessions, you and Maria work closely on the above skills, while Ms. L buys a medical bracelet for Maria to wear which will inform other adults in the case of an emergency that she has a peanut allergy. Maria successfully attends the sought-after sleepover without any concerns, and she reports that she was successful in talking with her friends about her peanut allergy.

6.6 Chronic Pain

Chronic pain is thought to impact approximately one-third of children and adolescents, with a higher proportion of females typically being affected than males (King et al., 2011). Pediatric pain is typically designated as chronic if the duration of pain has exceeded 3 months (Fisher et al., 2014).

Chronic pain appears to negatively impact pediatric patients' overall academic and social functioning. Academic functioning tends to be impacted by the rates of high school absenteeism, as approximately half of adolescents with chronic pain will miss at least 25% of school days in a month (Logan et al., 2008). This impact on functioning tends to extend to social functioning as pediatric chronic pain is associated with a decreased number of friends and decreased participation in activities with peers (Forgeron et al., 2010). This finding of decreased social functioning is logical given that patients' ability to develop social skills will naturally be inhibited by fewer opportunities in which to practice them. As such, clinicians may find it advantageous to include social skills training as part of their treatment plan should their patient exhibit difficulties with social isolation, as well as to help patients begin to increase their daily functioning despite the continued presence of chronic pain.

Pediatric chronic pain appears not only to adversely impact the patient's quality of life and impair multiple areas of functioning but to also potentially impact the psychological health of patients and their parents. For instance, depression and anxiety disorders tend to be more prevalent in mothers of children with chronic pain (Campo et al., 2007). To assist with all of these concerning findings regarding the impact of pediatric chronic pain on patients and their families, research has mostly focused on cognitive behavioral interventions (Fischer et al., 2014).

Furthermore, biofeedback has been found to be effective in assisting with improving physical functioning due to its mechanism of providing the patient with feedback about their physiological status, which in turn leads to increased control over physiological arousal (Achterberg et al., 1981; Coakley & Wihak, 2017). Of interest to most clinicians who work with children, biofeedback also appears to be well accepted by children, which is attributed to the hypothesis that the visual nature of biofeedback is typically appealing to children (Coakley & Wihak, 2017).

Overall, cognitive behavioral interventions for pediatric chronic pain are associated with decreased pain and depressive symptoms (Buenaver et al., 1996). In addition to traditional individual interventions, group interventions have been found to be an important alternative modality as the group format is thought to help with the provision of psychosocial support for children who may feel isolated due to their chronic pain (Forgeron et al., 2010).

In comparison to traditional cognitive behavioral therapy approaches, "third wave" cognitive behavioral therapies tend to emphasize the importance of assisting people in changing the "function" of events experienced rather than trying to unsuccessfully change the actual events (Hayes et al., 2006). This can be a particularly effective approach for pediatric patients with chronic pain in that in many cases, the etiology or antecedents of the chronic pain itself cannot be decreased or relieved, but clinicians can help patients "reframe" how they view the role of chronic pain in their life and overall identity. This framework fits well with the goal of attempting to have patients return to their previous functioning as much as possible, such as returning to school and other activities in spite of chronic pain, and improving their quality of life rather than trying to actively decrease the pain itself.

Acceptance and commitment therapy (ACT) has been established as an effective treatment that differs slightly from other treatments in that the focus is on participating in values-based activities and not on the engagement in seemingly unproductive efforts to avoid or control pain (McCracken et al., 2004). This overall "acceptance of chronic pain is associated with reports of less pain, psychological distress, and physical and psychological disability" (p. 159).

One empirically supported tool that can be utilized to help assess the pediatric patient's acceptance of chronic pain is the Chronic Pain Acceptance Questionnaire (CPAQ) (McCraken et al., 2004). It is important for clinicians to assess the patient's pain acceptance as lower levels of pain acceptance are associated with higher rates of in-patient hospitalizations and prescription medication use (Clementi et al., 2018). For readers, the Chronic Pain Acceptance Questionnaire (McCraken et al., 2004) has been graciously provided by its authors and is listed in the "Reproducible Resources" section.

Clinical Vignette: The Avoidant Academic

Luke is a 10-year-old Caucasian male who was referred by his neurologist for impaired academic functioning related to chronic migraines. During the intake, Luke's father, Mr. G, indicates that Luke is currently failing his classes due to having missed the last month of school. Mr. G. reports feeling confused and concerned about how to proceed given that Luke reports being unable to attend school due to chronic migraines. He is worried that Luke will be in trouble soon for truancy as his neurologist will no longer provide further medical excuses for school absences for migraines in the future.

Luke reports that he has missed the last month of school as his pain is a "10 out of 10!" When queried about whether he has attempted to go to school despite the pain, Mr. G reported, "Luke tried once, but the school nurse called one hour later and I had to go pick him up." When asked about what he does during the day when he has been home from school over the past month, Luke noted that he enjoys playing video games and eating lunch with his father, as his father recently transitioned to working from home approximately 2 months ago. During the intake, a release of information is obtained to speak to Luke's neurologist to assist with collaborative care and to speak with school personnel at his school. Following this initial session, Luke's neurologist reports that the patient's migraines should be well managed on his current treatment regimen, that no changes to his current plan were being considered, and that there were no medical restrictions for the patient to return to school.

During the first psychotherapy session, psychoeducation is provided on the role of avoidance and family accommodation in perpetuating functional disability associated with chronic pain. Mr. G was receptive to the observation that Luke's reported pain level did not appear consistent with his observed behavior (i.e., Luke consistently rates his pain as a level "10" but remains able to play video games when he is home from school). Emphasis is then placed on validating Luke's perception of chronic pain, while also supporting Luke's self-efficacy in attending school consistently. With support from his school, an initial plan is created for Luke to sequentially begin to spend 1 hour per day at school before returning home and to subsequently receive reinforcement via a favorite snack while playing video games with his father for 20 minutes. Each week, Luke is required to spend more and more time at school in order to earn his reward, and he is prevented from playing video games until he has attended school for the required length of time each day.

During subsequent psychotherapy sessions, you assist Luke and his father in modifying the rewards and target behaviors (i.e., length of time at school each day) each week. You also work individually with Luke on utilizing a headache diary to identify triggers for migraine. With this work, impaired sleep and academic stress are identified as common antecedents for migraines, so sessions subsequently focus on relaxation training and the implementation of sleep hygiene principles. Over time, Luke is able to consistently attend school for the entire school day, and both he and his father report increased quality of life following this clinical intervention.

6.7 Epilepsy

In the United States, approximately 1 in 150 children will be diagnosed with epilepsy by age 10, with most diagnoses occurring during infancy (Aaberg et al., 2017). Across most settings, pediatric epilepsy "has usually been defined as ≥ 2 unprovoked seizures separated by at least 24 hours" (Camfield & Camfield, 2015, p. 118). Although the actual causes of childhood epilepsy are unidentified in approximately 50% of patients, some cases have an identified trigger and there is a decreased chance of recurrent seizures once the triggering factor (e.g., fever or closed head injury) has been resolved (Camfield & Camfield, 2015).

For pediatric epilepsy, treatments typically involve aspects of the following: antiepileptic medication, vagus nerve stimulation, surgery, and changes in diet (Wagner et al., 2011). A patient's treatment regimen may have a substantial impact on the patient's overall quality of life as pediatric quality of life is associated with factors such as the number of anti-epileptic medications and side effects associated with these medications (Modi et al., 2011; Ferro et al., 2013).

In comparison to their same-aged peers without epilepsy, pediatric patients with epilepsy tend to exhibit higher rates of anxiety and suicidal ideation, with the most common psychiatric diagnosis being anxiety (Jones et al., 2007). Similarly, cognitive symptoms may be more predominant within this population as patients may exhibit increased problems with attention and memory when seizures are not well controlled, and this risk is increased in temporal lobe epilepsy and when patients experience longer duration of refractory seizures (Nolan et al., 2004).

Children and adolescents diagnosed with epilepsy are not the only members of family that may be impacted by this condition, as parents of children with epilepsy tend to exhibit higher rates of anxiety and depression (Lv et al., 2009). Due to this anxiety, many parents may exhibit overprotectiveness. This can interfere with the developmental task of adolescents to become more autonomous, which in turn can negatively impact the patient's self-efficacy (Spangenberg & Lalkhen, 2006).

Some parents may experience particularly heightened anxiety and possibly fear that their child is dying when they witness their child experiencing a seizure. They may subsequently respond to this fear by taking the child to a hospital, calling for an ambulance, or performing mouth-to-mouth resuscitation (Besag et al., 2005). To help balance this natural fear, it may be helpful to ensure that families and other individuals who may witness a seizure have basic information about how to respond in the event of an emergency. Given that seizures can be a frightening event to witness and leave most people feeling unsure of how best to respond, a reproducible "First Aid for Seizures" handout (Edmonton Epilepsy Association, 2011) is listed in the "Reproducible Resources" section.

In addition to the impact of epilepsy and treatments on pediatric patients and families, patients and families also have to contend with stigma associated with epilepsy, as "research on lay attitudes towards people with epilepsy has revealed that they are perceived as sexually deviant, antisocial, aggressive, potentially violent, mentally ill and unattractive" (Spangenerg & Lalkhen, 2006, p. 60). One study reported that in a survey of adolescents, 40% of participants were not sure if people with epilepsy were dangerous and 31% indicated that they would not personally date someone who had been diagnosed with epilepsy (Austin et al., 2002).

Despite the well-documented impact on patients of additional stressors, medication, and stigma associated with epilepsy, there is a relative lack of randomized clinical trials for psychosocial interventions for this population (Wagner & Smith, 2007). From the research that has been conducted on pediatric epilepsy, cognitive behavioral therapy that primarily emphasizes self-management strategies has shown some efficacy in reducing pediatric depressive symptoms (Martinovic, Simonovic, & Djokic, 2006). One such program that integrates cognitive behavioral therapy and self-management strategies provides separate groups for caregivers and patients (Wagner et al., 2010). This program ("Coping Openly and Personally with Epilepsy") emphasizes the use of primary and secondary coping strategies, with results indicating that participating parents observed an increased utilization of coping skills in patients and that patients reported increased self-efficacy in being able to manage seizures.

6.8 Cancer

Pediatric cancer is the leading cause of death past infancy in children in the United States (National Cancer Institute, 2014). Cancer remains a leading cause of death despite significant medical advances that have led to increased survival rates in children, with more than 80% of children diagnosed with cancer before age 20 surviving past 5 years between 2004 and 2010. This is particularly inspiring since the cancer mortality rate has declined by approximately 50% since 1975 (National Cancer Institute, 2014). Given this increased survivorship, emphasis has shifted from surviving cancer to managing the sequelae of cancer and its treatment, as survivors of pediatric cancer are at greater risk for other significant medical problems such as secondary cancers or neurocognitive damage from the cancer or treatments for it (Butler & Mulhern, 2005; National Cancer Institute, 2014).

Unfortunately, the late effects of cancer survivorship can occur long after remission has been achieved. Most survivors will experience some physical late effects, such as cardiomyopathy and obesity, and are at an 11-fold risk of death 5 years after the end of treatment (Eiser, 2007). These late effects, as well as the need to remain vigilant to detect the recurrence of cancer, are important reasons for continued medical follow-up. In addition to medical problems and neurocognitive concerns, pediatric cancer survivorship is associated with difficulty in certain life domains later in adulthood, particularly social withdrawal, educational and occupational problems, and relationship problems, as well as possible psychiatric concerns, including but not limited to depression, anxiety, posttraumatic stress, and suicidal ideation (Children's Oncology Group, 2018).

While most cancer survivors exhibit good psychological adjustment in both the long-term and the active cancer phase, approximately 10–25% of pediatric patients experience elevated psychological symptoms related to anxiety and depression (Germann et al., 2015). As such, it is good clinical practice for mental health clinicians to screen for these concerns as well as other psychiatric concerns that may arise. One recommended screening tool is the Brief Symptom Inventory-18 (BSI-18), which is a screening tool commonly utilized in pediatric cancer survivorship due to its emphasis on assessing a broad range of symptoms and its normative data from an oncology sample (Derogatis, 2001).

In addition to screening for psychological concerns, mental health clinicians can help patients and their families learn about the late effects of cancer and associated treatments, reduce risk behaviors associated with cancer such as smoking and excess exposure to ultraviolet light, and assist in promoting a greater quality of life (Eiser, 2007). In pediatric cancer, a patient's feelings of hope have been linked with healthier psychological adjustment, as people with higher levels of hopefulness are more likely to use active coping strategies rather than passive, less beneficial strategies. The role of hope has been found to be a mediating factor in improving quality of life and reducing anxiety and depression symptoms (Germann et al., 2015). According to hope theory, it can be helpful to strengthen a person's belief in their ability to achieve their goals. To achieve this end, clinicians can work from a variety of approaches (e.g., acceptance and commitment therapy, motivational interviewing, and problem-solving), with the main premise being for the clinician to help the patient identify their goals, reach their goals, and then reflect on their success in reaching their goals (Germann et al., 2015).

Clinical Vignette: Cara's Crusade

Cara is a 12-year-old African American female who is a survivor of acute lymphoblastic leukemia (ALL). As part of her medical care, Cara was treated with chemotherapy intermittently from ages 5 to 7. Since this time, Cara had been in remission and had been attending school regularly. You first began working with Cara a year ago when she was attending the fifth grade and having difficulty academically and socially. You had been instrumental in working with her school counselor in creating a Section 504 plan to assist with academic accommodations, as neuropsychological testing indicated deficits in processing speed and verbal comprehension, which is thought to be related to the adverse effects of chemotherapy. With appropriate academic accommodations in place, Cara had begun to perform better academically. Unfortunately, 1 month ago, she was found to have a recurrence of the same cancer and her parents pulled her from school due to the intensity of the medical treatments and resultant side effects.

When seeing Cara for the first time since she learned about the recurrence of cancer, you observe that she has a depressed affect and responds to queries with minimal phrases, which is vastly different from her typically bright affect and voluble presentation. Cara endorses feelings of hopelessness and helplessness regarding her medical situation and endorses other symptoms consistent with a major depressive episode. During a recent hospitalization, Cara had been started on an antidepressant and is currently being followed by a pediatric psychiatrist. In session today, you discuss with Cara and her father the efficacy of the combined treatment of evidence-based psychotherapy and psychotropic medication in the treatment of pediatric depression, and you gain permission to collaborate as needed with her psychiatrist.

In reviewing the pediatric oncology literature, you decide to incorporate hope-building exercises as part of your cognitive behavioral treatment plan. You ask Cara to identify past instances in which she has overcome difficult situations and then subsequently identify personal strengths she utilized to help overcome these situations. Cara identifies her sense of humor and religious faith as sources of strength she has utilized previously when dealing with cancer, tough math tests, and difficult peer situations. For between-session homework, she makes a collage of images that fill her with hope and remind of her times when she has demonstrated personal resilience. During following sessions, you incorporate other hope-building exercises into helping her utilize cognitive restructuring to help examine and reframe automatic dysfunctional thoughts and core beliefs.

6.9 Human Immunodeficiency Virus

Human immunodeficiency virus (HIV) is a disease that is unique in its ability to create fear and resultant stigma in a community. In addition to the significant medical, neurological, and functional impact that HIV can have on a patient's life, the resulting social implications can precipitate other significant hurdles for patients. Regarding medical impact, HIV creates "profound immune deficiency, particularly cell-mediated immune dysfunction" (American Psychiatric Association, 2000, p. 12). Despite medical advances that have led to an overall decrease in deaths attributed to acquired immunodeficiency syndrome (AIDS), the rate of HIV infection has remained fairly stable, with African American, Latinx, and gay and bisexual communities being disproportionately affected (Society of Pediatric Psychology, 2016c).

HIV can be transmitted both vertically and horizontally, with vertical transmission being characterized as transmission from mother to child in utero or via breastfeeding, and horizontal transmission occurring from risk behaviors such as sexual contact and needle sharing. It is estimated that approximately 39% of new infections occur each year between people ages 13–29 (Society of Pediatric Psychology, 2016c). The mode of transmission is of clinical significance as the progression from HIV to AIDS is affected by whether HIV was acquired via vertical or horizontal transmission, as vertical transmission is associated with a faster progression to AIDS.

Pediatric HIV is associated with multiple physical problems, including neurological problems, cardiac concerns, and vision and hearing problems (Lindegren et al., 2006). Of note, pediatric patients must constantly be alert to the concern of myriad life-threatening conditions that can result from opportunistic infections. This vigilance and "need to know" about circulating infections and viruses at a school must be weighed against the concerns associated with disclosing a student's HIV status. Clinicians can play an integral role in assisting families in working with schools and in this decisional balance of weighing confidentiality versus increased information about resources that could fundamentally benefit the patient, both medically and academically. Laws and policies regarding confidentiality about HIV status vary among school districts, but for the most part, HIV status is not mandated to be disclosed to the school and families are protected by federal law to prevent discrimination should they decide to disclose a student's HIV status to the school (Pozen, 1995).

A family's disclosure to a child's school about their child's HIV or AIDS status not only can be helpful for needed medical assistance while the child is at school and for ongoing awareness of opportunistic infections occurring within the school, but it can also help with the provision of any indicated accommodations for neurological and/or psychiatric concerns. Neurological impairment associated with HIV/AIDS can lead to regression in developmental milestones or a decline in motor skills, and schools can help assist with accommodations based on the patient's changing needs (Olson et al., 1988). A patient's ability to succeed in the classroom may also be impacted by psychiatric concerns that require accommodations, as 30% of children and adolescents with HIV have a diagnosable mood disorder and 35% meet criteria for attention-deficit/hyperactivity disorder (American Psychiatric Association, 2000).

In working clinically with pediatric patients with HIV or AIDS, a main emphasis of intervention should be on treatment adherence as "95% adherence to treatment was associated with complete viral suppression but … failure rates increased sharply with less than 95% adherence" (American Psychiatric Association, 2000). This can be particularly important when guiding adolescents through the transition of becoming responsible for their own medical care in adulthood. In clinical practice with adolescents diagnosed with HIV, motivational enhancement therapy has been found to be an effective means of intervening to reduce alcohol use and viral load in adolescents with HIV (Naar-King et al., 2008). This intervention employs typical motivational interviewing techniques, such as decisional balance exercises, and emphasizes behavioral change, but is unique in that goal-setting is prioritized based on a patient's identification of which specific problem behaviors they want to work on as part of the intervention (i.e., substance use, sexual risk, or health behaviors). Despite only being a four-session intervention, clinical effects appear to be maintained for approximately 9 months (Naar-King et al., 2008).

As part of a holistic approach to care, it may be advisable to be aware of how parental HIV status can impact the pediatric patient. There is an added complexity of working with pediatric patients when they have other family members diagnosed with HIV or AIDS, as there may be different prevailing values in the family regarding diagnosis disclosure and confidentiality. Depending on the families' dynamics, there may be a culture of silence in which the diagnosis is not discussed among family members. Research suggests that in families where parents have HIV or AIDS, many children may worry about discussing their parent's diagnosis due to concerns about upsetting their parent, while parents, on the other hand, may be concerned about a child's ability to understand the illness (Corona et al., 2009).

When a parent has HIV, they may be reluctant to disclose their diagnosis to their child, but this disclosure may be helpful with anticipatory grieving, particularly if the child is aware of physical symptoms experienced by a parent. Similar to the decision to disclose or discuss other significant family concerns, developmental age plays a factor in how and when a parent discloses a diagnosis. For most families, it appears that the typical age of disclosure is around age 10 (Armistead et al., 2001). The decision to disclose should be weighed individually by each family with a thorough exploration of the possible negative and positive ramifications, including that the child may be expected to preserve family secrecy about the disclosure with people outside the family but that disclosure may help increase communication within the family. Current research does not suggest that child functioning is impacted significantly either positively or negatively by the decision to disclose, although more research on the long-term impact of disclosure is needed (Armistead et al., 2001).

There are several key psychotherapeutic issues to be aware of when conducting psychotherapy with a pediatric patient diagnosed with HIV or AIDS. According to Pollock and Thompson (1995), it is vital for the psychotherapist to help in "1) developing a sense of safety in the therapeutic setting as a component of a working alliance, 2) understanding the child's perception of the illness, 3) sensitive handling of the disclosure of the diagnosis, and 4) understanding of the impact of HIV/AIDS on the psychotherapeutic process" (p. 128).

While all therapy sessions require that a sense of safety has been developed in order for a true working alliance to occur, this recommendation by Pollock and Thompson emphasizes this concept due to the shame and secrecy that children with HIV/AIDS may feel in connection to discussing their illness with someone outside the family. These feelings of shame may be exacerbated by losses experienced by the child in connection with their disease, such as bereavement and foster care placement. Once a sense of safety has been developed in the psychotherapeutic setting, clinicians must ascertain the child's understanding of their illness, including their awareness of how they contracted the disease, why they attend medical appointments, and their reaction to the physical symptoms they may be experiencing in comparison to their non-infected peers (Pollock & Thompson, 1995).

As previously discussed, disclosing a diagnosis of HIV/AIDS is an extremely difficult issue that must be weighed carefully by each family. In disclosing a diagnosis to the child, it is recommended to attempt to begin this discussion during relatively calm periods when there is not an acute medical event occurring and after a positive therapeutic alliance with the psychotherapist has been established (Pollock & Thompson, 1995). Following the initial disclosure, it is important to "keep the conversation going" to help ensure that the patient has accurate understanding and is working through the complex emotions that have been triggered as a result of disclosure. This influences the final recommendation by Pollock and Thompson of understanding the impact of the disease on the therapeutic process.

In their work with children and adolescents with HIV/AIDS, mental health clinicians may face frequent dilemmas about how best to proceed with discussing some of the toughest issues encountered in psychotherapy, such as a discussion of the progressive nature of the disease, concern for the child's death and dying, traumatic loss of loved ones, and difficult emotions regarding how the child was infected. Additionally, psychotherapists are human. Despite their commitment to maintaining an objective and nonjudgmental stance in their work with patients, it can be extremely difficult to maintain objectivity as the "patient, a victim in so many dimensions, can become symbolic of social injustice" (Pollock & Thompson, 1995, p. 139). As such, clinicians must be mindful of their own self-care and need for periodic consultation in light of their own conflicting (and very human) emotions during their work with pediatric patients with HIV/AIDS.

6.10 Congenital Heart Disease

Congenital heart disease is the most common birth defect in the United States, and although the majority of children survive, they may face difficulties related to neurodevelopmental problems, decreased quality of life for parents and patients, and other concerns (Brosig, 2012). Congenital heart disease refers to a group of diverse structural heart defects that are typically diagnosed in infancy and childhood. Most patients diagnosed with congenital heart disease will have an operation or interventional catheterization (Karsdorp et al., 2007). Medical advances have led to increased survival rates; however, patients are still at risk for premature death and comorbid medical conditions (e.g., pulmonary and renal conditions).

With congenital heart disease, there is an increased risk of decreased cognitive functioning in association with some defects, particularly hypoplastic left heart syndrome and transposition of the great arteries. This decrease in cognitive functioning typically affects perceptual organization, but is not associated with all heart defects seen in congenital heart disease, as evidenced by the lack of associated cognitive decreases in atrium septum defects or ventricular septum defects (Karsdorp et al., 2007). In addition to the type of defect influencing cognition, decreased oxygenation associated with surgical procedures and/or chronic heart disease is also associated with higher rates of cognitive concerns. Overall, more complicated medical courses with organ rejection and infections are also more regularly linked with these concerns (Todaro et al., 2000).

Many children with congenital heart disease will require a medical intervention, including cardiac surgeries and other procedures. For these more medically serious cardiac surgeries, families need more than just information and resources to help with coping with a cardiac surgery. Research by Campbell and colleagues found that adding a preoperative emphasis on learning active coping skills in addition to information and resources was helpful (1995). Specifically, this intervention resulted in increased adaptive behavior observed in the child in various settings following cardiac surgery and an increased sense of competency in caregivers. This presurgical intervention consisted of information and resources provided by other multidisciplinary members, while a psychologist worked with families on learning emotion-focused techniques with an emphasis on relaxation techniques. For preschool children, caregivers were first trained and then they were taught to "coach" their child. The psychologist taught both the caregiver and child simultaneously if the child was of school age (Campbell et al., 1995).

This intervention demonstrates the importance of clinicians involving primary caregivers as part of treatment to help provide the most effective care. With many congenital heart disease patients being diagnosed prenatally or in early childhood, the mental health of parents in managing this stress should not be neglected, as research shows that maternal mental health is particularly affected by severe congenital heart disease (Solberg et al., 2012). The stress from surgical interventions and postoperative problems appears to exacerbate anxiety and depressive symptoms in mothers of patients with congenital heart disease. Given that research has shown that maternal mental psychiatric symptoms play a large factor in bonding, it can be hypothesized that the anxiety and depressive symptoms associated with stress from surgical operations may have an adverse impact on mother–infant bonding and attachment.

The stress of a cardiac surgery on parents cannot be underappreciated as approximately one-third of parents will experience trauma symptoms associated with acute stress disorder following their infant's cardiac surgery (Franich-Ray et al., 2013). Given the acuity of these symptoms during an already stressful time in a parent's life, it is important for clinicians to help normalize this trauma-related reaction and to help monitor parental coping following surgery. This not only helps the parent but also can greatly impact a child's adjustment following cardiac surgery.

Most pediatric patients will adjust well psychologically within 1 year posttransplant, but approximately 20–24% of patients will experience elevated difficulties in areas such as anxiety, depression, and self-concept (Todaro et al., 2000). It may be intuitive to think that the risk of a child experiencing greater difficulty adjusting after cardiac surgery is influenced by the severity of their congenital heart disease; however, this premise is not accurate. What is accurate is that a child's adjustment is strongly associated with the mother's perceptions of parenting competence and internal locus of control (DeMaso et al., 1991). Research has shown that approximately 33% of variability in adjustment in one study was accounted for by maternal perceptions in comparison to 3% in variability that was accounted for by the actual medical severity (DeMaso et al., 1991).

Clinical Vignette: Henry's Heart

Ms. Johnson presents with her 5-year-old son, Henry, for their first psychotherapy appointment. In the previous intake session, you learned that Henry has congenital heart disease that will require a major cardiac surgery in 5 weeks. In session today, you spend half of the time with Ms. Johnson providing psychoeducation from the research literature about the importance of parental perceptions of recovery on Henry's overall adjustment following surgery. Ms. Johnson is surprised but gratified to find that some research indicates that she does have a greater impact on his psychological adjustment than the actual severity of his medical conditions. With this in mind, you teach Ms. Johnson basic relaxation techniques not only for her own anxiety management, but also to help her in modeling and teaching these techniques to Henry. In the second half of the session, you coach Ms. Johnson on teaching Henry how to perform deep breathing, as you know that very young children learn best when their caregiver acts as the teacher. This also helps confirm your perception that Ms. Johnson has adequately understood herself how to perform the relaxation exercises.

Over the next several sessions, you assist Ms. Johnson and Henry in learning more adaptive coping skills in preparation for the surgery, which they practice daily in between psychotherapy sessions. Sessions also focus on normalizing for Ms. Johnson the potential occurrence of trauma-related symptoms for herself following the surgery and providing family support resources for both Ms. Johnson and Henry's father.

Following Henry's successful cardiac surgery, he remains in the hospital for several days during his recovery. One week later, he and Ms. Johnson present for their psychotherapy appointment. Henry was proud to show off his new scar and appeared minimally troubled by the surgery. However, Ms. Johnson confided that she was having frequent nightmares, insomnia, and an overall depressed mood. With her consent, you refer Ms. Johnson to her own adult psychotherapist while you continue working with Henry on processing his hospital experience through stories and drawing.

Summary

Working with pediatric patients who are experiencing complications from complex and life-changing medical conditions requires perseverance and a dedication to remaining abreast of the current research literature in order to provide evidence-based care. With constantly updating guidelines and recommendations from different medical societies and groups, it can be challenging (and intimidating) for mental health clinicians to be knowledgeable about specific medical diagnoses faced by their patients. This chapter is meant to be used as a means of pointing clinicians toward the most relevant issues and challenges they will likely face regarding differing diagnoses. Resources have been provided in the "Recommended Websites, Books, and Other Resources" section should readers desire to expand their knowledge base about a specific condition.

Each diagnosis comes with its own unique challenges, as well as sharing similar challenges with other illnesses. Below are five main "takeaways" for each medical diagnosis to help guide clinicians:

Cystic Fibrosis

- Cystic fibrosis is a progressive lung disease typically diagnosed at birth/infancy, with the average life expectancy having increased recently to 47 years old.
- Cystic fibrosis may be complicated by comorbid medical conditions (i.e., CF-related diabetes, pancreatic insufficiency, constipation).
- Patients and parents are at elevated risk for anxiety and depression.
- Strict infection protocols prevent patients with cystic fibrosis from being within 6 feet of each other due to the concern of passing pathogens to each other.
- Clinicians should encourage physical activity to assist with both mental and physical health, while being mindful of safety guidelines for physical activity with cystic fibrosis.

Diabetes Mellitus, Type 1

- Time-intensive daily regimens make adherence a challenge for many patients.
- Significant short-term consequences (e.g., dizziness) and long-term consequences (e.g., vision loss, limb amputation) can be experienced without consistent glycemic control.
- Daily fluctuations based on diet, illness, and other factors require frequent modifications and calculations of dosage adjustments (insulin).
- Patients are at increased risk for depression, cognitive processing concerns, and disordered eating.
- Research typically recommends a family-systems approach as part of clinical treatment.

Obesity

- Prevalence rates of obesity continue to rapidly increase within the United States.
- Obesity may be related to a variety of different factors that should be considered during treatment planning, including environmental/lifestyle causes, medical conditions, and medication side effects.
- When attempting to help patients make behavioral changes, it is important to include the family as part of the treatment process as parents' lifestyle and weight status influence the patient's weight.
- Setting family goals (e.g., walking together several times per week) and the use of stimulus control strategies (e.g., limiting electronics time and removing high-calorie foods from the home) can be tools to help families make lifestyle changes.
- Mental health clinicians should work collaboratively with other medical providers (e.g., pediatricians, bariatric specialists) in order to help with providing consistent treatment recommendations for physical activity and dietary consumption, as well as to ensure the patient's physical health and safety.

Asthma

- Although treatment regimens will vary from patient to patient, most regimens include allergen avoidance and medications.
- The prevalence of asthma is higher in lower-income and in ethnic minority communities, and this discrepancy has been attributed to health care disparities and genetic factors.
- Clinicians can assist in preventing school absences by ensuring that patients have an asthma action plan in place at their school.

- Stress can exacerbate asthma symptoms for some patients; thus, relaxation and stress management techniques may be beneficial.
- Many interventions identified in the research literature with this patient population tend to emphasize problem-solving and family-based interventions.

Food Allergies

- Food allergies are most prevalent in very young children, and some allergies will dissipate once the patient is between ages 4 and 6.
- Food allergies are the most frequent cause of anaphylaxis, which requires immediate medical attention.
- Clinicians should collaborate with medical providers in helping families to learn about allergen avoidance, early warnings signs of an allergic reaction, and how to respond in the event of an emergency.
- Many parents may be unaware of how to administer epinephrine correctly or may not be carrying (unexpired) epinephrine at all times.
- Many patients and parents may become fearful of eating away from home due to fears of having an allergic reaction. Clinicians can assist families in ensuring that vigilance does not extend to hypervigilance and subsequent avoidant behavior by the patient and/or family.

Chronic Pain

- Pain is identified as chronic after a pediatric patient has been experiencing pain for at least 3 months.
- Chronic pain is associated with impairments in social and academic functioning, which may in part be attributed to high rates of school absenteeism.
- An important therapeutic goal when working with pediatric patients with chronic pain is to help restore functioning and quality of life, rather than focusing on decreasing the actual pain itself.
- Cognitive behavioral techniques, including biofeedback, have been found to help decrease pain and depressive symptoms.
- "Third wave" therapies such as acceptance and commitment therapy have strong empirical support with pediatric chronic pain.

Epilepsy

- The cause of approximately 50% of pediatric epilepsy cases is unknown, while for others, seizures may decrease or cease once the identifying factor has been treated, such as a fever or closed head injury.
- Treatment interventions can include intervention such as antiepileptic medications, vagus nerve stimulation, dietary changes, and surgery.
- Pediatric epilepsy is associated with elevated rates of anxiety, suicidal ideation, and cognitive concerns.
- Parents of patients with pediatric epilepsy are also at increased risk for anxiety and depression.
- Cognitive behavioral techniques that emphasize self-management are recommended within the research literature for patients with this condition.

Cancer

- Cancer is the leading cause of death past infancy in the United States; however, medical advances have led to significantly improved survival rates.
- Cancer survivorship is associated with increased risk for late physical effects and neurocognitive impairments associated with the cancer itself and/or treatment side effects.
- Most pediatric patients exhibit positive psychological adjustment after cancer, but approximately 10–25% of patients will exhibit elevated anxiety and depressive symptoms.
- Given the risk of cancer recurrence, it is important for clinicians to help patients reduce risky behaviors such as cigarette smoking and excess exposure to ultraviolet light.
- Active coping strategies that emphasize hopefulness are effective in improving quality of life and decreasing symptoms associated with anxiety and depression.

Human Immunodeficiency Virus (HIV)

- HIV is an incurable disease that has been linked with immune deficiency and myriad other physical concerns, and the prevalence rate of this disease is higher in African American, Latinx, gay, and bisexual communities.
- HIV can be acquired both vertically (i.e., in utero and/or breastfeeding) or from horizontal transmission from risk behaviors (e.g., needle sharing, sexual relations).
- When or if families should disclose the patient's diagnosis to their school should be weighed carefully due to the inherent risks in confidentiality as well as the potential gain from school resources, including increased awareness of opportunistic infections occurring at the school and academic accommodations if needed for the student.
- The promotion of treatment adherence is a critical therapeutic goal, as 95% adherence to treatment is linked with complete viral suppression.
- When helping families disclose a diagnosis of HIV to the patient, it is important for clinicians to help families to view disclosure as a process rather than as a singular event, which should begin during a relative period of calm for the family and after therapeutic rapport has been established.

Congenital Heart Disease

- Congenital heart disease is the most common birth defect in the United States and is typically diagnosed during infancy or childhood.
- Patients with congenital heart disease are at increased risk for comorbid medical conditions, premature death, and decreased cognitive functioning.
- Most patients with congenital heart disease will have a medical intervention, such as cardiac surgery, which is associated with increased risk for trauma-related symptoms in parents.
- Prior to surgery, it may be helpful for clinicians to focus on teaching patients active coping skills, with an emphasis on relaxation strategies.
- Parental coping after cardiac surgery should be assessed and monitored given that parental coping appears to significantly influence the patient's psychological adjustment following cardiac surgery.

References

Aaberg, K., Gunnes, N., Bakken, I., Søraas, C., Berntsen, A., Magnus, P., Lossius, M., Stoltenberg, C., Chin, R., & Surén, P. (2017). Incidence and prevalence of childhood epilepsy: a nationwide cohort study. *Pediatrics, 139*(5). doi: 10.1542/peds.2016-3908.

Achterberg, J., McGraw, P., & Lawlis, G. (1981). Rheumatoid arthritis: a study of relaxation and temperature biofeedback training as an adjunctive therapy. *Applied Psychophysiology and Biofeedback, 6,* 207–223.

AllerMates. (n.d.). Asthma Action Plan. Retrieved April 2, 2018, from https://cdn.shopify.com/s/files/1/0773/2859/files/MedimatesActionPlan.pdf.

American Academy of Pediatrics. (2017). Allergy and Anaphylaxis Emergency Plan. Retrieved May 4, 2018, from www.aap.org/en- us/Documents/AAP_Allergy_and_Anaphylaxis_Emergency_Plan.pdf.

American Academy of Pediatrics. (2018). Seizures and Epilepsy in Children. Retrieved April 26, 2018, from www.healthychildren.org/English/health-issues/conditions/head-neck-nervous- system/Pages/Seizures-Convulsions-and-Epilepsy.aspx.

American Diabetes Association. (2011). Standards of medical care in diabetes – 2011. *Diabetes Care,* 34, S11–S61.

American Diabetes Association. (n.d.). New to Type 1 Diabetes? Retrieved February 3, 2018, from www.diabetes.org/living-with-diabetes/recently-diagnosed/type-1-kit.html.

American Psychiatric Association. (2000). Practice Guideline for the Treatment of Patients with HIV/AIDS. Retrieved February 12, 2019, from https://psychiatryonline.org/pb/assets/raw/sitewide/practice_guidelines/guidelines/hivaids.pdf.

Anddit. (2018). Hope Portal. Retrieved February 14, 2019, from www.anddit.com/hope-portal.

Association of Clinicians for the Underserved. (2018). Comprehensive Asthma Resource List. Retrieved April 2, 2018, from http://clinicians.org/comprehensive-asthma-resource-list/.

Armistead, L., Tannenbaum, L., Forehand, R., Morse, E., & Morse, P. (2001). Disclosing HIV status: are mothers telling their children? *Journal of Pediatric Psychology, 26* (1), 11–20.

Austin, J., Shafer, P., & Deering, J. (2002). Epilepsy familiarity, knowledge, and perceptions of stigma: report from a survey of adolescents in the general population. *Epilepsy and Behavior, 3,* 368–375.

Barlow, S. (2007). Expert committee recommendations regarding the prevention, assessment, and treatment of child and adolescent overweight and obesity: summary report. *Pediatrics, 120,* S164–S192.

Bernard, R. & Cohen, L. (2004). Increasing adherence to cystic fibrosis treatment: a systematic review of behavioral techniques. *Pediatric Pulmonology, 37*(1), 8–16.

Besag, F., Nomayo, A., & Pool, F. (2005). The reactions of parents who think that their child is dying in a seizure – in their own words. *Epilepsy and Behavior, 7*(3), 517–523.

Bhogal, S., Zemek, R., & Ducharme, F. (2009). Written action plans for asthma in children. *Cochrane Database of Systematic Reviews, 3.* doi: 10.1002/14651858.CD005306.pub2.

Bollinger, M., Dahlquist, L., Mudd, K., Sonntag, C., Dillinger, L., & McKenna, K. (2006). The impact of food allergy on the daily activities of children and their families. *Allergy, Asthma and Immunology, 96,* 415–421.

Bostic, E. (n.d.). Food Allergy Aware Letter to Parents. Retrieved May 9, 2018, from http://thrivingwithallergies.blogspot.com/2016/08/food-allergy-aware-letter-to- parents.html.

Boyce, J., Assa'ad, A., Burks, A., Jones, S., Sampson, H., Wood, R, Plaut, M., Cooper, S., Fenton, M., Arshad, S., Bahna, S., Beck, L., Byrd-Bredbenner, C., Camargo, C., Eichenfield, L., Furuta, G., Hanifin, J., Jones, C., Kraft, M., Levy, B., Lieberman, P., Luccioloi, S., McCall, K., Schneider, L., Simon, R., Simons, F., Teach, S., & Yawn, B. (2011). Guidelines for the diagnosis and management of food allergy in the United States: summary of the NIAID-sponsored expert panel report. *Nutrition Research (New York, N.Y.), 31*(1), 61–75.

Branum, A. & Lukacs, S. (2008). Food Allergy among U.S. children: Trends in Prevalence and Hospitalizations. NCHS data brief, no. 10. Hyattsville, MD: National Center for Health Statistics.

Brosig, C. (2012). Commentary: the use of health and behavior codes in a pediatric cardiology setting. *Journal of Pediatric Psychology, 37*(5), 514–518.

Buenaver, L., McGuire, L., & Haythornthwaite, J. (1996). Cognitive-behavioral self-help for chronic pain. *Journal of Clinical Psychology, 62*, 1389–1396.

Butler, R. & Mulhern, R. K. (2005). Neurocognitive interventions for children and adolescents surviving cancer. *Journal of Pediatric Psychology, 30*(1), 65–78.

Camfield, P. & Camfield, C. (2015). Incidence, prevalence, and aetiology of seizures and epilepsy in children. *Epileptic Disorders, 17*(2), 117–123.

Campbell, L., Kirkpatrick, S., Berry, C., & Lamberti, J. (1995). Preparing children with congenital heart disease for cardiac surgery. *Journal of Pediatric Psychology, 20*(3), 313–328.

Campo, J., Bridge, J., Lucas, A., Savorelli, S., Walker, L., Di Lorenzo, C., & Brent, D. (2007). Physical and emotional health of mothers of youth with functional abdominal pain. *Archives of Pediatrics and Adolescent Medicine, 161*(2), 131–137.

Center for Pediatric Pain Research. (n.d.). For Health Professionals. Retrieved May 4, 2018, from http://pediatric-pain.ca/for-health-professionals/.

Centers for Disease Control and Prevention. (2013). Asthma Prevalence Percents, by Age, United States. National Health Interview Survey (NHIS) Data. Retrieved from www.cdc.gov/asthma/nhis/2013/data/htm.

Centers for Disease Control and Prevention. (2017a). Childhood Overweight and Obesity. Retrieved February 2, 2018, from www.cdc.gov/obesity/childhood/.

Centers for Disease Control and Prevention. (2017b). Childhood Obesity Facts. Retrieved February 20, 2018, from www.cdc.gov/obesity/data/childhood.html.

Centers for Disease Control and Prevention. (2017c). Most Recent National Asthma Data. Retrieved on July 25, 2019, from www.cdc.gov/asthma/most_recent_national_asthma_data.htm.

Childhood Cancer Guides. (2019). Our Books. Retrieved February 14, 2019, from www.childhoodcancerguides.org/our-books/.

Children's Diabetes Foundation. (2017). Pink Panther Books. Retrieved February 17, 2018, from www.childrensdiabetesfoundation.org/books/.

Children's Hospital Association. (2012). Expert Guidelines: Role of Psychologist in Assessment and Treatment of Obese Youth. Retrieved February 20, 2018, from www.childrenshospitals.org/ /media/Files/CHA/Main/Issues_and_Advocacy/Key_Issues/Child_Health/Obesity/FFF/fff_psychology_guidelines010112.pdf.

Children's Oncology Group. (2018). Long-Term Follow-up Guidelines for Survivors of Childhood, Adolescent, and Young Adult Cancers, Version 5.0. Monrovia, CA: Children's Oncology Group. Retrieved February 14, 2019, from http://survivorshipguidelines.org/pdf/2018/COG_LTFU_Guidelines_v5.pdf.

Clementi, M., Kao, G., & Monico, E. (2018). Pain acceptance as a predictor of medical utilization and school absenteeism in adolescents with chronic pain. *Journal of Pediatric Psychology, 43*(3), 294–302.

Coakley, R. & Wihak, T. (2017). Evidence-based psychological interventions for the management of pediatric chronic pain: new directions in research and clinical practice. *Children (Basel), 4*(2). doi:10.3390/children4020009.

Cooperman, N. (2003). Nutrition management of overweight and obesity. In N. Nevin-Folino (ed.), *Pediatric Manual of Clinical Dietetics*, 2nd ed. Chicago: American Dietetic Association.

Corona, R., Cowgill, B., Bogart, L., Parra, M., Ryan, G., Elliot, M., Park, S., Patch, J., &

Schuster, M. (2009). Brief report: a qualitative analysis of discussions about HIV in families of parents with HIV. *Journal of Pediatric Psychology, 34*(6), 677–680.

Crocker, M. & Yanovski, J. (2009). Pediatric obesity: etiology and treatment. *Endocrinology Metabolism Clinics of North America, 38*(3), 525–548.

Cystic Fibrosis Foundation. (2018). Individualized Education Programs (IEPs) and 504 Plans. Retrieved November 15, 2018, from www.cff.org/Life-With-CF/Caring-for-a- Child-With-CF/Working-With-Your-Childs-School/Individualized-Education-504-Plans/.

Davidson, J. (2014). Diabulimia: how eating disorders can affect adolescents with diabetes. *Nursing Standard, 29*(2), 44–49.

Davis, C., Delamater, A, Shaw, K., La Greca, A., Eidson, M., Perez-Rodriguez, J., & Nemery, R. (2001). Parenting styles, regimen adherence, and glycemic control in 4- to 10-year-old children with diabetes. *Journal of Pediatric Psychology, 26*(2), 123–129.

DeMaso, D., Campis, L., Wypij, D., Bertram, S., Lipshitz, M., & Freed, M. (1991). The impact of maternal perceptions and medical severity on the adjustment of children with congenital heart disease. *Journal of Pediatric Psychology, 16*(2), 137–149.

Derogatis, L. (2001). Brief Symptom Inventory (BSI)-18. Administration, Scoring, and Procedures Manual. Minneapolis: NCS Pearson, Inc.

Dinakar, C. (2012). Anaphylaxis in children: current understanding and key issues in diagnosis and treatment. *Currenty Allergy and Asthma Reports, 12.*

Duff, A. & Latchford, G. (2010). Motivational interviewing for adherence problems in cystic fibrosis. *Pediatric Pulomonology, 45,* 211–220.

Edmonton Epilepsy Association. (2011). Epilepsy: A Guide for Parents. Retrieved May 2, 2018, from www.edmontonepilepsy.org/documents/Epilepsy%20- %20A%20Guide%20For%20Parents.pdf.

Eiser, C. (2007). Beyond survival: quality of life and follow-up after childhood cancer.

Journal of Pediatric Psychology, 32(9), 1140–1150.

Epilepsy Foundation. (n.d.a). First Aid Resources. Retrieved April 27, 2018, from www.epilepsy.com/learn/seizure-first-aid-and-safety/adapting-first-aid-plans/first- aid/first-aid-resources.

Epilepsy Foundation. (n.d.b). Model Section 504 Plan for a Student with Epilepsy. Retrieved April 26, 2018, from www.epilepsynorcal.org/wp- content/uploads/2015/07/Sample_504.pdf.

Ferro, M., Camfield, C., Levin, S., Smith, M., Wiebe, S., Zou, G., & Speechley, K. (2013). Trajectories of health-related quality of life in chidren with epilepsy: a cohort study. *Epilepsia, 54*(11), 1889–1897.

Fischer, E., Heathcote, L., Palermo, T., Williams, A., Lau, J., & Eccleston, C. (2014). Systematic review and meta-analysis of psychological therapies for children with chronic pain. *Journal of Pediatric Psychology, 39*(8), 763–782.

Food Allergy Research and Education. (n.d.). Retrieved May 4, 2018, from www.foodallergy.org/.

Forgeron, P., King, S., Stinson, J., Mcgrath, P., Macdonald, A., & Chambers, C. (2010). Social functioning and peer relationships in children and adolescents with chronic pain: a systematic review. *Pain Research and Management, 15,* 27–41.

Franich-Ray, C., Bright, M., Anderson, V., Northam, E., Cochrane, A., Menahem, S., & Jordan, B. (2013). Trauma reactions in mothers and fathers after their infant's cardiac surgery. *Journal of Pediatric Psychology, 38*(5), 494–505.

Germann, J., Leonard, D., Stuenzi, T., Pop, R., Stewart, S., & Leavey, P. (2015). Hoping is coping: a guiding theoretical framework for promoting coping and adjustment following pediatric cancer diagnosis. *Journal of Pediatric Psychology, 40*(9), 846–855.

Gupta, N., Mueller, W., Chan, W., & Meininger, J. (2002). Is obesity associated with poor sleep quality in adolescents? *American Journal of Human Biology, 14,* 762–768.

Hayes, S., Luoma, J., Bond, F., Masuda, A., & Lillis, J. (2006). Acceptance and commitment therapy: model, processes, and outcomes. *Behavior Research and Therapy, 44,* 1–26.

Holmes, C. & Richman, L. (1985). Cognitive profiles of children with insulin-dependent diabetes. *Developmental and Behavioral Pediatrics, 6,* 323–326.

Huizinga, M., Elasy, T., Wallston, K., Cavanaugh, K., Davis, D., Gregory, R., Fuchs, L., Malone, R., Cherrington, A., DeWalt, D., Buse, J., Pignone, M., & Rothman, R. (2008). Development and validation of the Diabetes Numeracy Test (DNT). *BMC Health Services Research, 8*(1–8), 96.

Hunninghake, G., Weiss, S., & Celedon, J. (2006). Asthma in Hispanics. *American Journal of Respiratory and Critical Care Medicine, 173,* 143–163.

Instruction Manual: Instructions for Patient Health Questionnaire (PHQ-9) and GAD-7 Measures. (n.d.). Retrieved March 18, 2018, from https://phqscreeners.pfizer .edrupalgardens.com/sites/g/files/g10016261/ f/201412/instructions.pdf.

Jacobs, A., Vermeulen, F., Boeck, K., Casteels, K., & Proesmans, M. (2016). Clinical outcomes of CF patients with CF related diabetes: do we need to change our policy? *Open Journal of Pathology, 6,* 32–40.

Jandasek, B. & Fedele, D. (2014). Pediatric asthma. In M. Roberts, B. Aylward, & Y. Wu (eds.), *Clinical Practice of Pediatric Psychology.* New York: Guilford Press.

Jelalian, E., Stark, L., Reynolds, L., & Seifer, R. (1998). Nutrition intervention for weight gain in cystic fibrosis: a meta-analysis. *Journal of Pediatrics, 132,* 486–492.

Joke, A., Hunfeld, C., Perquin, H., Duivenvoorden, A., Hazebroek-Kampschreur, J., Passchier, J., van Suijlekom-Smit, L., & van der Wouden, J. Chronic pain and its impact on quality of life in adolescents and their families. *Journal of Pediatric Psychology, 26*(3), 145–153.

Jones, J., Watson, R., Sheth, R., Caplan, R., Koehn, M., Seidenberg, M., & Hermann, B. (2007). Psychiatric comorbidity in children with new onset epilepsy. *Developmental Medicine and Child Neurology, 49,* 493–497.

Karsdorp, P., Everaerd, W., Kindt, M., & Mulder, B. (2007). Psychological and cognitive functioning in children and adolescents with congenital heart disease: a meta-analysis. *Journal of Pediatric Psychology, 32*(5), 527–541.

King, S., Chambers, C., Huguet, A., MacNevin, R., McGrath, P., Parker, L., & MacDonald, A. (2011). The epidemiology of chronic pain in children and adolescents revisited: a systematic review. *Pain, 152,* 2729–2738.

Knibb, R. (2015). Effectiveness of cognitive behaviour therapy for mothers of children with food allergy: a case series. *Healthcare, 3,* 1194–1211.

Kroenke, K. & Spitzer, R. (2002). The PHQ-9: a new depression diagnostic and severity measure. *Psychiatric Annals, 32,* 509–521.

LeBovidge, J., Strauch, H., Kalish, L., & Schneider, L. (2009). Assessment of psychological distress among children and adolescents with food allergy. *Journal of Allergy and Clinical Immunology, 124*(6), 1282–1288.

Lindegren, M., Hammett, T., & Bulterys, M. (2006). The epidemiology of pediatric HIV disease. In S. Zeichner & J. Read (eds.), *Handbook of Pediatric HIV Care.* Cambridge: Cambridge University Press.

Little Hearts, Inc. (n.d.). Welcome to Little Hearts, Inc. Retrieved February 20, 2019, from www.littlehearts.org/Default.asp.

Logan, D., Simons, L., Stein, M., & Chastain, L. (2008). School impairment in adolescents with chronic pain. *The Journal of Pain, 9,* 407–416.

Loghmani, E. (2005). Diabetes mellitus: type 1 and type 2. In J. Stang & M. Story (eds.), *Guidelines for Adolescent Nutrition Services.* Minneapolis, MN: Center for Leadership, Education, and Training in Maternal and Child Nutrition.

Lv, R., Wu, L., Jin, L., Lu, Q., Wang, M., Qu, Y., & Liu, H. (2009). Depression, anxiety, and quality of life in parents of children with epilepsy. *Acta Neurologica Scandinavica, 120*(5), 335–341.

Marshall, B. (2017). Surviving Trending Upward but What Does This Really Mean? Retrieved February 27, 2018, from www.cff.org/

CF-Community-Blog/Posts/2017/Survival-Trending-Upward-but-What-Does-This-Really-Mean/.

Martinovic, Z., Simonovic, P., & Djokic, R. (2006). Preventing depression in adolescents with epilepsy. *Epilepsy and Behavior, 9,* 619–624.

McCracken, L., Vowles, K., & Eccleston, C. (2004). Acceptance of chronic pain: component analysis and a revised assessment method. *Pain, 107,* 159–166.

McQuaid, E. & Abramson, N. (2009). Pediatric asthma. In M. Roberts & R. Steele (eds.), *Handbook of Pediatric Psychology*, 4th ed. (pp. 254–270). New York: Guilford Press.

McQuaid, E., Walders, N., Kopel, S., Fritz, G., & Klinnert, M. (2005). Pediatric asthma management in the family context: the Family Asthma Management System Scale. *Journal of Pediatric Psychology, 30*(6), 492–502.

Modi, A., Ingerski, L., Rausch, J., & Glauser, T. (2011). Treatment factors affecting longitudinal quality of life in new onset pediatric epilepsy. *Journal of Pediatric Psychology, 36,* 466–475.

Mullen, M. & Shield, J. (2003). *Childhood and Adolescent Overweight: The Health Professional's Guide to Identification, Treatment, and Prevention.* Chicago: American Dietetic Association.

Mulvaney, S., Lilley, J., Cavanaugh, K., Pittel, E., & Rothman, R. (2013). Validation of the Diabetes Numeracy Test with adolescents. *Journal of Health Communication, 18*(7). doi:10.1080/10810730.2012.757394.

Muraro, A., Werfel, T., Hoffmann-Sommergruber, K., Roberts, G., Beyer, K., Bindslev-Jensen, C., Cardona, V., Dubois, A., duToit, G., Eigenmann, P., Fernandez Rivas, M., Halken, S., Hickstein, L., Høst, A., Knol, E., Lack, G., Marchisotto, M., Niggemann, B., Nwaru, B., Papadopoulos, N., Poulsen, L., Santos, A., Skypala, I., Schoepfer, A., Van Ree, R., Venter, C., Worm, M., Vlieg-Boerstra, B., Panesar, S., de Silva, D., Soares-Weiser, K., Sheikh, A., Ballmer-Weber, B., Nilsson, C., de Jong, N., & Akdis, C. (2014b). EAACI food allergy and anaphylaxis guidelines: diagnosis and management of food allergy. *Allergy, 69,* 1008–1025.

Naar-King, S., Lam, P., Wright, K., Parsons, J., & Frey, M. (2008). Brief report: maintenance of effects of motivational enhancement therapy to improve risk behaviors and HIV-related health in a randomized controlled trial of youth living with HIV. *Journal of Pediatric Psychology, 33*(4), 441–445.

National Cancer Institute. (2014). Cancer in Children and Adolescents. Retrieved February 14, 2019, from www.cancer.gov/types/childhood-cancers/child-adolescent-cancers-fact-sheet#q1.

National Diabetes Education Program. (n.d.). Diabetes Medical Management Plan. Retrieved February 3, 2018, from http://main.diabetes.org/dorg/PDFs/living-with-diabetes/diabetes-medical- management.pdf.

National Sleep Foundation. (2018). Sleep Hygiene. Retrieved February 27, 2018, from https://sleepfoundation.org/sleep-topics/sleep-hygiene.

Nichols, L., Barton, P., Glazner, J., & McCollum, M. (2007). Diabetes, minor depression, and health care utilization and expenditures: a retrospective database study. *Cost Effectiveness and Resource Allocation, 5*(4). doi:10.1186/1478-7547-5-4.

Nolan, M., Redoblado, M., Lah, S., Sabaz, M., Lawson, J., Cunningham, A., Bleasel, A., & Bye, A. (2004). Memory function in childhood epilepsy syndromes. *Journal of Paediatrics and Child Health, 40,* 20–27.

Nowak-Wegrzyn, A., Conover-Walker, M., & Wood, R. (2001). Food-allergic reactions in schools and preschools. *Archives of Pediatrics and Adolescent Medicine, 155,* 790–795.

Ogden, C., Carroll, M., Curtin, L., Lamb, M., & Flegal, K. (2010). Prevalence of high body mass index in US children and adolescents. *JAMA, 303,* 242–249.

Olson, R., Huszti, H., Mason, P., & Seibert, J. (1988). Pediatric AIDS/HIV infection: an emerging challenge to pediatric psychology. *JPP, 14*(1), 1–21.

Pain Associates in Nursing. (n.d.) Oucher!™. Retrieved May 4, 2018, from www.oucher.org/index.html.

Philpott, J., Houghton, K., & Luke, A. (2010). Physical activity recommendations for children with specific health conditions: juvenile idiopathic arthritis, hemophilia, asthma, and cystic fibrosis. *Paediatrics and Child Health, 15*(4), 213–218.

Platts-Mills, T., Blumenthal, K., Perzanowski, M., & Woodfolk, T. (2000). Determinants of clinical allergic disease: the relevance of indoor allergens to the increase in asthma. *American Journal of Respiratory and Critical Care Medicine, 162*, S128–S133.

Pollock, S. & Thompson, C. (1995). The HIV-infected child in therapy. In N. Boyd-Franklin, G. Steiner, & M. Boland (eds.), *Children, Families, and HIV/AIDS* (pp. 127–141). New York: Guilford Press.

Polonsky, W., Fisher, L., Esarles, J., Dudl, R., Lees, J., Mullan, J., & Jackson, R. (2005). Assessing psychosocial distress in diabetes: development of the Diabetes Distress Scale. *Diabetes Care, 28*, 626–631.

Pozner, A. (1995). HIV/AIDS in schools. In N. Boyd-Franklin, G. Steiner, & M. Boland (eds.), *Children, Families, and HIV/AIDS* (pp. 233–255). New York: Guilford Press.

Quittner, A., Abbott, J., Georgiopoulos, A., Goldbeck, L., Smith, B., Hempstead, S., Marshall, B., Sabadosa, K., & Elborn, S. (2016). International Committee on Mental Health in Cystic Fibrosis: Cystic Fibrosis Foundation and European Cystic Fibrosis Society consensus statements for screening and treating depression and anxiety. *Thorax, 71*, 26–34.

Quittner, A., Barker, D., Marciel, K., & Grimley, M. (2009). Cystic fibrosis. In M. Roberts and R. Steele (eds.), *Handbook of Pediatric Psychology*, 4th ed. (pp. 130–152). New York: Guilford Press.

Rothman, R., Huizinga, M., Elasy, T., Wallston, K., Cavanaugh, K., Davis, D., Gregory, R., Wolff, K., Fuchs, L., Malone, R., Cherrington, A., DeWalt, D., Buse, J., & Pignone, M. (2009). Literacy and Numeracy Toolkit for Diabetes Provider's Manual. Retrieved March 31, 2018, from www.mc.vanderbilt.edu/documents/CDTR/files/dlnet- instructions%5B1%5D.pdf.

Ryan, C., Vega, A., Longstreet, C., & Drash, A. (1984). Cognitive deficits in adolescents who developed diabetes early in life. *Pediatrics, 75*, 921–927.

Saiman, L., Siegel, J., LiPuma, J., Brown, R., Bryson, E., Chambers, M., Downer, V., Filege, J., Hazle, L., Jain, M., Marshall, B., O'Malley, C., Pattee, S., Bynoe, G., Reid, S., Robinson, K., Sabadosa, K., Schmidt, J., Tullis, E., Webber, J., & Weber, D. (2014). Infection prevention and control guidelines for cystic fibrosis: 2013 update. *Infection Control and Hospital Epidemiology, 35*(S1), S1–S67. Retrieved March 4, 2018, from www.jstor.org/stable/pdf/10.1086/676882.pdf.

Sampson, H. (2000). Food allergy: from biology toward therapy. *Hospital Practice, 35*(5), 67–83.

Sicherer, S., Forman, J., & Noone, S. (2000). Use assessment of self-administered epinephrine among food-allergic children and pediatricians. *Pediatrics, 105*(2), 359–362.

Smart, C., Annan, F., Bruno, L., Higgins, L., & Acerini, C. (2014). ISPAD Clinical Practice Consensus Guidelines 2014 Compendium: nutritional management in children and adolescents with diabetes. *Pediatric Diabetes, 15*, 135–153.

Society of Pediatric Psychology. (2016a). Allergic Diseases Special Interest Group. Retrieved April 15, 2018, from www.societyofpediatricpsychology.org/node/739.

Society of Pediatric Psychology. (2016b). Epilepsy Special Interest Group. Retrieved April 15, 2018, from www.societyofpediatricpsychology.org/epilepsy_sig.

Society of Pediatric Psychology. (2016c). Fact Sheet: HIV/AIDS in Children and Adolescents. Retrieved February 13, 2019, from www.societyofpediatricpsychology.org/hiv_aids.

Society of Pediatric Psychology. (2016d). Cardiology Special Interest Group. Retrieved February 20, 2019, from www.societyofpediatricpsychology.org/Cardiology.

Society of Pediatric Psychology. (2016e). Fact Sheet: Cardiovascular Disease in Children and Adolescents. Retrieved February 20, 2019, from www .societyofpediatricpsychology.org/ cardiovascular_disease.

Solberg, M., Grønning, D., Holmstrøm, H., Eskedal, L., Landolt, M., & Vollrath, M. (2012). Trajectories of maternal mental health: a prospective study of mothers of infants with congenital heart defects from pregnancy to 36 months postpartum. *Journal of Pediatric Psychology, 37*(6), 687–696.

Spangenberg, J. & Lalkhen, N. (2006). Children with epilepsy and their families: psychosocial issues. *South African Family Practice, 48*(6), 60–63.

Spitzer, R., Kroenke, K., Williams, J., & Löwe B. (2006). A brief measure for assessing generalized anxiety disorder: the GAD-7. *Archives of Internal Medicine, 166,* 1092–1097.

Stark, L., Clifford, L., Towner, E., Filigno, S., Zion, C., Bolling, C., & Rausch, J. (2012). A pilot randomized controlled trial of a behavioral family-based intervention with and without home visits to decrease obesity in preschoolers. *Journal of Pediatric Psychology, 39*(3), 1001–1012.

Stark, L., Jelalian, E., & Miller, D. (1995). Cystic fibrosis. In M. Roberts (ed.), *Handbook of Pediatric Psychology*, 2nd ed. (pp. 241–262). New York: Guilford Press.

Steege/Thomson Communications. (n.d.). Pediatric Asthma. Retrieved April 15, 2018, from www.pediatricasthma.org/about.

Switzer, S., Moser, E., Rockler, B., & Garg, S. (2012). Intensive insulin therapy in patients with type 1 diabetes mellitus. *Endocrinology Metabolism Clinics of North America, 41,* 89–104.

Taveras, E., Gillman, M., Kleinman, K., Rich-Edwards, J., & Rifas-Shiman, S. (2013). Reducing racial/ethnic disparities in childhood obesity: the role of early life factors. *JAMA Pediatrics, 167*(8), 731–738.

Todaro, J., Fennell, E., Sears, S., Rorigue, J., & Roche, A. (2000). Cognitive and psychological outcomes in pediatric heart transplantation. *Journal of Pediatric Psychology, 25*(8), 567–576.

US Department of Health and Human Services. (2008). 2008 Physical Activity Guidelines for Americans. Washington, DC: US Department of Health and Human Services.

Wagner, J. & Smith, G. (2007). Psychological services in a pediatric epilepsy clinic: referral patterns and feasibility. *Epilepsy and Behavior, 10,* 129–133.

Wagner, J., Modi, A., & Smith, G. (2011). Commentary: pediatric epilepsy: a good fit for pediatric psychologists. *Journal of Pediatric Psychology, 36*(4), 461–465.

Wagner, J., Smith, G., Ferguson, P., Bakergem, K., & Hrisko, S. (2010). Pilot study of an integrated cognitive-behavioral and self-management intervention for youths with epilepsy and caregivers: Coping Openly and Personally with Epilepsy (COPE). *Epilepsy and Behavior, 18,* 280–285.

Walders, N., Drotar, D., & Kercsmar, C. (2000). The allocation of family responsibility for asthma management tasks in African-American adolescents *Journal of Asthma, 37,* 89–99.

Wicksell, R., Melin, L., & Olsson, G. (2007). Exposure and acceptance in the rehabilitation of adolescents with idiopathic chronic pain – a pilot study. *European Journal of Pain, 11,* 267–274.

Wilfley, D., Tibbs, T., Van Buren, D., Reach, K., Walker, M., & Epstein, L. (2007). Lifestyle interventions in the treatment of childhood overweight: a meta-analytic review of randomized controlled trials. *Health Psychology, 26,* 521–532.

Williams, C., Benden, C., Stevens, D., & Radtke, T. (2010). Exercise and training in adolescents with cystic fibrosis: theory into practice. *International Journal of Pediatrics.* Article ID 670640. doi:10.1155/2010/670640.

Wright, D., Groisman-Perelstein, A., Wylie-Rosett, J., Vernon, N., Diamantis, P., & Isasi, C. (2010). A lifestyle assessment and intervention tool for pediatric weight management: the HABITS questionnaire. *Journal of Human Nutrition and Dietetics, 24,* 96–100.

Wysocki, T., Harris, M., Greco, P., & Buckloh, L. (2001). Behavioral Family Systems Therapy for Adolescents with a Chronic Illness [Treatment and Implementation Manual].

Wysocki, T., Harris, M., Buckloh, L., Mertlich, D., Lochrie, A., Taylor, A., Sadler, M., Mauras, N., & White, N. (2006). Effects of behavioral family systems therapy for diabetes on adolescents' family relationships, treatment adherence, and metabolic control. *Journal of Pediatric Psychology, 31*(9), 928–938.

Yau, M. & Sperling, M. (2017). Treatment of diabetes mellitus in children and adolescents. In L. De Groot, G. Chrousos, K. Dungan, et al. (eds.), *Endotext* [Internet]. South Dartmouth, MA: MDText.com, Inc. Retrieved March 20, 2018, from www.ncbi.nlm.nih.gov/books/NBK279087/.

Yocum, M., Butterfield, J., Klein, J., Volcheck, G., Schroeder, D., & Silverstein, M. (1999). Epidemiology of anaphylaxis in Olmstead County: a population-based study. *Journal of Allergy Clinical Immunology, 104,* 452–456.

Young-Hyman, D. & Davis, C. (2010). Disordered eating behavior in individuals with diabetes. *Diabetes Care, 33*(3), 683–689.

Young-Hyman, D., Groot, M., Hill-Briggs, F., Gonzalez, J., Hood, K., & Peyrot, M. (2016). Psychosocial care for people with diabetes: a position statement of the American Diabetes Association. *Diabetes Care, 39,* 2126–2140.

Zemek, R., Bhogal, S., & Ducharme, F. (2008). Systematic review of randomized controlled trials examining written action plans in children. *Archives of Pediatric and Adolescent Medicine, 162*(2), 157–163.

Ziaian, T., Sawyer, M., Reynolds, K., Carbone, J., Clark, J., Baghurst, P., Couper, J., Kennedy, D., Martin, A., Staugas, R., French, D. (2006). Treatment burden and health-related quality of life of children with diabetes, cystic fibrosis, and asthma. *Journal of Paediatrics and Child Health, 42,* 596–600.

Reproducible Resources

PATIENT HEALTH QUESTIONNAIRE-9 (PHQ-9)

Over the last 2 weeks, how often have you been bothered by any of the following problems? (Use "☒" to indicate your answer)	Not at all	Several days	More than half the days	Nearly every day
1. Little interest or pleasure in doing things	0	1	2	3
2. Feeling down, depressed, or hopeless	0	1	2	3
3. Trouble falling or staying asleep, or sleeping too much	0	1	2	3
4. Feeling tired or having little energy	0	1	2	3
5. Poor appetite or overeating	0	1	2	3
6. Feeling bad about yourself — or that you are a failure or have let yourself or your family down	0	1	2	3
7. Trouble concentrating on things, such as reading the newspaper or watching television	0	1	2	3
8. Moving or speaking so slowly that other people could have noticed? Or the opposite — being so fidgety or restless that you have been moving around a lot more than usual	0	1	2	3
9. Thoughts that you would be better off dead or of hurting yourself in some way	0	1	2	3

FOR OFFICE CODING ___0___ + _____ + _____ + _____

=Total Score: _____

If you checked off any problems, how difficult have these problems made it for you to do your work, take care of things at home, or get along with other people?

Not difficult at all	Somewhat difficult	Very difficult	Extremely difficult
☐	☐	☐	☐

Figure 6.1 Patient Health Questionnaire-9 (PHQ-9) (Kroenke & Spitzer, 2002).
Retrieved March 18, 2018, from https://phqscreeners.pfizer.edrupalgardens.com/sites/g/files/g10016261/f/201412/instructions.pdf.
Developed by Drs. Robert L. Spitzer, Janet B. W. Williams, Kurt Kroenke, and colleagues, with an educational grant from Pfizer Inc.

GAD-7

Over the last 2 weeks, how often have you been bothered by the following problems? (Use "✔" to indicate your answer)	Not at all	Several days	More than half the days	Nearly every day
1. Feeling nervous, anxious or on edge	0	1	2	3
2. Not being able to stop or control worrying	0	1	2	3
3. Worrying too much about different things	0	1	2	3
4. Trouble relaxing	0	1	2	3
5. Being so restless that it is hard to sit still	0	1	2	3
6. Becoming easily annoyed or irritable	0	1	2	3
7. Feeling afraid as if something awful might happen	0	1	2	3

(For office coding: Total Score T____ = ____ + ____ + ____)

Figure 6.2 Generalized Anxiety Disorder-7 (GAD-7) (Spitzer, Kroenke, Williams, &, Löwe, 2006). Retrieved March 18, 2018 from https://phqscreeners.pfizer.edrupalgardens.com/sites/g/files/g10016261/f/201412/instructions.pdf. Developed by Drs. Robert L. Spitzer, Janet B. W. Williams, Kurt Kroenke, and colleagues, with an educational grant from Pfizer Inc.

Recommendations for Most Patients

Specific recommendations for patients
1. Use of a hunger scale (a patient-friendly scale to assist in determining level of hunger at any given time, typically 10-point scale with faces reflecting different levels of hunger/discomfort) and awareness of hunger versus boredom or emotional eating
2. Provide education about metabolism and factors affecting metabolic rate such as the negative effects of skipping breakfast
3. Review the importance of sleep hygiene and impact on hunger, fatigue, health, and behavior
   a. sleep in cool (68 degrees F), dark, quiet environment
   b. no eating 1 – 2 hours prior to bed
   c. no caffeine 6 – 8 hours prior to bedtime
   d. no electronics for 30 minutes prior to bed or turned on in the room while sleeping
   e. consistent bedtime, consistent wake time
   f. no pets in bed or in the bedroom while sleeping
   g. use the bed only for sleeping
   h. consistent bedtime routine for 30 – 60 minutes with low lights, low movement, low stimulation
   i. consider relaxation training
   j. no naps unless developmentally appropriate
   k. developmentally appropriate sleep duration
4. Review the impact of teasing/bullying on patient; provide education on school policies related to bullying; support caregivers in making changes in the home and school environment to reduce or eliminate teasing/bullying
5. Recommend eating slowly, shaping toward appropriate portion sizes
6. Recommend need for 5 small meals/snacks a day, shaping toward that goal
7. Recommend leaving the table after normal portion size/meal size and wait 20 minutes before second servings (only of fruits/vegetables); review delay in satiation communicated to the brain
8. Review benefits of regular exercise, shaping toward moderate/vigorous exercise
9. Recommend reduced screen time and other sedentary behaviors, working toward fewer than 2 hours a day

Figure 6.3 Recommendations for Most Patients.
Adapted (from a much larger list) from *Expert Guidelines: Role of Psychologist in Assessment and Treatment of Obese Youth* (Children's Hospital Association, 2012)

10. Recommend reduced caffeine intake to less than 1 8-oz serving a day, to avoid diminishment of hunger signals
11. Recommend increasing variety of fruits/vegetables through tasting opportunities, pairing with liked foods (dips), repeated presentations, shaping serving size over time, caregiver modeling
12. Provide psychotherapy to address coping with chronic illness, functional impairment, body image
13. Consider self-monitoring or caregiver monitoring (daily food or exercise log)
14. Consider using pedometer to log steps
15. Review pros/cons of packing lunch versus eating school lunch
16. Recommend only zero-calorie drinks with the exception of skim or 1% milk
17. Recommend working toward reducing fast food intake to only twice a week or less
18. Discuss healthy snack options and how to reinforce choosing those over unhealthy options

Specific recommendations for caregivers
1. Teach management of health-related behaviors including using Premack principle and reinforcement to increase frequencies of desired health-related behaviors, using distraction, alternate behaviors, and negative reinforcement to reduce frequencies of undesired health-related behaviors
2. Teach anger control strategies, positive coaching techniques
3. Specifically discuss alternative reward options rather than using food as a reward
4. Discuss the importance of showing love, nurturance, caregiving in a way that does not involve food provision
5. Recommend family-based treatment, in which all family members eat healthier foods, exercise regularly, and provide a supportive and validating atmosphere such that caregivers avoid negative comments about the patient's eating habits or body
6. Recommend targeting family-based weight loss and/or improving health-related behaviors of all family members
7. Discuss caregiver role as positive coach in all the patient recommendations above
8. Review meal planning, budgeting for healthy foods
9. Recommend parents not purchase foods that their child typically overeats
10. Recommend parents have a consistent time when the kitchen is "closed" and eating stops in the evening
11. Recommend eating together as a family at a table without distractions, problem-solve barriers to this plan
12. Discuss how to develop a positive family culture regarding eating
13. Review importance of routine and its impact on healthy habit development

Toddlers Through Preschool

Specific recommendations for caregivers
1. Recommend 4 oz max of juice for this age child and work toward eliminating sugared beverages
2. Discuss how to transition from bottle to cup by age 12 months
3. Recommend no eating or drinking at night (except water) to protect teeth from cavities and reduce perception of hunger at night and promote sleep quality; recommend shaping and behavioral techniques over time to achieve this goal if needed
4. Recommend active play with dancing strongly encouraged and high activity levels normative
5. Recommend working toward no screen time under age 2 and less than two hours for preschoolers
6. Discuss overfeeding practices if present
7. Recommend capitalizing on absence of food preferences early in life, trying new foods, presenting wide variety of foods
8. Recommend capitalizing less on a tendency to be influenced by environmental cues

Figure 6.3 (cont.)

(e.g., go with self-regulation, internal hunger and satiety cues) at this age

9. Recommend whole family physical activity with caregiver modeling of physical activity
10. Recommend using behavioral techniques to work toward child sleeping independently
11. Recommend individual treatment with a strong level of caregiver participation; consider adding a group, multidisciplinary, multicomponent treatment although efficacy studies are limited for this age group

School Age

Specific recommendations

1. Strongly consider group multidisciplinary, multicomponent treatment with caregiver participation, and the following behavioral strategies:

   a. Caregiver monitoring of food and activities (with child involvement increasing as child matures)
   b. Positive reinforcement (not food) by caregivers and teachers
   c. Stimulus control
   d. Problem solving
   e. Preplanning
   f. Consider targeting caregiver weight change as well
   g. Length of treatment--no evidence but 6 months is most common

2. Recommend attempts to prevent decline in sports participation that happens after 13; attention to sports options for K – Grade 5 children, quality of coaching, and with particular attention to pre-adolescent girls
3. Recommend active play as a good option for this age group
4. Recommendations to increase physical activity:
   a. Immediate and genuine praise for effort rather than outcome
   b. Teach and practice skills
   c. Promote self-efficacy
   d. Promote caregiver involvement
   e. Link physical activity to peer and/or family involvement rather than solo
2. Address not eating breakfast at home and at school ; discuss impact on metabolism; utilize shaping procedures if needed to increase intake at those times
3. Facilitate building positive body image

Adolescents

Specific recommendations

1. As in school-age population, strongly consider group multicomponent intervention including caregiver participation (either simultaneous with the teens or parallel); no consensus regarding length, but 14 – 16 weeks is most common
2. Consider adding peer-enhanced intervention (group challenging activities such as ropes course, mazes) to standard CBT (cognitive behavioral therapy) for greater effect
3. Recommend support for gradually increasing autonomy in health behaviors and increased responsibility for diet and physical activity while maintaining caregiver monitoring, education, and involvement
4. Watch for and address a decline in participation in sports after age 13
5. Problem solving to increase time available for physical activity and to address self-perception and self-efficacy
6. For boys and girls—assess and treat negative body image and appearance-related self-esteem issues that increase in prevalence in adolescence
7. Recommend caregiver support and involvement in physical activity, including providing transportation and encouragement

Figure 6.3 *(cont.)*

8. Consider technology-facilitated (Internet, texting, phone apps) behavioral intervention options
9. Review and emphasize sleep issues noted in general section above (Developmentally, adolescents need more sleep than younger patients but tend to get less resulting in greater sleep debt. Further, adolescents are prone to sleep phase problems that require behavioral intervention.)
10. Recommend increased patient involvement in planning for meals/snacks and physical activity including planning for eating in peer/social situations
11. Address particular issue of skipping meals: Why are they skipping?; What are the effects on metabolism?; How to increase ability to tolerate eating early in the morning?
12. Consider peer support interventions

Figure 6.3 (*cont.*)

	Monday	Tuesday	Wednesday	Thursday	Friday	Saturday	Sunday
Sleep							
What did you to relax before bed?							
TV/phone/radio computer screen on?							
Caffeine after 5pm?							
Time Went to Bed							
Time Fell Asleep							
Number of Times Woke Up During Night							
Time Work Up							
Time Got Up							
Rate Quality of Sleep (1-10)							
Rate Mood (1-10)							

	Monday	Tuesday	Wednesday	Thursday	Friday	Saturday	Sunday
Exercise							
What time did you exercise? (ex. 9:00am)							
What type of exercise? (ex. walking)							
How long did you exercise?							
Rate Mood Before Exercise (1-10)							
Rate Mood After Exercise (1-10)							

Figure 6.4 Sleep and exercise log.

+ asthma action plan

+ Name: _____

My Personal Best Peak Flow is : _____

Date of birth: _____	**My Triggers**
Doctor name: _____	
Doctor phone: _____	☐ pollen ☐ exercise ☐ mold ☐ cold/flu
Emergency contact: _____	☐ dust mites ☐ weather ☐ animals ☐ air pollution
Emergency phone: _____	☐ smoke ☐ food ☐ other_____

If exercise or playing sports triggers your asthma take :

Medicine: _____

How much: _____

When: _____

Additional instructions: _____

GREEN ZONE — HEALTHY

Symptoms

Breathing is Easy
No Cough or Wheeze
Can Do Usual Activities
Can Sleep through the Night

Peak Flow from _____ to _____

My Daily Control Medications

Medicine	How Much	How Often / When

YELLOW ZONE — CAUTION

Symptoms

Some Shortness of Breath
Cough, Wheeze or Chest Tightness
Some Difficulty Doing Usual Activities
Sleep Disturbed by Symptoms
Symptoms of a Cold or Flu

Peak Flow from _____ to _____

The Caution Zone Plus Quick Relief

Medicine	How Much	How Often / When

Call your Doctor if

RED ZONE — EMERGENCY

Symptoms

Severe Breathing Problems
Cannot Do Usual Activities
Difficulty Walking and Talking
Rescue Medicine is Not Helping

Peak Flow from _____ to _____

The Danger Zone Take this Medicine and Call the Doctor Now!

Medicine	How Much	How Often / When

Take these medicines **NOW** and **CALL 911** immediately!

This information has been reviewed by:
Allergy & Asthma Specialists, P.C.
82 East Allendale Road,
Saddle River, NJ 07456

AllerMates
Safeguarding Kids

Figure 6.5 Asthma Action Plan.
Reprinted from https://cdn.shopify.com/s/files/1/0773/2859/files/MedimatesActionPlan.pdf by AllerMates. Copyright 2009–2013 by Awearables, LLC

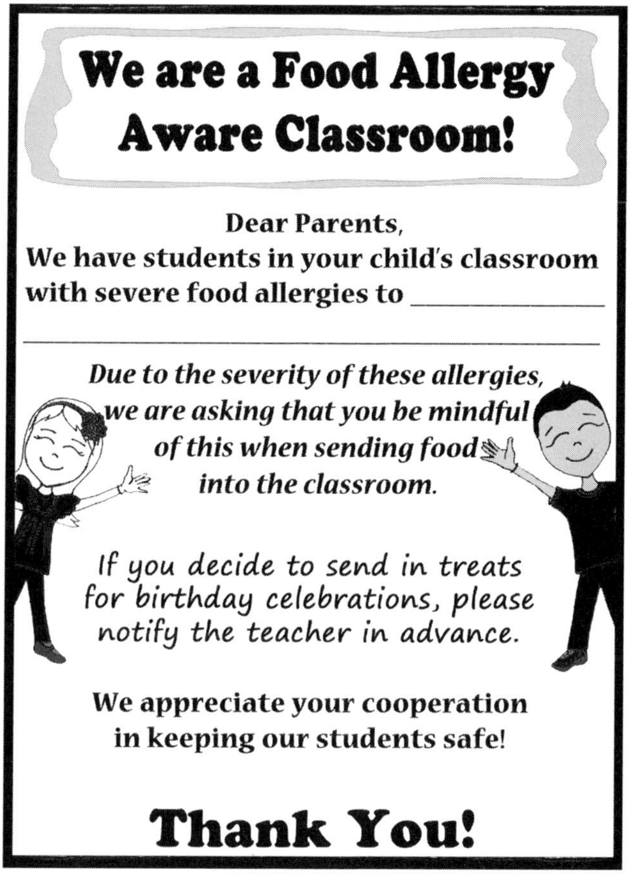

We are a Food Allergy Aware Classroom!

Dear Parents,
We have students in your child's classroom with severe food allergies to ______________

____

Due to the severity of these allergies, we are asking that you be mindful of this when sending food into the classroom.

If you decide to send in treats for birthday celebrations, please notify the teacher in advance.

We appreciate your cooperation in keeping our students safe!

Thank You!

Figure 6.6 Food Allergy Awareness Letter to Parents. Reprinted from Bostic, E. (n.d.). Food Allergy Aware Letter to Parents. Retrieved May 9, 2018, from http://thrivingwithallergies.blogspot.com/2016/08/food-allergy-aware-letter-to-parents.html

Chronic Pain Acceptance Questionnaire (CPAQ)

*Reprinted with permission from Lance McCracken, PhD

McCraken, L. M., Vowles, K. E. & Eccleston, C. (2004). Acceptance of chronic pain: component analysis and a revised assessment method. Pain, 107, 159-166.

Directions: below you will find a list of statements. Please rate the truth of each statement as it applies to you. Use the following rating scale to make your choices. For instance, if you believe a statement is 'Always True' you would write a 6 in the blank next to that statement.

0	1	2	3	4	5	6
Never true	Very rarely true	Seldom true	Sometimes true	Often true	Almost always true	Always true

1. I am getting on with the business of living no matter what my level of pain is ………
2. My life is going well, even though I have chronic pain ………
3. It's OK to experience pain ………
4. I would gladly sacrifice important things in my life to control this pain better ………
5. It's not necessary for me to control my pain in order to handle my life well ………
6. Although things have changed, I am living a normal life despite my chronic pain ………
7. I need to concentrate on getting rid of my pain ………
8. There are many activities I do when I feel pain ………
9. I lead a full life even though I have chronic pain ………
10. Controlling pain is less important than any other goals in my life ………
11. My thoughts and feelings about pain must change before I can take important steps in my life ………
12. Despite the pain, I am now sticking to a certain course in my life ………
13. Keeping my pain level under control takes first priority whenever I'm doing something ………
14. Before I can make any serious plans, I have to get some control over my pain ………
15. When my pain increases, I can still take care of my responsibilities ………
16. I will have better control over my life if I can control my negative thoughts about pain ………
17. I avoid putting myself in situations where my pain might increase ………
18. My worries and fears about what pain will do to me are true ………
19. It's a relief to realize that I don't have to change my pain to get on with my life ………
20. I have to struggle to do things when I have pain ………

Scoring:
Activities engagement: Sum items 1, 2, 3, 5, 6, 8, 9, 10, 12, 15, 19.
Pain willingness: reverse score items 4, 7, 11, 13, 14, 16, 17, 18, 20 and sum.
Total: activity engagement + pain willingness.

Figure 6.7 Chronic Pain Acceptance Questionnaire (CPAQ).
Reprinted from McCraken, Vowles, & Eccleston. 2004. Acceptance of chronic pain: component analysis and a revised assessment method. Pain, 107, 159–166. https://journals.lww.com/pain/Abstract/2004/01000/Acceptance_of_chronic_pain__component_analysis_and.22.aspx.

First Aid for Seizures

What To Do If Someone Has A <u>Non-Convulsive</u> Seizure
(staring blankly, confused, not responding, movements are purposeless)

1   Stay with the person. Let the seizure take its course. Speak calmly and explain to others what is happening.

2   Move dangerous objects out of the way.

3   DO NOT restrain the person.

4   Gently guide the person away from danger or block access to hazards.

5   After the seizure, talk reassuringly to the person. Stay with the person until complete awareness returns.

What To Do If Someone Has A <u>Convulsive</u> Seizure
(characterized by stiffening, falling, jerking)

1   Stay calm. Let the seizure take its course.

2   Time the seizure.

3   Protect from injury. If necessary, ease the person to the floor. Move hard or sharp objects out of the way. Place something soft under the head.

4   Loosen anything tight around the neck. Check for medical identification.

5   DO NOT restrain the person.

6   DO NOT put anything in the mouth. The person will not swallow his or her tongue.

7   Gently roll the person onto his or her side as the convulsive seizure subsides to allow saliva or other fluids to drain away and keep the airway clear.

8   After the seizure, talk to the person reassuringly. Do not leave until the person is re-oriented. The person may need to rest or sleep.

Figure 6.8 First Aid for Seizures.
Reprinted from www.edmontonepilepsy.org/documents/Epilepsy%20-%20A%20Guide%20For%20Parents.pdf. Copyright 2011 by Edmonton Epilepsy Association

Recommended Websites, Books, and Other Resources

Diabetes

"Pink Panther" diabetes books by Peter Chase & David Maahs, www.childrensdiabetesfoundation.org/books/

Diabetes Medical Management Plan (DMMP), http://main.diabetes.org/dorg/PDFs/living-with-diabetes/diabetes-medical-management.pdf

"Courage-Wisdom-Hope Kit" for newly diagnosed patients from American Diabetes Association, order free kit online

Literacy and Numeracy Toolkit for Providers Training Manual by Vanderbilt University, www.mc.vanderbilt.edu/documents/CDTR/files/dlnet-instructions%5B1%5D.pdf

Obesity

Clinical Resources

Mullen, M. & Shield, J. (2003). *Childhood and Adolescent Overweight: The Health Professional's Guide to Identification, Treatment, and Prevention.* Chicago: American Dietetic Association.

Barlow, S. (2007). Expert *Committee Recommendations Regarding the Prevention, Assessment, and Treatment of Child and Adolescent Overweight and Obesity: Summary Report.* Retrieved February 27, 2018, from http://pediatrics.aappublications.org/content/120/Supplement_4/S164.

Sleep Hygiene

National Sleep Foundation. (2018). Sleep Hygiene. Retrieved February 27, 2018, from https://sleepfoundation.org/sleep-topics/sleep-hygiene.

Cystic Fibrosis

Cystic Fibrosis Foundation, www.cff.org

Infection Control Guidelines

Saiman, L., Siegel, J., LiPuma, J., Brown, R., Bryson, E., Chambers, M., Downer, V., Filege, J., Hazle, L., Jain, M., Marshall, B., O'Malley, C., Pattee, S., Bynoe, G., Reid, S., Robinson, K., Sabadosa, K., Schmidt, J., Tullis, E., Webber, J., & Weber, D. (2014). Infection prevention and control guidelines for cystic fibrosis: 2013 update. *Infection Control and Hospital Epidemiology, 35*(S1), S1–S67. Retrieved March 4, 2018, from www.jstor.org/stable/pdf/10.1086/676882.pdf.

Mental Health Guidelines

Quittner, A., Abbott, J., Georgiopoulos, A., Goldbeck, L., Smith, B., Hempstead, S., Marshall, B., Sabadosa, K., & Elborn, S. (2016). International Committee on Mental Health in Cystic Fibrosis: Cystic Fibrosis Foundation and European Cystic Fibrosis Society consensus statements for screening and treating depression and anxiety. *Thorax, 71*, 26–34.

School Accommodations

Individualized Education Programs (IEPs) and 504 Plans, www.cff.org/Life-With-CF/Caring-for-a-Child-With-CF/Working-With-Your-Childs-School/Individualized-Education-504-Plans/

PHQ-9 and GAD-7 Scoring

Instruction Manual: Instructions for Patient Health Questionnaire (PHQ-9) and GAD-7 Measures. (n.d.). Retrieved March 18, 2018, from https://phqscreeners.pfizer.edrupalgardens.com/sites/g/files/g10016261/f/201412/instructions.pdf.

Recommended Book for Parents

Cline, F. & Greene, L. (2007). *Parenting Children with Health Issues*. Golden, CO: Love and Logic Institute.

Asthma

Asthma Resources for Clinicians, http://clinicians.org/comprehensive-asthma-resource-list/

Pediatric Asthma Initiative, www.pediatricasthma.org/resources

Food Allergies

Society of Pediatric Psychology's Allergic Diseases Special Interest Group, www.societyofpediatric psychology.org/node/739

Food Allergy Research and Education, www.foodallergy.org/

Allergy and Anaphylaxis Emergency Plan, www.aap.org/en-us/Documents/AAP_Allergy_and_Anaphylaxis_Emergency_Plan.pdf

Chronic Pain

OucherTM Pain Scale for Children, www.oucher.org/index.html

Center for Pediatric Pain Research, http://pediatric-pain.ca/for-health-professionals/

Epilepsy

Society of Pediatric Psychology's Epilepsy Special Interest Group, www.societyofpediatric psychology.org/epilepsy_sig

Parent Information, www.healthychildren.org/English/health-issues/conditions/head-neck-nervous-system/Pages/Seizures-Convulsions-and-Epilepsy.aspx

Sample 504 Plan for Students with Epilepsy, www.epilepsynorcal.org/wp-content/uploads/2015/07/Sample_504.pdf

Seizure First Aid Guide, www.epilepsy.com/learn/seizure-first-aid-and-safety/adapting-first-aid-plans/first-aid/first-aid-resources

Cancer

Long-Term Follow Up Guidelines for Survivors of Childhood, Adolescent, and Young Adult Cancers, http://survivorshipguidelines.org/pdf/2018/COG_LTFU_Guidelines_v5.pdf

Recommended Books for Families, www.childhoodcancerguides.org/our-books/

Resource Directory for Families, www.anddit.com/hope-portal

HIV/AIDS

Clinical Resources

Zeichner S. & Read, J. (eds.). (2006). *Handbook of Pediatric HIV Care*. Cambridge: Cambridge University Press.

Boyd-Franklin, N., Steiner, G., & Boland, M. (eds.). (1995). *Children, Families, and HIV/AIDS*. New York: Guilford Press.

Clinician Fact Sheet, www.societyofpediatricpsychology.org/hiv_aids

Congenital Heart Disease

Society of Pediatric Psychology's Cardiology Special Interest Group, www.societyofpediatric psychology.org/Cardiology

Clinician Fact Sheet, www.societyofpediatricpsychology.org/cardiovascular_disease

Family Support Resources Little Hearts, Inc., www.littlehearts.org/Default.asp

Special Populations in Pediatric Psychology

7.1 Rural Populations

In working with children and adolescents both with and without chronic illnesses, clinicians should be mindful of the role culture, socioeconomic status, and other contextual factors play in impacting psychological and physical health. In rural settings, children and adolescents may face greater health disparities and may exhibit a higher prevalence of unhealthy lifestyle behaviors, including greater substance use, more sedentary behavior, and poor nutrition (Polaha et al., 2011). Rural children also tend to exhibit higher rates of obesity and unintentional injury rates. They are less likely to have regular physician visits but are more likely to use emergency room services in comparison to children in more urban areas (Janicke & Davis, 2011). These factors are significant when considering that approximately 20% of the United States population is considered to live in a rural area.

Much of the pediatric literature on rural populations focuses on the higher rates of children who are overweight or clinically obese. Researchers point to higher calorie consumption, increased screen time, and lower physical activity as probable causes for this prevalence, as well as the influence of typically lower levels of education and financial means in comparison to urban groups (Davis et al., 2012). In examining rural parental beliefs and expectations regarding this phenomenon, one qualitative study indicated that some rural parents may believe that their child weight's loss will be unsuccessful due to family history and genetics, as many of the parents themselves were overweight or obese. Parents also indicated concerns due to the lack of access to a pediatric weight-loss program in their community, difficulty obtaining healthy foods, and limited access to sports equipment due to financial limitations (Davis et al., 2012).

Of course, these increased risks for obesity and other health concerns are not an indication that every child in a rural area will experience any of these difficulties, but this data does indicate that specific screening may be warranted when working with this population. This is particularly salient given that rural populations tend to experience increased difficulty with access to mental health specialists due to a shortage of mental health providers as well as potentially increased stigma around mental health (Polaha et al., 2011). As a result of stigma, help-seeking may be more directed to primary care services rather than specialist mental health clinics.

Cultural values in rural populations can be incredibly diverse and require mental health clinicians to be knowledgeable about the local culture. For example, Appalachian regions tend to face higher rates of unemployment and poverty, and their cultural values emphasize seeking support from friends, family, and religious community rather than from professional sources (Owens et al., 2007). Seeking professional help may be more associated with privacy concerns, overall distrust, and a fear of being judged. In particular, Owens and colleagues point to "significant distrust related to confidentiality and corporal punishment" (p. 190). Given this distrust, it may be helpful to include parents as "co-leaders" in treatment and to emphasize early on in the therapeutic process clear information about reporting laws and mandated disclosure.

Mental health practitioners may face new difficulties and barriers when working with a rural population in comparison to working with patients located in more suburban or urban populations. Due to the smaller population, mental health providers face a greater likelihood of dual relationships and there may be fewer local specialists to whom to refer patients. This may force many providers to act more as a generalist at times, as well as potentially being tasked with providing more education about psychotherapy roles and expectations due to decreased understanding about this treatment model in rural culture (Smalley et al., 2010).

To combat these difficulties, clinicians treating pediatric patients in rural areas may need to be willing to utilize other treatment-delivery models such as school-based or telehealth models and to find creative ways to reduce stigma (e.g., having concealed parking or being co-located within a medical clinic). These logistical considerations can help combat some of the barriers associated with rural mental health care, but, most importantly, clinicians should be aware of the cultural nuances and unwritten rules that guide their local population. Clinicians should also be mindful that rural patients may be more likely to seek treatment at a later time when symptoms are more serious, and that strong partnerships with schools and physicians in primary care settings can be helpful when providing mental health services in a rural community (Smalley et al., 2010).

To better understand the attitudes and barriers to mental health services in their community, it may be helpful for clinicians to utilize the Child and Adolescent Services Assessment (CASA). The CASA was created to help clinicians understand the use of mental health services by children between the ages of 8 and 18 and helps provide information about attitudes toward treatment and perceived barriers to treatment (Burns et al., 2008). The authors of this instrument provide information to mental health providers regarding the use of this assessment and training opportunities for utilizing this assessment appropriately. For further information, refer to the website identified in the "Recommended Websites, Books, and Other Resources" section at the end of this chapter.

Clinical Vignette: "Hopeful but Hesitant"

Mary Anne is a 12-year-old Caucasian female from a rural area who was referred by her pediatrician for depressive symptoms. She presented with her mother for the intake session and both appeared visibly nervous and ill at ease. After introducing yourself and providing information about standard clinic policies, you begin the discussion about informed consent, including information about mandated reporting for child abuse. Being aware of the corporal punishment practices of many of the parents in the local area, you spend more time than usual carefully explaining the differences between child abuse and nonreportable corporal punishment. You frame this in the context of being aware that corporal punishment is practiced in many families, and that you want to be transparent about mandated reporting in order to ensure a positive working relationship.

Mary Anne's mother still appears tense and notes that the patient's father does not want them to seek psychological treatment as this "is for crazy people" and, therefore, has chosen to remain in the lobby. She indicated that he had chosen to park in the back of the building so that other people in the community would not know they were being seen by a "shrink." Having faced this concern before, you spend time discussing the family's concerns about privacy and note that your care of individuals in an outpatient setting is for "normal" people who are wanting to improve their quality of life. They both appear to outwardly relax when you discuss the prevalence of depression in adolescence, and they are both engaged when you discuss the plan for evidence-based treatment to focus on helping Mary Anne to build skills to help with depression.

At the next session, you meet with Mary Anne's parents together prior to meeting with Mary Anne, and, similar to the intake session, you spend time discussing the parents' awareness of the expectations of psychotherapy and discussing any misconceptions they might have regarding it. You invite both parents to be instrumental as "co-leaders" in helping Mary Anne learn skills to help manage depression, and both parents appear interested in this idea. After meeting with both parents, you and Mary Anne identify famous people she knows who have been open about their own struggles with depression, including several well-known teenage celebrities who have been open about their own mental health treatment.

Over the next several sessions, you include the parents in treatment as "co-leaders" whenever possible while conducting cognitive behavioral therapy for depression. One morning when you pull into the parking lot, you notice that the family has parked in the front of the clinic for the first time.

7.2 Ethnic Minority Populations

The United States is becoming more ethnically diverse over time due to shifting demographics (McQuaid, 2008). Similar to rural and low-income populations, ethnic minority populations also face significant health disparities. Care for this population is likewise complicated by factors such as a potential lack of cultural competency by providers and limited access to care. Health care disparities are seen in various aspects of health care for ethnic minority populations, starting with prenatal and maternal care, and resulting in higher rates of chronic diseases, such as asthma and obesity (McQuaid, 2008).

Just as rural cultures should not all be "lumped together" when looking at different cultural elements and other factors, so too are there significant differences both between and within ethnic minority groups. For example, in comparison to the majority ethnic population as well as other ethnic minority groups, the American Indian population exhibits elevated risk of alcohol abuse and the highest injury death rates of all groups in the United States, with American Indian adolescent males having the highest suicide rates of all age and ethnic groups (Gray & Winterowd, 2002). While there are some known between-group differences with regard to mental health considerations and diagnostic prevalence, each patient and family should be assessed individually with great respect paid to within-group differences.

When working with patients from ethnic minority groups, it is important to be cognizant of the fact that much of the information that the field of psychology has gained through its research is based on assessment and treatment protocols normed on Caucasian populations. This can lead to misdiagnosis or the view of behaviors within cultural norms as psychopathological given the way that culture impacts presentation of symptoms and parenting practices. For instance, in some African American families, increased parental stress related to poverty and a greater likelihood of being raised in a single-parent home in comparison to Caucasian patients can have a strong impact on parenting techniques

(McNeil et al., 2002). As such, some African American parents may exhibit different parenting strategies that may not be addressed by parenting programs normed on Caucasian populations.

This concern about most of psychology's research stemming from data normed on a Caucasian population is also predominant with regard to assessment. The concern about health disparities in the assessment of ethnic minority children is warranted as response bias has been observed in the phrasing of assessment questions (Alegria et al., 2010). This can lead to disparity in diagnosis as well as an overall potential delay in the timing of a mental health diagnosis in comparison to the timing of diagnoses for Caucasian children (Alegria et al., 2010).

To assist with this well-documented concern about the use of Caucasian-normed treatment protocols with ethnic minority populations, attempts have been made to add culturally responsive elements to evidence-based protocols for treating ethnic minority youth (Huey & Polo, 2010). Culturally responsive elements that have been added include but are not limited to ethnic matching between therapist and patient, the use of cultural themes and language matching in therapy, and having a family resource specialist help therapists learn about certain cultures. Unfortunately, it is still unclear whether this cultural adaptation has led to more positive treatment outcomes. For instance, only a correlational positive effect has been found with therapist–patient ethnic matching (Huey & Polo, 2010).

Despite the above efforts to address barriers in mental health care for ethnic minority populations, ethnic minority pediatric patients still exhibit increased rates of premature termination of mental health care and lower utilization rates (Huey & Polo, 2010). Similarly, communications between medical providers and ethnic minority patients continues to be more problematic as a whole than that observed in Caucasian populations, which is important given that positive interactions and communications are linked with improved health outcomes (Valenzeula & Smith, 2016).

To assist with this observed communication problem, clinicians should make cultural competence a professional priority. Cultural competence is an important professional mandate that can help ensure equitable treatment is available for patients from all ethnic groups. Cultural competence is an ongoing process rather than an "end process" and requires careful cultivation by clinicians. Readers are urged to assess their cultural competence with the use of the Cultural Competence Self-Evaluation Form graciously made available to readers by Dr. Anthony Marsella (Marsella et al., 2000; Multicultural Mental Health, 2013), which is listed in the "Reproducible Resources" section at the end of this chapter.

Although many clinicians may be aware of the importance of having transparent dialogues with patients about race and ethnicity, some mental health clinicians may refrain from initiating these conversations due to concerns about accidentally saying something offensive, being unsure of how to have the conversation, or preferring to wait for a patient to bring it up (Cardemil & Battle, 2003). However, these types of conversations can help strengthen the therapeutic alliance when handled correctly.

Researchers provide the following recommendations for having a positive dialogue about ethnicity and race with patients: directly asking about a patient's ethnicity early in the psychotherapy process instead of making assumptions based on visible physical characteristics, using the same terminology that is used by the patient (e.g., white, black, Caucasian, African American), becoming aware of a patient's acculturation and racial identity rather than blindly having assumptions about a patient's similarity to preconceived beliefs about an entire ethnic group, and discussing their perception about how they view mental health services, their communication style, and how they relate/interact with their family (Cardemil & Battle, 2003).

7.3 Sexual and Gender Minorities

The term "sexual and gender minorities" refers to "lesbian, gay, bisexual, and transgender populations, as well as those whose sexual orientation, gender identity and expressions, or reproductive development varies from traditional, societal, cultural, or physiological norms" (National Institute on Minority Health and Health Disparities & Director's Office, 2016). For children and adolescents, understanding and accepting their gender and sexual orientation is a process that is best fostered by affirmation and family support.

In the United States, working with sexual and gender minorities in a pediatric setting brings forth ethical dilemmas and concerns that are heavily influenced by the family's values and beliefs, as well as the clinician's own beliefs. Due to the complexity of how these different contextual and personal factors play a role in sexuality, some clinicians may attempt to avoid discussing gender and sexuality with a pediatric patient unless this issue was brought as a presenting concern or otherwise organically arose during the course of psychotherapy.

To assist with this unease or hesitancy, certain recommendations have been made to help clinicians facilitate these important discussions. Specifically, it is recommended that mental health clinicians discuss sexuality and gender individually with the patient, including questions that ask about attraction, sexual behavior, and whether the patient identifies with a certain gender, sexual orientation, or pronoun (Smith, 2016). Given the risk factors associated with being a sexual and gender minority in the United States, clinicians should also be mindful of screening for trauma, depression, and body image concerns.

To provide a more affirmative environment for patients who identify as lesbian, gay, bisexual, transsexual, or queer (LGBTQ), clinicians may want to consider environmental modifications such as having known symptoms of affirmation (e.g., rainbow flag) placed in visible spots in the clinic or having policies visible that allow patients to identify their bathroom based on their self-identified gender rather than their assigned sex at birth (Hadland et al., 2016). Similarly, clinicians may want to ensure that health promotion materials regarding healthy sexuality or relationships are not heteronormative in approach. Formal LGBTQ competency trainings as well as having a referenceable list of affirming/inclusive terminology for the clinician to refer to may also be of assistance in daily practice. For a list of sample affirming/inclusive terminology, see the LGBTQ-Inclusive Language Dos and Don'ts listed in the "Reproducible Resources" section.

In addition to making changes for the patient, clinicians may want to focus on providing family support as family support is strongly related to a pediatric patient's risk for depressive symptoms. Specifically, transgender patients and other sexual minority populations appear to be impacted positively by parent support (Simons et al., 2013). Research conducted with transgender patients, or patients who self-identify with a gender that is different from what was assigned at birth, are at higher risk for depressive symptoms and suicidal ideation; however, parent support has been shown to be protective against these concerns and is associated with greater perceived life satisfaction (Simons et al., 2013).

In addition to this higher risk for depressive symptoms and suicidal ideation, lesbian, gay, and bisexual (LGB) adolescents have higher prevalence rates of cigarette smoking

(Rosario et al., 2010). This increased risk is thought to be associated with these adolescents attempting to utilize smoking as a coping strategy for high stress, as LGB adolescents tend to report higher levels of stress, more problematic social relationships, higher levels of victimization, and lower levels of social support (Rosario et al., 2010). Unfortunately, despite the reason why LGB adolescents may be smoking cigarettes, research suggests that smoking may actually be linked to increasing psychological distress rather than alleviating it, as well as smoking's association with numerous serious medical concerns. However, similar to the previously identified protective role that parental support can play, social support appears to be a key factor in successful smoking cessation (Rosario et al., 2010).

Affirmative psychotherapy is recommended for transgender youth not because identifying as transgender is suggestive of mental illness, but rather to help affirm and support the youth during this process (Olson et al., 2011). Affirmative mental health treatments are recommended to help patients explore gender identity and to discuss gender transitioning, whether this is via social transitioning and/or hormonal therapy. Social transitioning involves the process of beginning to outwardly express and disclose their gender identity. Each patient may prefer to approach this process differently, as some patients might want to discuss this with family and close friends prior to being open about their gender identity with larger populations (e.g., school peers). In addition to being verbally open about their gender identity, social transitioning often is accompanied by visible changes in appearance and other means of gender expression.

The actual process of medically transitioning is ethically complex and requires working closely with skilled medical teams. While hormone therapy before puberty is not recommended, some aspects of the medical transition can be reversible (Olson et al., 2011). Reversible treatment typically begins with the suppression of gonadotropin-releasing hormone analogues, and partially reversible treatments refer to cross-gender hormone therapy (e.g., testosterone or estrogen therapy). Once a patient has decided to make an irreversible medical transition, medical procedures such as jaw shaping, vaginoplasty, mastectomy, and phalloplasty are typically utilized to help the patient physically transition into their identified gender (Olson et al., 2011).

Another special population that falls under the category of sexual and gender minorities is that of patients who have been diagnosed with a disorder of sexual development (DSD). DSD refers to a collection of disorders in which there are atypical aspects of sex determination or differentiation, and this is seen in approximately 1 in 100 live births (Sandberg, Pasterski, & Callens, 2017). These congenital conditions are typically diagnosed at birth or at puberty when symptoms such as a lack of menstrual cycle indicate a concern. Learning that their child has DSD can be extremely stressful for parents, as they may be forced to make early decisions about sex reassignment and other surgeries when they may still be coping with the stressors associated with new parenthood. Additionally, stigma about DSD may make it hard for parents to talk about the diagnosis or to find support from their usual support system.

Medical professionals working with patients with DSD may find themselves in ethically complex situations, particularly in situations with conflicting family dynamics, divergent cultural or religious values, and complicated state laws. Current guidelines suggest that it can be advantageous to try to delay gender assignment surgeries until the patient can help in the decision-making process (Intersex Society of North America, 2006). This is contrary to the historical viewpoint that early surgeries to confirm initial sex assignment would help prevent later psychosocial problems; however, there has been no substantial evidence to support this approach as there does not appear to be an increased risk for psychosocial problems if a patient does not have early gender assignment surgery (Intersex Society of North America, 2006).

As part of clinical care for patients with DSD, many patients will have to endure routine genital exams, which can be particularly frightening for patients and families who are already distressed by the diagnosis of DSD. There has been limited research into clinical guidelines on how to help prepare families and patients for genital exams when there is a diagnosis of DSD. As such, most recommendations for genital exams have been extrapolated from the child sexual abuse literature (Tishelman et al., 2017).

Prior to an anticipated genital exam, clinicians can help prepare both the parent and child by discussing what will occur during the exam and helping to determine ways in which the patient can be given "control" when possible during the exam, such as reducing the number of people in the exam room or requesting that a certain provider perform the exam (Tishelman et al., 2017). Reducing the number of people in the exam room may be particularly important as it would not be implausible for extraneous medical trainees to be in attendance to gain experience with a relatively uncommon diagnosis.

Mental health clinicians can help to lessen the impact of stigma associated with DSD by helping parents learn how to discuss the diagnosis with their support system, as well as their child. Although it is understandable that many parents may be unsure or uncomfortable about beginning this discussion with their child due to a fear of causing distress, clinically, it is recommended that the child is provided with developmentally appropriate information as they grow, rather than waiting to defer these discussions until they are an adult (Tishelman et al., 2017). To help teach parents to discuss the diagnosis, clinicians should be mindful of avoiding language that may be stigmatizing, such as "hermaphrodite," and using gender-neutral language whenever possible as part of modeling appropriate communication for the parents. Refer to Figure 7.2 in the "Reproducible Resources" section for a handout with guidelines about using LGBTQ-inclusive language (The Safe Project Zone, 2019).

Clinical Vignette: Adam's Journey

Abigail is a 12-year-old Caucasian female who was referred by her pediatrician for body image concerns and disordered eating. She presents as a slightly underweight, adolescent dressed in baggy athletic clothes. In speaking with Abigail's parents, they disclose that their daughter began losing weight 6 months ago when she began to restrict her caloric intake, and they express concern that she has an eating disorder. Around this same time frame, her parents indicated that she also made significant changes to her physical appearance via cutting her hair very short and dressing in baggy athletic clothes.

When queried about these changes in a one-on-one setting, Abigail stated, "I don't want to look like a girl. I'm not a girl – not really." Further questioning revealed that Abigail started her menstrual cycle 6 months ago, which she identified was traumatic for her. She reported that she had decided to lose weight to try to prevent the development of breasts. She denied actually liking the other changes in her body that had resulted from the weight loss, as she stated that she now had "chicken legs" and was not performing well in sports as a result of her decreased energy and strength. Abigail denied that her parents were aware of her distress over these pubertal changes, nor were they aware that she identified as male. She noted that several of her friends knew and were calling her "Adam" as requested. Abigail reported that she preferred the name "Adam" and the use of the pronouns "he" and "him."

Adam expressed anxiety about discussing his gender identity with his parents but gives permission for you to discuss this with his parents. As such, you meet separately with his parents and disclose Adam's gender identity to them in private. Additionally, you reframe their concern about his disordered eating in context of his pubertal concerns. Adam's parents become tearful at the news but do not appear overly shocked by this disclosure. You spend time with them grieving their perceived loss of a daughter while encouraging them to welcome their son.

Following this discussion, you reunite the family to help them process together their reactions to this disclosure. Adam's dad openly acknowledges that he is not ready to use the name "Adam" in public, but, like his mother, he reassures his son that he loves him. The following sessions focus on helping the family continue communicate about these changes and Adam's decision to continue to socially transition. You also provide resources about a local medical center with specialists who are trained in working with transgender youth.

7.4 Youth in the Juvenile Justice System

A significant number of children and adolescents who are involved in the juvenile justice system have mental health needs that are not being met. Mental health treatment has long been assessed as being inadequate in the juvenile justice system due to a lack of staff training, resources, and other systemic factors. This is particularly concerning given that approximately 50–75% of juvenile offenders meet criteria for a mental health disorder (Underwood & Washington, 2016).

Youth who have been adjudicated or otherwise engaged in some aspect of the juvenile justice system exhibit high prevalence rates of the following psychiatric diagnoses: attention-deficit/hyperactivity disorder, major depressive disorder, bipolar disorder, and disruptive behavior disorders (e.g., conduct disorder). Current research supports systemic treatments such as functional family therapy, multidimensional treatment foster care, and multisystemic therapy (Underwood & Washington, 2016). All of these psychological interventions emphasize the importance of collaborating with the family and community to support mental health and reduce delinquency-related behaviors, rather than just treating the patient as an isolated person without regard for whatever support systems they may already have in place.

This recommendation to incorporate family members extends beyond what may be traditionally considered as family (e.g., nuclear family members) and extends to other members not typically included in treatment, such as extended family members (e.g., grandparents, aunts, uncles) or close members of the community (e.g., neighbors, family friends, and religious leaders). Different from what many clinicians may consider typical therapeutic practice, it is recommended to "treat the whole family" with services such as crisis outreach, home-based services, and respite care, in a manner that highlights the strengths in each family and their culture (MacKinnon-Lewis et al., 2001).

The manner in which the juvenile justice system intersects with the mental health system is complex and will be different for each patient. For some patients, they may be given the option of a placement in the mental health system rather than probation or incarceration. Unfortunately, this option appears to be significantly impacted by specific factors that are not indicative of equal opportunity of placement for all patients, such as Caucasian ethnicity, female gender, younger age, and low incidence of prior offenses (Herz, 2001). Statistically, an African American male patient has the least likelihood of being granted a placement in the mental health system in comparison to patients of other ethnicities and gender. This discrepancy has been and continues to remain a strong cause for advocacy due to the disproportionate number of ethnic minority youths impacted by the juvenile justice system and concerns about equitable access to quality mental health care.

In detention settings, youth may be held for a finite period of time during the preadjudication phase due to the serious nature of the alleged crime, concerns that the youth will not attend mandated court appearances, and other concerns such as a parent's reported inability to control the youth's behavior (Desai et al., 2006). During this time, there is an opportunity for mental health services to reach at-risk youth. At a minimum, it is recommended during this transient time that a youth receive a mental health screening and assessment, case management, drug and alcohol treatment, cognitive behavioral therapy, and medication management. The modality of cognitive behavioral therapy appears to be a good fit for this setting given that it tends to be directive and time-limited in approach (Desai et al., 2006).

Once a youth has been released from incarceration, they are entering a pivotal period in their life, as reentry after a youth has been incarcerated is a very difficult process that appears critical in setting the course for the rest of the youth's life. Specifically, youth exhibit much better outcomes regarding recidivism if they are working or enrolled in school shortly (i.e., within approximately 6 months) after release from incarceration (Clark & Unruh, 2010). Mental health and substance abuse treatment appear to be essential for an effective transition from incarceration and should be part of an individualized transition plan to help with reentry. Similar to the recommended use of cognitive behavioral therapy in detention settings, researchers recommend that cognitive behavioral therapy should be continued following reentry to help with the transfer of skills (e.g., self-regulation skills, decision-making skills, and social skill training) to "real world" settings (Clark & Unruh, 2010).

When working with youth who have been engaged in some capacity with the juvenile justice system, clinicians should be mindful that these patients tend to have higher rates of having experienced adverse childhood experiences (ACE), which are typically experiences of child maltreatment (e.g., physical abuse or neglect) and traumatic childhood events (e.g., incarceration of a parent) (Wolff et al., 2017). Of note, higher ACE scores are associated with higher rates of incarceration and involvement in violence, so it stands to reason that "treating the trauma" is an important part of clinical care of at-risk youths.

For this reason, trauma-focused cognitive behavioral therapy (TF-CBT) has been utilized with many youths (Cohen et al., 2016). This evidence-based intervention has been shown to be effective not only with youths who have experienced trauma and exhibit conduct problems, but also with youth who have experienced different types of trauma and may be residing in different types of treatment settings, including residential treatment settings. TF-CBT appears to help with symptoms of posttraumatic stress disorder as well as behavior problems, with sessions primarily focusing on skills such as relaxation skills, trauma narration with subsequent processing, and joint youth–parent sessions (Cohen et al., 2016).

Clinical Vignette: An Adjudicated Alliance

Jeremiah is a 15-year-old African American male who was referred for court-mandated psycho-therapy following his release 2 weeks ago from a juvenile detention center after a burglary conviction. Jeremiah has had multiple "run-ins" with the juvenile justice system, and his maternal grandmother expresses fear that he will continue on this same path of behavior despite her best efforts. During the intake session, you screen Jeremiah for a history of trauma, and he and his grandmother note that he has experienced multiple adverse childhood experiences (ACE), including neglect from his biological mother (which led to his grandmother becoming his legal guardian at age 8) and the incarceration of his biological father.

During subsequent psychotherapy sessions, you provide psychoeducation to Jeremiah and his grandmother about the importance of working collaboratively as a team with his probation officer and local school district to help create an individualized transition plan. As part of this transition plan, it is mutually agreed that you will collaborate with the school to enroll Jeremiah in school as soon as possible, as you are mindful of the impact of early engagement in work or school on recidivism rates.

As you assist with this collaboration, you also focus on discussing Jeremiah's perception of psychotherapy, particularly when it is court-mandated, as well as processing his views about working with a female and Caucasian mental health provider. In response to his observation, "You can't really understand what my life is like because you're white," you reply, "You make a good point. I do not have your lived experience and can't fully understand everything. As we work together, can I rely on you to help point out when you think I have misunderstood something or don't understand the full context due to these differences?" A wide-eyed Jeremiah pauses before responding softly, "I guess . . . we can try."

Each week, Jeremiah and his grandmother continue to arrive promptly for psychotherapy. As the therapeutic alliance is established, treatment segues from aspects of case management and psychoeducation to following a formal TF-CBT protocol. As promised, Jeremiah helps clarify when he believes that you have missed an important cultural aspect regarding his current lifestyle and behavior. As therapy continues, Jeremiah's approach to psychotherapy changes and he becomes active in performing the assigned between-session homework activities.

Summary

For many children and adolescents, aspects of their identity or systemic influences in their environment influence their access to and utilization of mental health care in the United States. In rural settings, children and adolescents tend to exhibit greater health disparities, such as higher prevalence rates of obesity and substance use. These health disparities are further highlighted by the acknowledged difficulty with access to mental health specialists due to a shortage of mental health providers as well as potentially increased stigma around mental health in rural areas.

To work productively with children and adolescents in rural areas, mental health clinicians have to become knowledgeable about the local culture of their patients and be creative in overcoming barriers inherent with working in less populated settings. For example, mental health clinicians may be more likely to have to contend with the ethical dilemmas of dual relationships in small communities, as well as dilemmas regarding scope of practice given that there may be fewer specialists to whom to refer patients. Given the risk of increased stigma about mental health in rural communities, mental health providers may also find it advantageous to utilize alternative treatment-delivery models (e.g., tele-psychology or co-location within a primary care clinic).

Similar to children and adolescents in rural populations, pediatric patients from ethnic minorities groups are at increased risk for significant health disparities. Despite the United States becoming increasing more ethnically diverse over time, the field of psychology is still behind in ensuring that the research literature is representative of current population demographics. Currently, most assessment and treatment protocols have been normed on Caucasian populations, which adds to the probability of response bias in the assessment of ethnic minority children and concern that treatment interventions may not be equally effective for all patients.

While some researchers and clinicians have attempted to add culturally responsive elements to evidence-based protocols for treating ethnic minority youth, it is still unclear whether this cultural adaptation is associated with more positive treatment outcomes. What we do know is that given higher incidences of communication problems with clinicians and other concerns, clinicians should make cultural competence an ongoing professional priority and should prioritize having ongoing positive dialogues about ethnicity and race with their patients as part of the therapeutic process.

Another special population of children and adolescents that clinicians can be instrumental in helping are pediatric patients who identify as a sexual or gender minority. Continuing stigma and ignorance in the United States regarding sexuality and gender orientation, particularly in young patients, can cause many ethical dilemmas and concerns in the clinical setting. Regardless of whether a patient identifies as lesbian, bisexual, gay, transgender, intersex, or another identity, recommended clinical practices emphasize that the acceptance of their sexual or gender orientation is a process that is best fostered by affirmation and family support. This family support is associated with a decreased risk for depressive symptoms, and overall social support appears to be key in helping adolescents quit smoking.

As a mental health clinician, it is important to help patients explore their sexual and gender identity by affirming and supporting the youth during this process. For families with a patient who identifies as transgender, or as a gender other than that assigned at birth, these discussions are important to help patients explore gender identity and gender transitioning. Education is an important part of clinical work particularly when families are scared and unsure of how to proceed when their loved one identifies as a different gender than that assigned at birth or when learning about a diagnosis of DSD and being confused about how to discuss this with their support system.

Lastly, another special population that is radically in need of increased access to quality mental health treatment are children and adolescents who are engaged in some capacity with the juvenile justice system. Recent estimates suggest that approximately 50–75% of juvenile offenders meet criteria for a mental health disorder and that a disproportionate number of ethnic minority youths are impacted by the juvenile justice system. Research indicates that preferred clinical interventions consist of systemic treatments that concentrate on collaborating with the family and community to support mental health and to reduce delinquency-related behaviors.

For youth who are reengaging with society after incarceration, an individualized transition plan that emphasizes mental health and/or substance abuse treatment as well as prompt engagement in academic or occupational settings is ideal. It is also recommended that cognitive behavioral therapy should be continued following reentry to help with the transfer of skills. Given that youth who have been engaged in the juvenile justice system tend to exhibit higher rates of having experienced adverse childhood experiences, trauma-focused cognitive behavioral therapy is an evidence-based treatment that should be considered following appropriate screening for suitability.

References

Alegria, M., Vallas, M., & Pumariega, A. (2010). Racial and ethnic disparities in pediatric mental health. *Child and Adolescent Psychiatric Clinics of North America, 19*(4), 759–774.

Burns, B., Angold, A., Magruder-Habib, K., Costello, E., & Patrick, M. (2008). The CASA. Retrieved March 6, 2019, from http://devepi.duhs.duke.edu/casa.html.

Cardemil, E. & Battle, C. (2003). Guess who's coming to therapy: getting comfortable with conversations about race and ethnicity in psychotherapy. *Professional Psychology: Research and Practice, 34*(3), 278–286.

Clark, H. & Unruh, D. (2010). Transition practices for adjudicated youth with E/BDs and related disability. *Behavioral Disorders, 36*(1), 43–51.

Cohen, J., Mannarino, A., Jankowski, K., Rosenberg, S., Kodya, S., & Wolford, G. II (2016). A randomized intervention study of trauma-focused cognitive behavioral therapy for adjudicated teens in residential treatment facilities. *Child Maltreatment, 21*(2), 156–157.

Davis, A., James, R., Curtis, M., Felts, S., & Daley, C. (2012). Pediatric obesity attitudes, services, and information among rural parents: a qualitative study. *Obesity, 16*(9), 2133–2140.

Desai, R., Goulet, J., Robbins, J., Chapman, J., Migdole, S., & Hoge, M. (2006). Mental health care in juvenile detention facilities: a review. *Journal of the American Academy of Psychiatry and the Law, 34*(2), 204–214.

Gray, J., & Winterowd, C. (2002). Health risks in American Indian adolescents: a descriptive study of a rural, non-reservation sample. *Journal of Pediatric Psychology, 27*(8), 717–725.

Hadland, S., Yehia, B., & Makadon, H. (2016). Caring for LGBTQ youth in inclusive and affirmative environments. *Pediatric Clinics of North America, 63*(6), 955–969.

Hanson, N., Pepitone-Arreola-Rockwell, F., & Greene, A. (2000). Multicultural competence: criteria and case examples. *Professional Psychology: Research and Practice, 31*(6), 652–660.

Herz, D. (2001). Understanding the use of mental health placements by the juvenile justice system. *Journal of Emotional and Behavioral Disorders, 9*(3) 172–181.

Huey, S. & Polo, A. (2010). Assessing the effects of evidence-based psychotherapies with ethnic minority youths. In J. R. Weisz & A. E. Kazdin (eds.), *Evidence-Based Psychotherapies for Children and Adolescents* (pp. 451–465). New York: Guilford Press.

Intersex Society of North America. (2006). Clinical Guidelines for the Management of Disorders of Sex Development in Childhood. Retrieved March 19, 2019, from www.dsdguidelines.org/files/clinical.pdf.

Janicke, D. & Davis, H. (2011). Introduction to the Special Section: Rural Health Issues in Pediatric Psychology. *Journal of Pediatric Psychology, 36*(6), 647–651.

MacKinnon-Lewis, C., Kaufman, M., & Frabutt, J. (2001). Juvenile justice and mental health: youth and family in the middle. *Aggressive and Violent Behavior, 7*, 353–363.

Marsella, A., Kaplan, A., & Suarez, E. (2000). Cultural considerations for understanding, assessing and treating depressive experience and disorder. In M. A. Reinecke & M. R. Davison (eds.), *Comparative Treatments of Depression*. New York: Springer.

McNeil, C., Capage, L., & Bennett, G. (2002). Cultural issues in the treatment of young African American children diagnosed with disruptive behavior disorders. *Journal of Pediatric Psychology, 27*(4), 339–350.

McQuaid, E. (2008). Introduction to Special Issue: *Journal of Pediatric Psychology* Statement of Purpose – Special Section on Diversity and Health Care Disparities. *Journal of Pediatric Psychology, 33*(1), 22–25.

Multicultural Mental Health. (2013). Cultural Competence Self Evaluation.

Retrieved March 11, 2019, from www.multiculturalmentalhealth.ca/training/self-assessment/.

National Center for Mental Health and Juvenile Justice. (2019). Retrieved March, 21, 2019, from www.ncmhjj.com/.

National Institute on Minority Health and Health Disparities & Director's Office. (October 6, 2016). Director's Message. Sexual and Gender Minorities Formally Designated as a Health Disparity Population for Research Purposes. Retrieved from www.nimhd.nih.gov/about/directors-corner/message.html.

Olson, J., Forbes, C., & Belzer, M. (2011). Management of the transgender adolescent. *Archives of Pediatric and Adolescent Medicine, 165*(2), 171–176.

Owens, J., Richerson, L., Murphy, C., Jageleweski, A., & Rossi, L. (2007). The parent perspective: informing the cultural sensitivity of parenting programs in rural communities. *Child Youth Care Forum, 36,* 179–194.

Polaha, J., Dalton, W., & Allen, S. (2011). The prevalence of emotional and behavior problems in pediatric primary care serving rural children. *Journal of Pediatric Psychology, 36*(6) 652–660.

Rosario, M., Schrimshaw, E., & Hunter, J. (2010). Cigarette smoking as a coping strategy: negative implications for subsequent psychological distress among lesbian, gay, and bisexual youth. *Journal of Pediatric Psychology, 36*(7), 731–742.

Rural Behavioral Health for Children, Youth, and Families. (n.d.). Retrieved March 6, 2019, from https://ruralbehavioralhealth.org/.

The Safe Project Zone. (2019). LGBTQ-Inclusive Language Dos and Don'ts. Retrieved April 3, 2019, from https://ayr1as72agcddsn3cyd41uu9-wpengine.netdna-ssl.com/wp-content/uploads/2018/09/LGBTQ-Inclusive-Dos-Donts.pdf.

Sandberg, D., Pasterski, V., & Callens, N. (2017). Introduction to the Special Issue: Disorders of Sex Development. *Journal of Pediatric Psychology, 42*(5), 487–495.

Simons, L., Schrager, S., Clark, L., Belzer, M., & Olson, J. (2013). Parental support and mental health among transgender adolescents. *Journal of Adolescent Health, 53*(6), 1–7.

Smalley, K., Yancey, C., Warren, J., Naufel, K., Ryan, R., & Pugh, J. (2010). Rural mental health and psychological treatment: a review for practitioners. *Journal of Clinical Psychology: In Session, 66*(5), 479–489.

Smith, J. (2016, March 12). Supporting Gender and Sexual Minority Adolescents. Invited presentation, Children's Hospital of WI Best Practice in Pediatrics Conference.

Society of Pediatric Psychology. (2016). Differences of Sex Development Special Interest Group. Retrieved March 3, 2019, from https://societyofpediatricpsychology.org/node/732.

Tishelman, A., Shumer, D., & Nahata, L. (2017). Disorders of sex development: pediatric psychology and the genital exam. *Journal of Pediatric Psychology, 42*(5), 530–543.

TransYouth Family Allies. (2017). Who Are TransYouth Family Allies? Retrieved March 7, 2019, from www.imatyfa.org/index.html.

The Trevor Project. (2019). Trevor Support Center. Retrieved March 7, 2019, from www.thetrevorproject.org/resources/trevor-support-center/#sm.0001356anf305fqnrby272mllzlwk.

Underwood, L. & Washington, A. (2016). Mental health and juvenile offenders. *International Journal of Environmental Research and Public Health, 13*(2), 228–242.

US Department of Justice. (2004). Screening and Assessing Mental Health and Substance Use Disorders among Youth in the Juvenile Justice System. Retrieved March 22, 2019, from https://files.eric.ed.gov/fulltext/ED484681.pdf.

Valenzuela, J. & Smith, L. (2016). Topical review: provider–patient interactions: an important consideration for racial/ethnic health disparities in youth. *Journal of Pediatric Psychology, 41*(4), 473–480.

Wolff, K., Baglivio, M., & Piquero, A. (2017). The relationship between adverse childhood experiences and recidivism in a sample of juvenile offenders in community-based treatment. *International Journal of Offender Therapy and Comparative Criminology, 61*(11), 1210–1242.

Yamada, A., Marsella, A., & Atuel, H. (2002). Deveopment of a cultural adaptation battery for Asian and Pacific Islanders in Hawai'i. *Asian Psychologist, 3,* 11–20.

Yamada, A., Marsalla, A., & Yamada, S. (1998). The development of the Ethnocultural Identity Behavior Index: psychometric properties and validation with Asian American and Pacific Islanders. *Asian American and Pacific Islander Journal of Health, 6,* 35–45.

Reproducible Resources

CULTURAL COMPETENCE SELF-EVALUATION FORM (CCSE)

Please Select Your Client's Ethnocultural Group: _____
(Then rate yourself on the following items of this scale to determine your "competence")

VERY TRUE OF ME 4	TRUE OF ME 3	SOMEWHAT TRUE OF ME 2	NOT TRUE OF ME 1	UNSURE ABOUT ME U

1. _____ Knowledge of group's history

2. _____ Knowledge of group's family structures, gender roles, dynamics

3. _____ Knowledge of group's response to illness (i.e., awareness, biases)

4. _____ Knowledge of help-seeking behavior patterns of group

5. _____ Ability to evaluate your view and group view of illness

6. _____ Ability to feel empathy and understanding toward group

7. _____ Ability to develop a culturally responsive treatment program

8. _____ Ability to understand group's compliance with treatment

9. _____ Ability to develop culturally responsive prevention program for group

10. _____ Knowledge of group's "culture-specific" disorders

11. _____ Knowledge of group's explanatory models of illness

12. _____ Knowledge of group's indigenous healing methods and traditions

13. _____ Knowledge of group's indigenous healers and their contact ease

14. _____ Knowledge of communication patterns and styles (e.g., non-verbal)

15. _____ Knowledge of group's language

16. _____ Knowledge of group's ethnic identification and acculturation situation

17. _____ Knowledge of how one's own health practices are rooted in culture

18. _____ Knowledge of impact of group's religious beliefs on health and illness

19. _____ Desire to learn group's culture

20. _____ Desire to travel to group's national location, neighborhood

TOTAL SCORE: _____ 80-65 = Competent; 65-40 = Near Competent; 40 Below = Incompetent

TOTAL # of U's: _____ (If this number is above 8, more self-reflection is need)

Your Age: _____ Your Gender: _____ Your Religion: _____ Your Ethnicity _____

Figure 7.1 Cultural Competence Self-Evaluation Form. Copyright: 2009 AJM, Atlanta, Georgia. Based on Hanson et al., 2000; Marsella et al., 2000; Yamada et al., 1998; 2002.

LGBTQ-INCLUSIVE LANGUAGE DOs and DON'Ts

AVOID SAYING...	SAY INSTEAD...	WHY?	EXAMPLE
"Hermaphrodite"	"Intersex"	Hermaphrodite is a stigmatizing, inaccurate word with a negative medical history.	"What are the best practices for the medical care of intersex infants?"
"Homosexual"	"Gay"	"Homosexual" often connotes a medical diagnosis, or a discomfort with gay/lesbian people.	"We want to do a better job of being inclusive of our gay employees."
"Born female" or "Born male"	"Assigned female/male at birth"	"Assigned" language accurately depicts the situation of what happens at birth	"Max was assigned female at birth, then he transitioned in high school."
"Female-bodied" or "Male-bodied"		"-bodied" language is often interpreted as as pressure to medically transition, or invalidation of one's gender identity	
"A gay" or "a transgender"	"A gay/transgender person"	Gay and transgender are adjectives that describe a person/group	"We had a transgender athlete in our league this year. "
"Transgender people and normal people"	"Transgender people and cisgender people"	Saying "normal" implies "abnormal," which is a stigmatizing way to refer to a person.	"This group is open to both transgender and cisgender people."
"Both genders" or "Opposite sexes"	"All genders"	"Both" implies there are only two; "Opposite" reinforces antagonism amongst genders	"Video games aren't just a boy thing -- kids of all genders play them."
"Ladies and gentlemen"	"Everyone," "Folks," "Honored guests," etc	Moving away from binary language is more inclusive of people of all genders	"Good morning everyone, next stop Picadilly Station."
"Mailman," "fireman," "policeman," etc.	"Mail clerk," "Firefighter," "Police officer," etc.	People of all genders do these jobs	"I actually saw a firefighter rescue a cat from a tree."
"It" when referring to someone (e.g., when pronouns are unknown)	"They"	"It" is for referring to things, not people.	"You know, I am not sure how they identify."

Figure 7.2 LGBTQ-Inclusive Language Dos and Don'ts. Reprinted from The Safe Project Zone. (2019). Retrieved April 3, 2019, from https://ayr1as72agcddsn3cyd41uu9-wpengine.netdna-ssl.com/wp-content/uploads/2018/09/LGBTQ-Inclusive-Dos-Donts.pdf

Recommended Websites, Book, and Other Resources
Rural Populations
Recommended Website
Rural Behavioral Health for Children, Youth, and Families, https://ruralbehavioralhealth.org/

Recommended Textbook
Stamm, B. (ed.). (2003). *Rural Behavioral Health Care: An Interdisciplinary Guide*. Washington, DC: American Psychological Association.

Recommended Assessment to Determine Barriers to Mental Health Care Child and Adolescent Services Assessment (CASA), http://devepi.duhs.duke.edu/casa.html

Ethnic Minority Populations
Professional Resources
Graves, S. Jr. & Blake, J. (eds.). (2016). *Psychoeducational Assessment and Intervention for Ethnic Minority Children: Evidence-Based Approaches*. Washington, DC: American Psychological Association.

Division 45 of the American Psychological Association
Society for the Psychological Study of Culture, Ethnicity, and Race, http://division45.org/

Sexual and Gender Minorities
Professional Group
Society of Pediatric Psychology, Differences of Sex Development Special Interest Group, https://societyofpediatricpsychology.org/node/732

Family Resources for Transgender Youth, www.imatyfa.org/index.html

Resource for LGBTQ Youth and Families: Trevor Support Center, www.thetrevorproject.org/resources/trevor-support-center/#sm.0001356anf305fqnrby272mllzlwk

Youth in the Juvenile Justice System
Clinician/Advocacy Resources
National Center for Mental Health and Juvenile Justice, www.ncmhjj.com/

Clinician Resources
Assessment Screening and Assessing Mental Health and Substance Use Disorders among Youth in the Juvenile Justice System, https://files.eric.ed.gov/fulltext/ED484681.pdf

Technological Applications and Pediatric Psychological Care

8.1 Technological Applications and Mental Health

Telemental health is "an intentionally broad term referring to the provision of mental health care from a distance" (American Telemedicine Association, 2013, p. 7). Telehealth includes different modalities and can assist with different facets of psychological services, including assessment, treatment, and education (American Telemedicine Association, 2013).

The field of psychology has historically worked with the field of technology to help reach underserved populations, to assist with improved communication between providers and patients, and to increase the efficiency of clinical services (Van Allen & Roberts, 2011). Additionally, the utilization of technological advances has been an area of study to help with increased overall access to mental health providers, as the need for children and adolescent clinicians is greater than the current supply of clinicians (American Telemedicine Association, 2017b).

In particular, pediatric psychology may be an area that could derive unique benefits from telehealth given that younger age groups tend to have greater comfort and familiarity with technology (Bennett et al., 2008). Moreover, technology can allow for providers with pediatric psychology training to reach children and adolescents who may not be geographically located near them. This is noteworthy given that "general-trained providers are particularly under-equipped to address child conditions showing relatively low base rates and/or conditions requiring more complex treatment regiments" (American Telemedicine Association, 2017b, p. 4).

Recent research has found that telehealth applications are relatively practical to implement in diverse areas of pediatric psychology, such as pediatric sleep, pediatric feeding disorders, and support for families of children with cancer (Bensink et al., 2008; Clawson et al., 2008; Witmans et al., 2008). In addition to the empirical evidence of the effectiveness of telehealth in psychological work with children and adolescents experiencing medical concerns, research suggests that telehealth has been well accepted by families and can reduce costs for families (Bensink et al., 2008; Clawson et al., 2008). These are not localized results specific to certain diseases as this reduction in the rates of acute services has been observed in other studies. For example, the overall utilization of urgent and emergency care was reduced by 77% when children and adolescents with diabetes played a video game at home that was focused on health education and disease management in comparison to patients who brought home a video game that was solely for entertainment (Brown et al., 1997).

In association with the benefits attributed to the use of telehealth with children and adolescents, telehealth and telemental health applications have also been established in the research literature as having unique advantages across different age groups, presenting concerns, and settings (Brignell et al., 2007; Nelson & Bui, 2010). A meta-analysis of 27 studies utilizing videoconferencing for adults with medical and/or mental health concerns found that videoconferencing decreased hospital days, decreased costs, and increased overall quality of life for caregivers (Mallow et al., 2016).

8.2 Utilization of Telehealth for Medical and Psychological Concerns

Telehealth has been utilized in various capacities across many different dimensions of patient care. Regarding overall telemental health practice, some centers like the University of Kansas Medical Center provide teleconsultation, individual psychotherapy, and multidisciplinary care for depression and obesity (Van Allen et al., 2011). In the field of pediatric psychology, telehealth and other technological interventions have focused on providing clinical assessment, behavioral interventions, management of medical conditions, and the promotion of health practices (Ritterband et al., 2003; Bradley et al., 2006; Cotterez et al., 2014).

There are various methods of assessment for pediatric interventions, including the use of web-based tools to help assess barriers to adherence for the daily oral use of hydroxyurea as part of the treatment for sickle cell disease (Crosby et al., 2012). In particular, diabetes care has been positively impacted by the use of assessment via web-based monitoring in which patients send information related to their current blood glucose levels allows physicians to have the real-time data needed to make adjustments to medications (Cotterez et al., 2014). Given the regular fluctuations inherent in diabetes mellitus, this real-time data is a vast improvement compared to relying on a patient's self-report or recall of diabetes-related information.

In addition to assessment, telehealth has also been used to help with overall medical management and behavioral training for common pediatric concerns such as encopresis. In particular, enhanced toilet training for encopresis is an evidence-based intervention for encopresis; however, medical or mental health providers typically do not have both the medical management and the behavioral intervention training that is necessary to provide comprehensive care for this condition (Ritterband et al., 2003). Moreover, many families may not seek in-person treatment due to the possible feelings of embarrassment associated with having to seek treatment for this type of condition. Use of online training modules was found to be a promising intervention in that there was a significant improvement in the number of accidents, declining from one accident per day to one accident every 2 weeks in the intervention group, in contrast to the control group where participants continued to have more than one accident per day (Ritterband et al., 2003).

Telehealth has also been linked with other targets of intervention in pediatric psychology, such as helping patients become engaged in health promotion activities (O'Donovan et al., 2014). Consistent engagement in physical activity, which has been associated with numerous improvements in physical health, mental health, and improved body image, is a notoriously difficult intervention to implement (Bradley et al., 2006). Like all behavioral changes in lifestyle, it can be particularly difficult for children and adolescents to consistently change their behavior, in contrast to relatively easier aspects of treatment regimens, such as taking a daily prescribed medication.

To assist with encouraging pediatric patients to exercise, it may be advantageous to think "outside the box" of typical activities, such as running, walking, or biking. Instead of viewing the growing pervasiveness of technology in all areas of life as a deterrent or barrier to increased physical activity, it may be helpful to include technology in planned exercise to improve adherence. Active video games, such as the Wii Fit Free Jogging, help provide moderate-intensity aerobic exercise, which may be more amenable to children and adolescents (O'Donovan et al., 2014).

Additionally, active video games provide an option for physical activity when other typical exercise options are unavailable due to factors such as an in-patient hospitalization (O'Donovan et al., 2014). For example, children and adolescents with cystic fibrosis are typically unable to leave the hospital room or unit due to infection control concerns; thus, active video games can help promote physical activity despite hospital room constraints. For other children and adolescents who are not hospitalized, active video games may still be beneficial as these children may not be able to regularly "go outside and play" for numerous reasons, including but not limited to unsafe neighborhoods, inclement weather, or a lack of transportation to available recreational areas. As such, active video games can help to mitigate some of these common barriers for physical activity.

Video games and virtual reality games have also been found be effective in helping pediatric patients cope with procedural pain (Gold et al., 2006). Virtual reality during intravenous (IV) line placement has been found to significantly reduce perceived pain by children, as children without the distraction of virtual reality reported a four-fold increase in pain in comparison to children who used virtual reality during IV line placement. Of importance, this intervention appeared to be well tolerated by patients and was perceived by patients as being satisfactory for pain management. This association between decreased pain and the use of technological games has been hypothesized as occurring due to the patient's engagement in virtual reality providing distraction as the "subjective experience of pain requires a person to attend to and process painful sensory inputs" (Gold et al., 2006, p. 208). In plain language, when a child's attention is diverted by something pleasurable and engaging such as a video game or virtual reality game, they are not attending to and thus processing the pain as directly as they might if their attention was not otherwise engaged.

Furthermore, video games have demonstrated some efficacy in improving children's self-concept, increasing health promotion, and increasing treatment adherence. Lieberman's research has shown that a patient's self-concept is strengthened after experiencing success in a video game (Lieberman, 1997). Children and adolescents are thought to actually undergo experiential learning while playing video games when character is asked to perform health-related behaviors and the patient subsequently sees the success of the video game character when it performs self-care behaviors (Lieberman, 2001). Of note, this research also indicates that patients may experience increased self-efficacy when they are able to "practice" asthma-related self-management skills in comparison to patients who had learned about self-management skills from a video rather than by "practicing" in a video game.

This hypothesis is borne out by research that indicates that a video game intervention (i.e., Re-Mission™) focused on behavior change and treatment adherence was more effective in combination with therapy than therapy alone (Kato et al., 2008). From this research, it was surmised that the knowledge gained via playing the video game in addition to psychotherapy had increased patient self-efficacy and thus resulted in the improved treatment adherence that was observed. Lepper and Gurtner (1989) also posit that children may experience increased knowledge acquisition about specific diseases and treatments as the interactive media associated with video games and other technological activities will motivate children who might typically be unmotivated to learn about this medical information in the more traditional manner.

In addition to video games, smartphone applications are another way in which technology can be utilized adjunctive to mental health interventions. Smartphone applications have been utilized in healthcare and can be used in a variety of ways in mental health treatment. Some applications can help with the coaching of therapeutic skills, provide feedback with physiological variables during relaxation training, and have other features such as the Global Positioning System (GPS) for help during exposure interventions (Luxton et al., 2011). It may be helpful when assigning between session homework to utilize a smartphone application to log completion of skills training, as adolescents in particular may find it more convenient and conducive to privacy to be able to use their smartphone rather than using traditional paper and pen logbooks to record their assignments. Similarly, some smartphone applications can help patients manage their treatment regimens by sending alerts to patients when it is time to take medications or order refills from pharmacies. For a list of phone applications specific to pediatric psychology, refer to the "Reproducible Resources" section at the end of this chapter.

Overall, research supports the effectiveness of using eHealth interventions to help produce or promote behavior change when behavioral principles, such as stimulus control and goal-setting, are used in addition to educational interventions (Cushing & Steele, 2010). Helping patients to create and maintain behavioral change is difficult for the best of clinicians, particularly when patients may not be seen as regularly as desired in clinic. eHealth interventions appear to be a novel way that can help clinicians and pediatric patients achieve this difficult goal, particularly given the younger generation's increased familiarity with technology in comparison to previous generations.

8.3 Telepsychotherapy

Telepsychotherapy has become a burgeoning field of interest for many mental health providers. Telepsychology via videoconferencing and other internet-based applications has been previously used in interventions for psychological concerns associated with myriad health conditions, such as obesity, asthma, congenital heart disease, and epilepsy (Glueckauf et al., 2002; Stinson et al., 2009). Telepsychology has been shown to have unique advantages over face-to-face interventions, such as increased engagement in services and overall continuity of care, which is particularly salient for patients who live in rural areas and/or have limited transportation options (American Telemedicine Association, 2017a). A patient may desire mental health treatment and be motivated to be engaged, but, due to geographical or logistical barriers, are unable to receive the evidence-based treatment they desire and deserve. It is thought that telepsychotherapy can help provide greater access to mental health by allowing these types of patients to engage in mental health services that were previously unavailable to them by nature of their location.

In addition to the overall benefits of telepsychotherapy, telepsychotherapy via videoconferencing has been identified as being particularly helpful for pediatric psychology. Videoconferencing is thought to be helpful with "chronic or recurrent conditions that require multiple treatment sessions and patient work between sessions" (Hicks et al., 2005, p. 724). When considering the logistics involved in managing pediatric chronic illness, an effective means of having consistent psychotherapy appointments without placing additional burden on families regarding transportation and other factors may be a wonderful option for many families.

Despite the effectiveness of telehealth in pediatric psychological services, there are numerous pitfalls and ethical concerns that are present with the utilization of telehealth in clinical services. Common pitfalls identified in a survey of psychologists and their use of technology include unauthorized access to confidential information and concerns about privacy and social networking (Van Ellens & Roberts, 2011).

At this time, the field of psychology has in place aspirational guidelines rather than enforceable guidelines regarding the practice of telepsychotherapy. Specifically, the Guidelines for the Practice of Telepsychology were created by the Joint Task Force for the Development of Telepsychology Guidelines for Psychologists to assist psychologists in the "consideration of legal requirements, ethical standards, telecommunication technologies, intra-and interagency policies, and other external constraints, as well as the demands of the particular professional context" (2013, p. 791).

These aspirational guidelines focus on psychologists' professional competence with the applicable technology, as well as particulars specific to telehealth regarding professional standards of care when providing telepsychological services, obtaining informed consent with specific consideration for concerns associated with telepsychology, awareness of relevant laws and regulations associated with informed consent, appropriate efforts to maintain confidentiality and security of data and other information, appropriate disposal of data and technologies to prevent unauthorized access, awareness of concerns associated with assessment via telepsychology, and awareness of legislation regarding the practice of telepsychology across borders.

8.4 Implementing Telepsychological Services

Preparation is a key factor when determining when and how to actually implement telepsychological services. Given the complexity and ever-changing nature of technology, telehealth providers should have "necessary education, training/orientation, licensure, and ongoing continuing education/professional development" (American Telemedicine Association, 2014, p. 6). Prior to implementing telepsychological services, providers must be aware of not only the clinical requirements but also the ethical considerations and technical recommendations required to implement telepsychological services in their clinical practice.

For new providers, core operational guidelines by the American Telemedicine Association provide technical and clinical recommendations for the overall provision of telehealth services from provider to patient, as well as specific guidelines for different clinical populations and clinical settings (American Telemedicine Association, 2013, 2014, 2017a). In addition to telemedicine guidelines, it is imperative for clinicians to review ethical guidelines from their specific governing body.

In conjunction with these aspirational guidelines, it is mandatory that psychologists and other mental health clinicians wishing to initiate telepsychotherapy services review their state's licensing board regulations about this subject, as states vary regarding eligibility to practice and rules regarding competence in delivering services in this modality. Refer to the American Psychological Association's "Telepsychology – 50 State Review" (2013) listed in the "Recommended Websites, Books, and Other Resources" section at the end of this chapter for more information about specifics regarding telepsychology for each state.

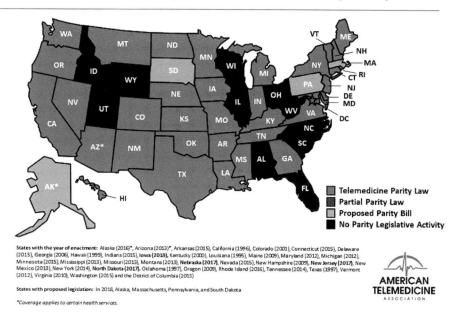

States with Parity Laws for Private Insurance Coverage of Telemedicine (2018)

Telemedicine Parity Law
Partial Parity Law
Proposed Parity Bill
No Parity Legislative Activity

States with the year of enactment: Alaska (2016)*, Arizona (2013)*, Arkansas (2015), California (1996), Colorado (2001), Connecticut (2015), Delaware (2015), Georgia (2006), Hawaii (1999), Indiana (2015), Iowa (2018), Kentucky (2000), Louisiana (1995), Maine (2009), Maryland (2012), Michigan (2012), Minnesota (2015), Mississippi (2013), Missouri (2013), Montana (2013), Nebraska (2017), Nevada (2015), New Hampshire (2009), New Jersey (2017), New Mexico (2013), New York (2014), North Dakota (2017), Oklahoma (1997), Oregon (2009), Rhode Island (2016), Tennessee (2014), Texas (1997), Vermont (2012), Virginia (2010), Washington (2015) and the District of Columbia (2013)

States with proposed legislation: In 2018, Alaska, Massachusetts, Pennsylvania, and South Dakota

*Coverage applies to certain health services.

AMERICAN
TELEMEDICINE
ASSOCIATION

Figure 8.1 States with Parity Laws for Private Insurance Coverage of Telemedicine (2018). Retrieved November 26, 2018, from www.americantelemed.org/policy-page/state-policy-resource-center. Copyright 2018 by the American Telemedicine Association

Specific to each state is the determination of whether private insurances must exhibit parity in reimbursing telehealth services at a rate equivalent to that of in-person services (see Figure 8.1). This mandate plays an enormous role in the sustainability of telepsychotherapy services, as this allows for the expectation of reimbursement from private insurance companies.

Prior to implementing telepsychotherapy services at a clinic, time for extensive preparation and deliberation should be dedicated to reviewing current guidelines and in creating standard operating procedures. As with any other medical intervention, it is important to be mindful of liability and risk management concerns associated with this modality. Standard operating procedures should include specific protocols to prevent or diminish concerns related to the telepsychotherapy modality, including but not limited to privacy and data security, informed consent and documentation standards, and emergency management plans.

Privacy and data security are two main concerns when deciding how to implement telepsychotherapy services. To help ensure that these areas of concern are prioritized, the American Telemedicine Association recommends, among other suggestions, that devices that are being used to participate in telepsychotherapy should have the ability to be remotely wiped if lost or stolen, that screens should have an inactivity timeout function, that security should be required for logging in to the device, and that encryption is point-to-point and meets standards for audio and video transmission security (American Telemedicine Association, 2013). These recommendations support the need to help maintain privacy and data security to the best of the clinician's and the current technology's ability.

Pursuant to traditional recommendations for informed consent, the informed consent for telepsychotherapy should also include a description of the differences between face-to-face and telehealth clinical services, billing, credentialing of telehealth provider, documentation for clinical encounters, and privacy and security risks (American Telemedicine Association, 2017a, p. 4). This additional information is important as many patients and families will be unfamiliar with the risks and benefits associated with telepsychotherapy, and they should be well educated so they can make an informed decision about available treatment options. For some families, the convenience of telepsychology might be more important for them compared with the risks, whereas other families might be more hesitant given the extra privacy and data security issues that may arise through the use of this technology.

Although mental health practitioners may not be well versed in technical specifications, it is important for basic technical guidelines to be adhered to in order to meet the minimum standard of care in implementing telepsychotherapy. Current specifications should be dependent on the videoconferencing application; however, basic recommendations include a minimum bandwidth of 384 Kbps or higher and a minimum resolution of 640 × 360 at 30 frames per second (American Telemedicine Association, 2013). Although these are minimum recommendations, it may be best for clinicians to "try out" different technologies and softwares in order to ensure that the technology allows for the standard of care or the session's equivalence in quality to face-to-face sessions to be met in delivering the intervention, as opposed to just relying on the technology meeting minimum standards.

While someone may be excited to implement telepsychotherapy for all of their patients due to the advantages associated with this modality, it is important to ensure that this is a "good fit" for each individual patient. The determination of fit for telepsychotherapy is particularly important when working with a patient in a clinically unsupervised setting, such as videoconferencing directly to the patient's home, as clinicians will have to have different methods for crisis intervention in comparison to standard practice in a face-to-face encounter. Each provider should be aware of the risks and benefits in utilizing telepsychotherapy with their specific patient population. For overall risk management purposes, it may be beneficial to have patients with the following factors engage in traditional face-to-face psychotherapy rather than telepsychotherapy: recent psychiatric hospitalizations, recent or current suicidal or homicidal ideation, current substance use, intellectual deficits, or language barriers. Overall, a clinician should utilize their own clinical judgment and expertise within their patient population, as well as consultation with other experienced professionals, in assessing likely candidates for telepsychotherapy.

In addition to these criteria, it is important that a patient has the aptitude and motivation to become comfortable using the selected technology. To meet the same standard of care as face-to-face psychotherapy, patients must be able to exhibit basic competence with the technology in order to prevent the quality of the session from being adversely impacted by technical confusion or concerns. For some patients, it may be helpful to have a "run through" with the technology in person to assure their competence in accessing the software for scheduled sessions, as well as having contact information if they have difficulty with the technology at a later date.

Particularly when working with patients in clinically unsupervised settings, it is good clinical practice to ensure that the patient has a "patient support person" who is available in case of an emergency (American Telemedicine Association, 2018). The patient support person should have previously agreed to an emergency management plan for how to respond in the event of a crisis, which clearly delineates their role and responsibilities, as well as providing direct contact information for local emergency services (Shore & Lu, 2015).

For more detailed information regarding standard operating procedures, informed consent, privacy and security recommendations, technical specifications, and other detailed information related to telepsychotherapy, refer to the "Recommended Websites, Books, and Other Resources" section for guidelines provided by the American Telemedicine Association, as well as a recommended book edited by Tuerk and Shore (2015) for more specific information related to clinical videoconferencing.

Clinical Vignette: Tommy the "Techie"

Dr. Reynolds recently began offering telepsychotherapy services to his patients within his private practice. This new offering has been well received by current patients and has led to several new referrals from the community due to word of mouth of this new offering. One of his patients, Tommy, is a 16-year-old male who was referred 2 months ago for difficulty emotionally adjusting to his new diagnosis of diabetes mellitus type 1 and for nonadherence to his treatment regimen. During the initial intake session, his mother indicates that she will have some difficulty attending sessions as often as clinically indicated due to the family sharing one car. Given this identified barrier, Dr. Reynolds indicates that telepsychotherapy via in-home videoconferencing may be an option instead of having the family travel to every appointment for a face-to-face session. Tommy immediately expresses interest in this modality by saying, "Cool! I can wear pajamas!" His mother laughs and indicates that Tommy loves being able to use technology whenever possible. She inquires for more information about telepsychotherapy as she has never heard the term before and is unaware of the logistics.

Dr. Reynolds provides brief psychoeducation about telepsychotherapy and reviews his current standard operating procedures, which necessitate the presence of an adult in the home at all times when telepsychotherapy is occurring. Given Tommy and his mother's continued interest, Dr. Reynolds conducts an assessment to determine suitability of fit, and due to the patient's low clinical risk and his family's apparent interest and support for this modality, Dr. Reynolds then reviews his telepsychotherapy informed consent form with both the patient and his mother. He is careful to explain both the benefits and risks inherent in telepsychotherapy and to ascertain that the mother will act as the patient support person in the event of an emergency. Further forms are reviewed and discussed, which provide detailed information about his emergency support plan should Tommy ever appear to be in crisis during telepsychotherapy.

Following the review of standard operating procedures and informed consent, Dr. Reynolds reviews the technology that will be utilized for videoconferencing, and indicates that he has signed a business associate agreement with the videoconferencing company in compliance with recommended guidelines for privacy and data security. Dr. Reynolds provides Tommy and his mother with a handout with "how to" instructions that detail how to log on to the videoconferencing platform should they forget the steps from this appointment, as well as contact information should they experience any technical difficulties. Prior to the first initial telepsychotherapy *session, Dr. Reynolds and Tommy schedule a "run through" to ensure Tommy's familiarity and comfort with the technology.*

During the first telepsychotherapy session, Tommy is asked to hold up his driver's license to help verify his identity. Then, Dr. Reynolds reviews the emergency contact plan, as well as Tommy's compliance with the policy of ensuring that he is in a room with a locked door and that his mother is available in the home at the time of the session. Following this review, the session continues as planned with Tommy and Dr. Reynolds communicating and working together via videoconferencing.

Summary

Telehealth has been utilized to provide different types of psychological services, including assessment, treatment, and education. Overall, research has found telehealth to be particularly helpful in providing care to underserved populations, assisting with improved communication between providers and patients, and increasing the efficiency of clinical services.

Telehealth applications have been a source of burgeoning interest in the pediatric psychology literature, and it appears that the younger age of the patients is associated with greater comfort and familiarity with technology.

Within the field of pediatric psychology, most telehealth applications have been focused on clinical assessment, behavioral interventions, management of medical conditions, and the promotion of health practices. Active video games have been shown to provide an option for helping to encourage physical activity in pediatric patients, while virtual reality games have also been used to help patients cope with procedural pain. Likewise, phone applications have demonstrated some effectiveness in helping to teach therapeutic skills, providing feedback with physiological variables during relaxation training, and helping to track medication and pharmacy refills.

Telepsychology has been shown to have unique advantages over face-to-face interventions, such as increased engagement in services and overall continuity of care, and videoconferencing has been identified as being particularly helpful for pediatric psychology. However, with these benefits comes additional risks and concerns that may not be as prominent with traditional face-to-face psychotherapy, such as concerns regarding data security. To help with these concerns, guidelines from the American Psychological Association and the American Telemedicine Association have been published to assist providers with becoming aware of clinical requirements, ethical considerations, and technical recommendations.

References

American Psychological Association. (2013). Telepsychology – 50 State Review. Retrieved from www.apaservices.org/practice/advocacy/state/telehealth-slides.pdf.

American Telemedicine Association. (2013). Practice Guidelines for Video-Based Online Mental Health Services. May. Retrieved July 20, 2018, from www.integration.samhsa.gov/operations-administration/practice-guidelines-for-video-based-online-mental-health-services_ATA_5_29_13.pdf.

American Telemedicine Association (2014). Core Operational Guidelines for Telehealth Services Involving Provider–Patient

Interactions. Retrieved from www.uwyo.edu/wind/_files/docs/wytn-doc/toolkit-docs/ata_core_provider.pdf.

American Telemedicine Association (2017a). Operating Procedures for Pediatric Telehealth. Retrieved from http://hub.americantelemed.org/resources/telemedicine-practice-guidelines.

American Telemedicine Association (2017b). Practice Guidelines for Telemental Health with http://hub.americantelemed.org/resources/telemedicine-practice-guidelines. Children and Adolescents. Retrieved from

American Telemedicine Association (2018). Best Practices in Videoconferencing-Based Telemental Health. Retrieved November 27, 2018, from https://higherlogicdownload.s3.amazonaws.com/AMERICANTELEMED/618da447-dee1-4ee1-b941-c5bf3db5669a/UploadedImages/APA-ATA_Best_Practices_in_Videoconferencing-Based_Telemental_Health.pdf.

BeHealthSolutions (2013). Retrieved December 20, 2017, from www.ucanpooptoo.com/.

Bennett, S., Maton, K., & Kervin, L. (2008). The "digital natives" debate. A critical review of the evidence. British Journal of Educational Technology, 39, 775–786.

Bensink, M., Armfield, N., Irving, H., Hallahan, A., Theodoros, D., Russell, T., Barnett, A., Scuffham, P., & Wootton, R. (2008). A pilot study of videotelephone-based support for newly diagnosed paediatric oncology patients and their families. Journal of Telemedicine and Telecare, 14, 315–321.

Bradley, J., Moran, M., & Elborn, J. (2006). Evidence for physical therapies (airway clearance and physical training) in cystic fibrosis: an overview of five Cochrane systematic reviews. Respiratory Medicine, 100, 191–201.

Brignell, M., Wootton, R., & Gray, L. (2007). The application of telemedicine to geriatric medicine. Age and Ageing, 36(4), 369–374.

Brown, S., Lieberman, D., Germany, B., Fan, Y., Wilson, D., & Pasta, D. (1997). Educational video game for juvenile diabetes: results of a controlled trial. Medical Informatics, 22(1), 77–89.

Clawson, B., Selden, M., Lacks, M., Deaton, A., Hall, B., & Bach, R. (2008). Complex pediatric feeding disorders: using teleconferencing technology to improve access to a treatment program: Pediatric Nursing, 34(3), 213–216.

Cotterez, A., Durant, N., Agne, A., & Cherrington, A. (2014). Internet interventions to support lifestyle modification for diabetes management: a systematic review of the evidence. Journal of Diabetes Complications, 28(2), 243–251.

Crosby, L., Barach, H., McGrady, M., Kalinyak, K., Eastin, A., & Mitchell, M. (2012). Integrating interactive web-based technology to assess adherence and clinical outcomes in pediatric sickle cell disease. Anemia, Article ID 492428.

Cushing, C. & Steele, R. (2010). A meta-analytic review of eHealth interventions for pediatric health promoting and maintaining behaviors. Journal of Pediatric Psychology, 35(9), 937–949.

Glueckauf, R., Fritz, S., Ecklund-Johnson, E., Liss, H., Dages, P., & Carney, P. (2002). Videoconferencing-based family counseling for rural teenagers with epilepsy: phase 1 findings. Rehabilitation Psychology, 47, 49–72.

Gold, J., Kim, S., Kant, A., Joseph, M., & Rizzo, A. (2006). Effectiveness of virtual reality for distraction during IV placement. CyberPsychology and Behavior, 9(2), 207–212.

Greatcall. (2017). MedCoach [Mobile Application Software]. Retrieved from https://play.google.com/store/apps/details?id=com.greatcall.medcoach.

Hicks, C., von Baeyer, C., & McGrath, P. (2005). Online psychological treatment for pediatric recurrent pain: a randomized evaluation. Journal of Pediatric Psychology, 31(7), 24–736.

Joint Task Force for the Development of Telepsychology Guidelines for Psychologists. (2013). Guidelines for the practice of telepsychology. American Psychologist, 68(9), 791–800.

Kato, P., Cole, S., Bradlyn, A., & Pollock, B. (2008). A video game improves behavioral outcomes in adolescents and young adults with cancer: a randomized trial. *Pediatrics, 122*, e305–e317.

Lepper, M. & Gurtner, J. (1989). Children and computers: approaching the twenty-first century. *American Psychologist, 44*(2), 170–178.

Lieberman, D. A. (1997). Interactive video games for health promotion: effects on knowledge, self-efficacy, social support, and health. In R. L. Street, W. R. Gold, & T. Manning (eds.), *Health Promotion and Interactive Technology: Theoretical Applications and Future Directions* (pp. 103–120). Mahwah, NJ: Lawrence Erlbaum Associates.

Lieberman, D. (2001). Management of chronic pediatric diseases with interactive health games: theory and research findings. *Journal of Ambulatory Care Management, 24*(1), 26–38.

Luxton, D., McCann, R., Bush, N., Mishkind, M., & Reger, G. (2011). mHealth for mental health: integrating smartphone technology in behavioral healthcare. *Professional Psychology: Research and Practice, 42*(6), 505–512.

Mallow, J., Petitte, T., Narsavage, G., Barnes, E., Theeke, E., Mallow, B., & Theeke, L. (2016). The use of video conferencing for persons with chronic conditions: a systematic review. *E-Health Telecommunication Systems and Networks, 5*, 39–56.

Mango Health. (2017). Mango Health [Mobile Application Software]. Retrieved from www.mangohealth.com/index.html.

McCaul, K. & Malott, J. (1984). Distraction and coping with pain. *Psychological Bulletin, 95*, 516–533.

Medisafe. (2017). Medisafe [Mobile Application Software]. Retrieved from https://medisafe.com/.

Modi, A., Crosby, L., Guilfoyle, S., Lemanek, K., Witherspoon, D., & Mitchell, M. (2009). Barriers to treatment adherence for pediatric patients with sickle cell disease and their families. *Children's Health Care, 38*(2), 107–122.

National Center for Telehealth and Technology. (2016). mHealth tools. Retrieved January 6, 2018, from http://t2health.dcoe.mil/sites/default/files/T2-TSWF-AIM-Client-Handout-Aug2016-web.pdf.

Nelson, E. & Bui, T. (2010). Rural telepsychology services for children and adolescents. *Journal of Clinical Psychology, 66* (5), 490–501.

O'Donovan, C., Greally, P., Canny, G., McNally, P., & Hussey, J. (2014). Active video games as an exercise tool for children with cystic fibrosis. *Journal of Cystic Fibrosis, 13*, 341–346.

Ritterband, L., Cox, D., Walker, L., Kovatchev, B., McKnight, L., & Patel, K. (2003). An internet intervention as adjunctive therapy for pediatric encopresis. *Journal of Consulting and Clinical Psychology, 71*(5), 910–917.

Shore, P. & Lu, M. (2015). Patient safety planning and emergency management. In P. Tuerk & P. Shore (eds.), *Clinical Videoconferencing in Telehealth: Program Development and Practice* (pp. 167–201). New York: Springer.

Stinson, J., Wilson, R., Gill, N., Yamada, J., & Holt, J. (2009). A systematic review of internet-based self-management interventions for youth with health conditions. *Journal of Pediatric Psychology, 160*(6), 457–460.

Swain, D. (2011). Quantity and quality of exercise for developing and maintaining cardiorespiratory, musculoskeletal, and neuromotor fitness in apparently healthy adults: guidelines for prescribing exercise. *Medicine and Science in Sports and Exercise, 43*, 1334–1359.

Van Allen, J. & Roberts, M. (2011). Critical incidents in the marriage of psychology and technology: a discussion of potential ethical issues in practice, education, and policy. *Professional Psychology: Research and Practice, 42*(6), 433–439.

Van Allen, J., Davis, A., & Lassen, S. (2011). The use of telemedicine in pediatric psychology: research review and current applications. *Child and Adolescent Psychiatric Clinics of North America, 20*, 55–66.

Witmans, M., Dick, B., Good, J., Schoepp, G., Dosman, C., Hawkins, M., Young, R., & Witol, A. (2008). Delivery of pediatric sleep services via telehealth: the Alberta experience and lessons learned. *Behavioral Sleep Medicine, 6*, 207–219.

Reproducible Resources

Table 8.1 Recommended pediatric psychology phone applications

General apps	Benefits	Limitations
MedCoach® (Greatcall, 2017)	• No cost to patient • Available for Android and iPhones • Logs which medications were taken and at what time • Able to refill medications via app • Medication reminder	• Parents are not alerted when a treatment task has been missed • Only tracks medications rather than all tasks (e.g., physiotherapy, blood glucose monitoring)
MediSafe® (Medisafe, 2017)	• No cost to patient • Available for Android and iPhones • Alerts parents/family when treatment task is missed • Helps manage multiple family members' prescriptions • Medication reminder • Able to send "diary" entry via email	• Only tracks medications rather than all tasks (e.g., physiotherapy, blood glucose monitoring)
Mango Health® (Mango Health, 2017)	• No cost to patient • Available for Android and iPhones • Logs steps per day • Alerts to refill medication • Reminders for health behaviors (e.g., drinking water, taking steps) • Provides information about medications, including drug interactions • Reminders to check blood glucose, blood pressure, etc. • Earn points toward rewards	• Parents are not alerted when a treatment task has been missed • Only tracks medications rather than all tasks (e.g., physiotherapy, blood glucose monitoring) • Unable to share information about adherence with provider

Recommended Websites, Books, and Other Resources
Telehealth Phone Applications

mHealth tools: Mobile Apps, http://t2health.dcoe.mil/sites/default/files/T2-TSWF-AIM-Client-Handout-Aug2016-web.pdf

Telepsychology

American Psychological Association, Guidelines for the Practice of Telepsychology, www.apa.org/practice/guidelines/telepsychology.aspx

American Telemedicine Association, Pediatric Telehealth Guidelines, http://hub.americantelemed.org/resources/telemedicine-practice-guidelines

American Telemedicine Association, Practice Guidelines for Video-Based Online Mental Health Services, https://higherlogicdownload.s3.amazonaws.com/AMERICANTELEMED/618da447-dee1–4ee1-b941-c5bf3db5669a/UploadedImages/Video-Based%20Online%20TMH%20Guidelines.final.new%20format.pdf

American Telemedicine Association, Practice Guidelines for Telemental Health with Children and Adolescents, http://hub.americantelemed.org/resources/telemedicine-practice-guidelines

American Telemedicine Association, Best Practices in Videoconferencing-Based Telemental Health, https://higherlogicdownload.s3.amazonaws.com/AMERICANTELEMED/618da447-dee1–4ee1-b941-c5bf3db5669a/UploadedImages/APA-ATA_Best_Practices_in_Videoconferencing-Based_Telemental_Health.pdf

American Psychological Association, Telepsychology – 50 State Review, www.apapracticecentral.org/advocacy/state/telehealth-slides.pdf

Incorporating Telepsychology into Clinical Practice

Tuerk, P. & Shore, P. (eds.). (2015). *Clinical Videoconferencing in Telehealth: Program Development and Practice.* New York: Springer.

American Telemedicine Association Learning Center, http://learn.americantelemed.org/diweb/start/

National Consortium of Telehealth Resource Centers, www.telehealthresourcecenter.org/

Index